JESS

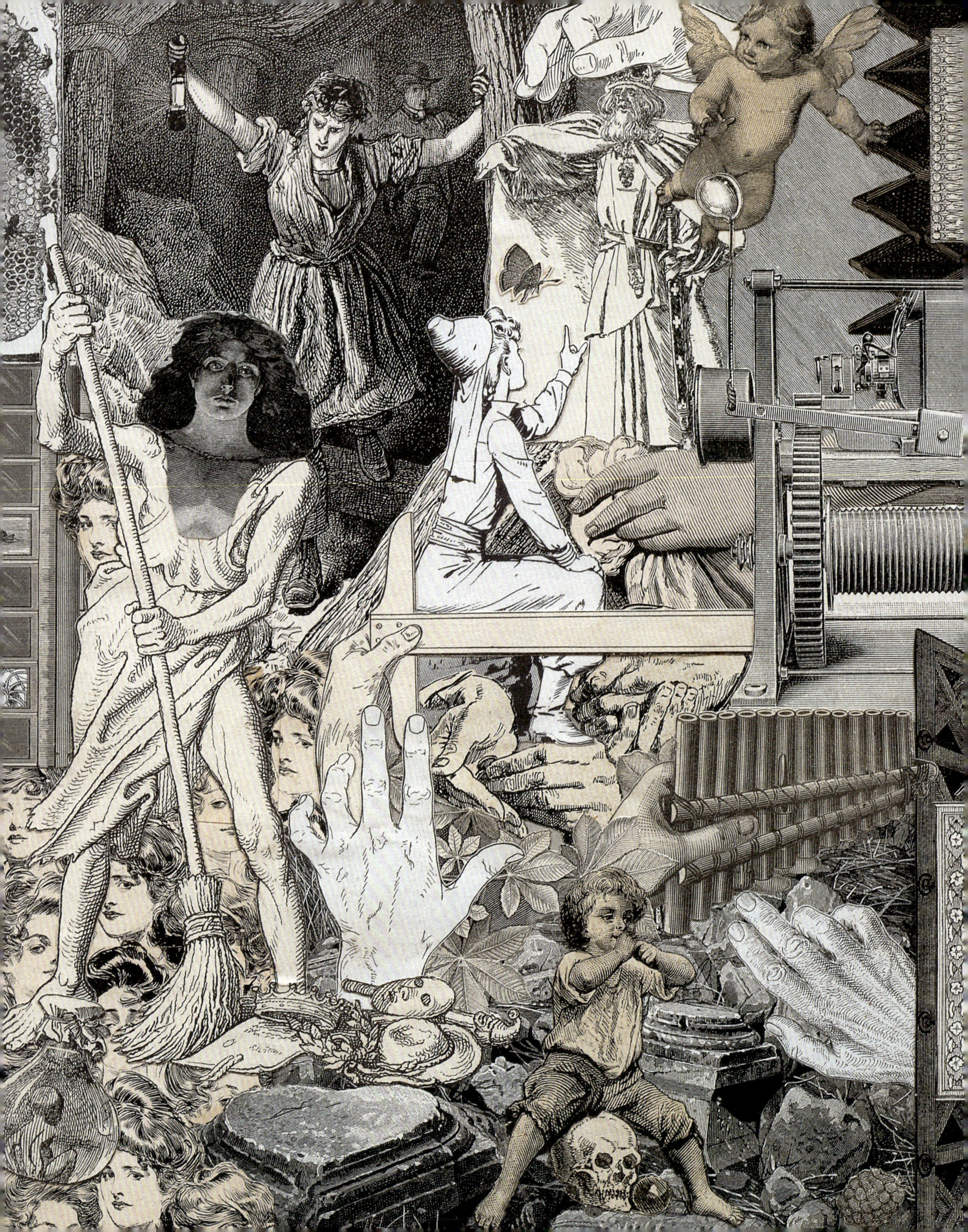

JESS

To and From
the Printed Page

Ingrid Schaffner

PROLOGUE BY JOHN ASHBERY

ESSAY BY LISA JARNOT

INDEPENDENT CURATORS INTERNATIONAL, NEW YORK

Published to accompany the traveling exhibition
Jess: To and From the Printed Page,
organized and circulated by iCI
(Independent Curators International), New York

Exhibition curated by Ingrid Schaffner

Exhibition Funders

The Andy Warhol Foundation for the Visual Arts
iCI Exhibition Partners
National Endowment for the Arts

Exhibition Itinerary

San Jose Museum of Art
San Jose, California
March 18–June 10, 2007

Madison Museum of Contemporary Art
Madison, Wisconsin
August 5–September 23, 2007

Pasadena Museum of California Art
Pasadena, California
October 14, 2007–January 6, 2008

Harry Ransom Humanities Research Center
The University of Texas at Austin
Austin, Texas
February 12–April 8, 2008

Douglas F. Cooley Memorial Art Gallery
Reed College
Portland, Oregon
April 21–June 17, 2008

The University of Iowa Museum of Art
Iowa City, Iowa
September 12–November 9, 2008

Cornell Fine Arts Museum
Rollins College
Winter Park, Florida
January 22–March 21, 2009

iCI
799 Broadway, Suite 205
New York, NY 10003
Tel: 212-254-8200 Fax: 212-477-4781
www.ici-exhibitions.org

Library of Congress Control Number: 2007921174
ISBN: 978-0-916365-75-2

Editor: Jennifer Liese
Designer: Bethany Johns
Printer: Transcontinental Litho Acme, Monteal, Canada
This book uses two fonts from Font Bureau, Inc. : Whitman, designed
by Kent Lew, and Antenna, designed by Cyrus Highsmith.

Cover: Jess, *Dyslecstasy* (detail), 1991. Collage, 36 x 24 in.
(91.4 x 61 cm). Private collection, San Francisco

Page 2: Jess, *Bookcover for Norma Cole (Mars)* (detail), 1993.
Collage, 8 1/4 x 12 3/4 in. (21 x 32.4 cm). Collection of Richard Harris

Page 6: **Fig. 1** Jess, *When My Ship Come Sin*, 1955. Collage, 25 x 30 in.
(63.5 x 76.2 cm). Gift of Federico and Odyssia Skouras Quadrani
(class of 1954 in honor of Professor Peter Viereck); Mount Holyoke
College Art Museum, South Hadley, Massachusetts

Paule Anglim

The Bancroft Library, University of California, Berkeley

Dodie Bellamy and Kevin Killian

Berkeley Art Museum, University of California

Anne and Robert Bertholf

Stephen D. Burton

Steve Dickison

di Rosa Preserve, Napa

Thomas Evans and Lisa Jarnot

Robert Glück

Richard Harris

Laree Hulshoff

Lawrence Jordan

The JPMorgan Chase Art Collection

Los Angeles County Museum of Art

Mount Holyoke College Art Museum, South Hadley,
    Massachusetts

Robert M. Murdock

The Museum of Modern Art, New York

Jim Newman and Jane Ivory

Odyssia Gallery, New York

Michael Palmer and Cathy Simon

Pennsylvania Academy of Fine Arts, Philadelphia

The Poetry Collection, State University of New York at Buffalo

Mr. and Mrs. Federico Quadrani

Jerome and Diane Rothenberg

Turtle Island Book Shop, Berkeley

Christopher Wagstaff

Weatherspoon Art Museum, University of North Carolina
    at Greensboro

Anonymous lenders

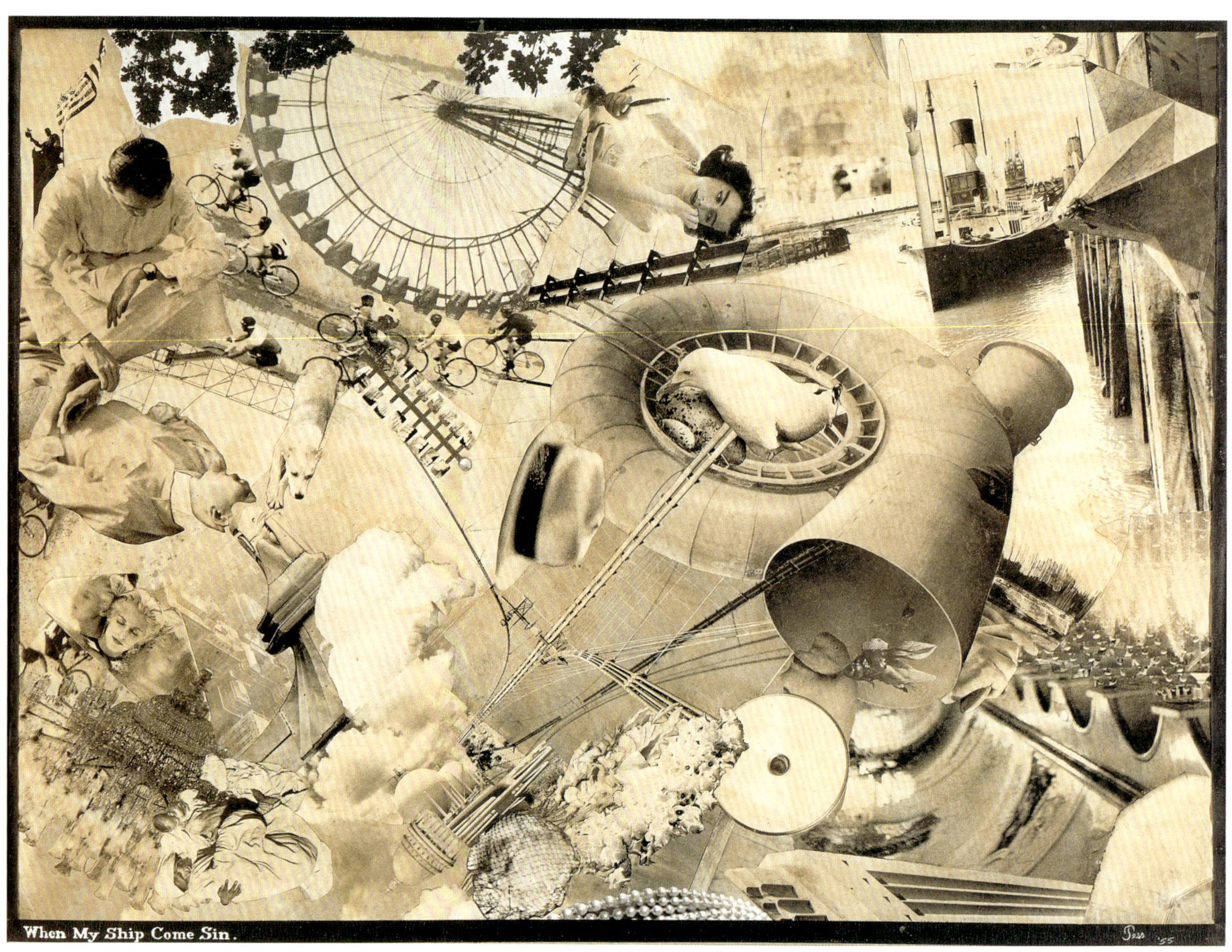
When My Ship Come Sin.

CONTENTS

8   **FOREWORD AND ACKNOWLEDGMENTS**
Judith Olch Richards

12   **PROLOGUE**
John Ashbery

14   **FOUND IN TRANSLATION**
Ingrid Schaffner

76   **JESS AND HIS LITERARY MILIEU**
Lisa Jarnot

88   **ON JESS: AN ASSEMBLED GLOSSARY**
Thomas Evans and Brandon Stosuy

102   **PUBLICATIONS WITH WORKS JESS MADE FOR REPRODUCTION**

106   **EXHIBITION CHECKLIST**

112   **iCI BOARD OF TRUSTEES**

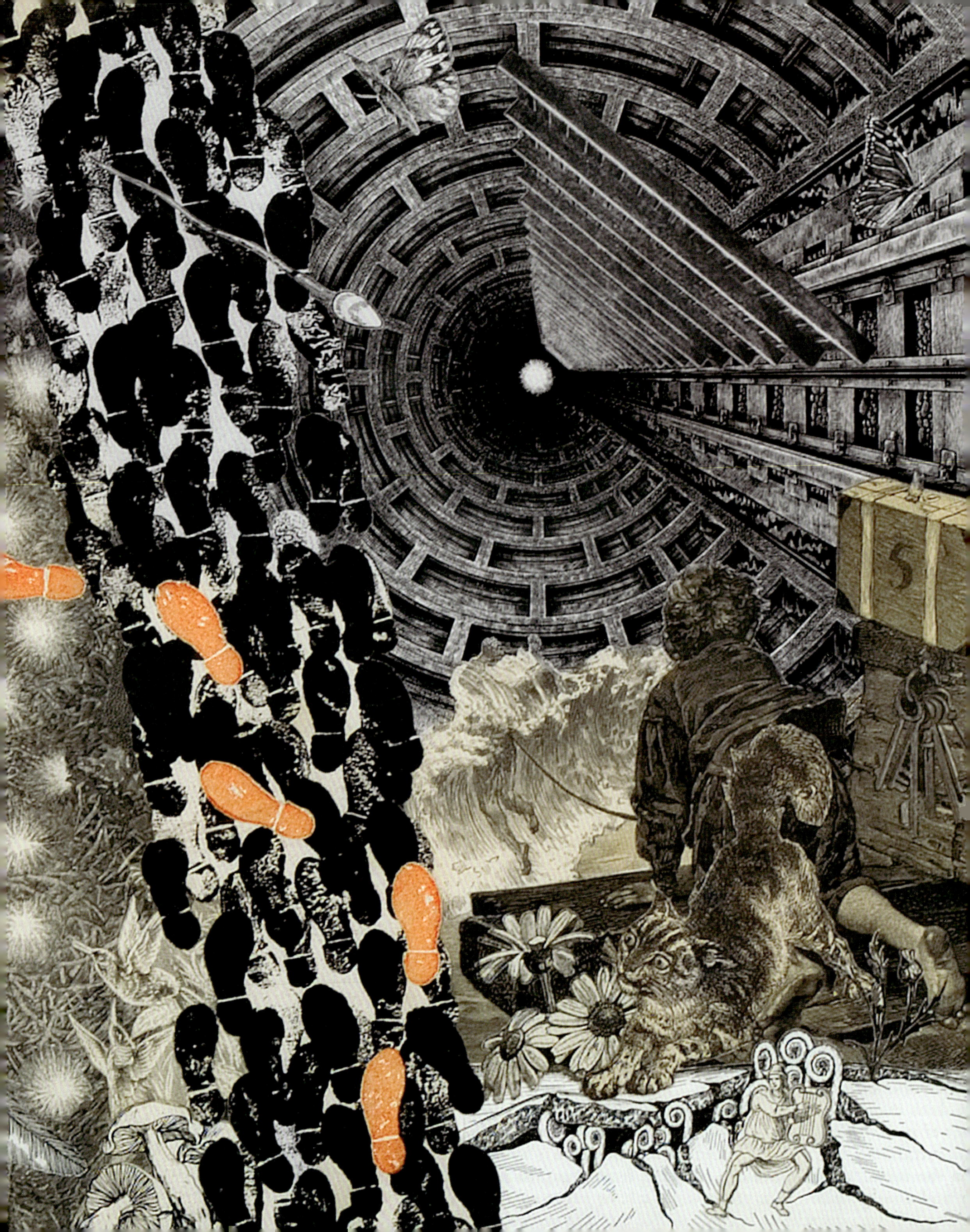

Jess: To and From the Printed Page explores one of the richest themes in the work of the influential artist known as Jess (1923–2004)—the ongoing dialogue between visual images and written words, which the artist derived from the poetry, literature, comics, and other printed matter that were integral to his oeuvre. Jess emerged from the context of San Francisco's thriving mid-century literary scene, and this compelling exhibition affords a view of the limited edition magazines and small presses with which he collaborated throughout his life. A most imaginative artist, Jess was steeped equally in the art and poetry of his time and in the modernist and Victorian literature he so treasured, and this project's multifaceted theme embraces his whole range of creative interests and activities.

Featuring some fifty original works of art and dozens of items of printed ephemera for which many of his original artworks were made, this exhibition enables viewers to imagine themselves in Jess's studio, immersed in the archival nature of his practice of reading and research, cutting and compiling, pinning and pasting. By entering into his process, one gains a greater understanding and appreciation of this "outsider" artist who, despite the following of passionate devotees, is still an unfamiliar name within the larger contemporary art community.

Finally, as Ingrid Schaffner highlights in her curatorial essay in these pages, Jess's art is strikingly timely: his intimate works on paper, collage-based practice, and densely layered images—an aesthetic of appropriation and diverse references—clearly resonate today, in a world that is ever more inundated by endless rivers of images and texts streaming in and out of our consciousness, as we struggle to make sense of it all.

This catalogue and traveling exhibition have been made possible through the dedicated efforts and generosity of a great many people. First and foremost, on behalf of iCI's Board of Trustees and staff, I extend our sincere thanks and appreciation to the exhibition's curator, Ingrid Schaffner, senior curator at the Institute of Contemporary Art, University of Pennsylvania, Philadelphia, with whom it is always a great pleasure to work. With exceptional scholarship, imagination, and sensitivity, she has established a new path into Jess's oeuvre, through both her focus on its literary or "bookish" aspects and her selection of an illuminating and provocative range of works. Moreover, her text gives us not only a better understanding of the objects on view, but a clear sense of Jess's unique approach to art making.

We are delighted and honored to open this book with a prologue by distinguished poet and longtime Jess fan John Ashbery, to whom we are most grateful for this contribution. We are also fortunate to include an essay by noted poet and literary scholar Lisa Jarnot, who so ably provides an essential overview of

Jess, *Cover for o·blēk* (detail), 1991. Collage, 10 1/2 x 14 1/2 in. (26.7 x 36.8 cm). Collection of Laree Hulshoff the literary milieu in which Jess created his visual works. I express our appreciation also to writers Thomas Evans and Brandon Stosuy for their unique glossary, which bridges the visual and literary worlds of the period, offering a guide to terms used or coined by Jess and his circle, as well as to the small presses that produced the books and other printed matter they authored.

The curator joins me in expressing our gratitude to Odyssia Skouras, whose longstanding commitment to Jess and his work and knowledge of his oeuvre were crucial to this project, as were her generous loans; and to Christopher Wagstaff of the Jess Collins Trust for his generous and enthusiastic involvement. We are indebted, as well, to all of the other lenders who have generously allowed their works to travel throughout the tour.

This exhibition and publication have been made possible, in part, through generous awards from The Andy Warhol Foundation for the Visual Arts and the National Endowment for the Arts, for which we are most grateful. Also crucial to the development of this exhibition are funds from the iCI Exhibition Partners.

On behalf of Ingrid Schaffner, I take pleasure in thanking those friends and supporters of Jess who extended their devotion to the artist and his work during his lifetime to supporting and inspiring these efforts. Schaffner thanks Michael Auping, chief curator, Modern Art Museum of Fort Worth, for meeting with her early on in this project and encouraging her work. His exhibitions and writings on Jess are foundations and standards of Jess scholarship. Appreciation is expressed as well to Dr. Hilde and David Burton and their son Stephen Burton, for sharing reminiscences of a lifetime of friendship with Jess and Robert Duncan. Thanks also for sharing their experiences and knowledge of Jess and his work to Paule Anglim and Ed Gilbert, of Gallery Paule Anglim, San Francisco; Michael Basinski, curator, and James Maynard, assistant to the Robert Duncan Archive, The Poetry Collection, University at Buffalo, The State University of New York; Robert Bertholf, Charles D. Abbott Scholar in Residence, SUNY Buffalo; Michael Duncan; Carol Eliel, curator, Los Angeles County Museum of Art; Adrian Fish, 871 Fine Arts, San Francisco; Ida Hodes; Constance Lewallen, senior curator, University of California, Berkeley Art Museum; Leah Levy; Julie Martin; Robert Murdock; John Hallmark Neff; Jim Newman; and John Ollman, Fleisher/ Ollman Gallery, Philadelphia. Schaffner corresponded and conversed with a number of poets and artists, writers and publishers, who as Jess's creative kin, may know his art best of all: Charles Bernstein, Robin Blaser, Norma Cole, Steven Clay, Tom Devaney, Steven Dickison, Clayton Eshleman, Thomas Evans, Robert Glück, Jane Hammond, Fran Herndon, Lisa Jarnot, Lawrence Jordan, Kevin Killian, Tim Maul, Bruce Posner, Brandon Stosuy, and Jerome Rothenberg.

Schaffner also thanks the curators and collectors who granted her access to Jess's art, including Jason Linetzky, The Anderson Collection, Menlo Park, California; Robert Haller and Andrew Lampert, Anthology Film Archives, New York; Dominic Angerame, Canyon Cinema, San Francisco; Charles Wylie, curator, and Victoria Scott, intern, Dallas Museum of Art; Michael Schwager, curator, di Rosa Preserve, Napa, California; Dan McLeod, editor, *The Georgia Straight*; Victoria Rowe, director, Nora Eccles Harrison Museum of Art, Utah State University, Logan; Alex Baker, curator, Pennsylvania Academy of the Fine Arts, Philadelphia; AA Bronson, director, Printed Matter, New York; and Anthony S. Bliss, curator, and Susan Snyder, Head of Public Services, The Bancroft Library, University of California, Berkeley. Finally, thanks to Marianne Doezema, director, and Wendy Watson, curator, at the Mount Holyoke College Art Museum, South Hadley, Massachusetts, for introducing sister alumna Ingrid Schaffner (class of 1983) and Odyssia Skouras (class of 1954), thereby making a college connection from which commenced this collage exhibition.

iCI extends well-earned appreciation to Bethany Johns for her design of this book, and to Jennifer Liese, the book's editor. It was a great pleasure to work with these superb professionals.

iCI's dedicated, knowledgeable, and enthusiastic staff deserves recognition for their work on every aspect of this project, from securing loans and images to obtaining crucial financial support, developing the tour, arranging for the packing and shipping, creating this publication, and promoting the project. Thanks for this work go especially to Susan Hapgood, director of exhibitions; Hedy Roma, director of development; Hilary Fry, grants and membership coordinator; Susan Callanan, registrar; Maia Gianakos, curatorial assistant; Sue Scott, communications and operations manager; and Ramona Piagentini, former curatorial assistant. Thanks also to Frances Wu, curatorial assistant; Collyn Hinchey, development assistant; Matt Hackett, exhibitions intern; and Alex Glauber, former exhibitions intern.

Finally, I extend my warmest appreciation to iCI's Board of Trustees for their steadfast support, enthusiasm, and commitment to all of iCI's activities. They join me in expressing our gratitude to everyone who has contributed to making possible this challenging and gratifying project.

Judith Olch Richards
Executive Director

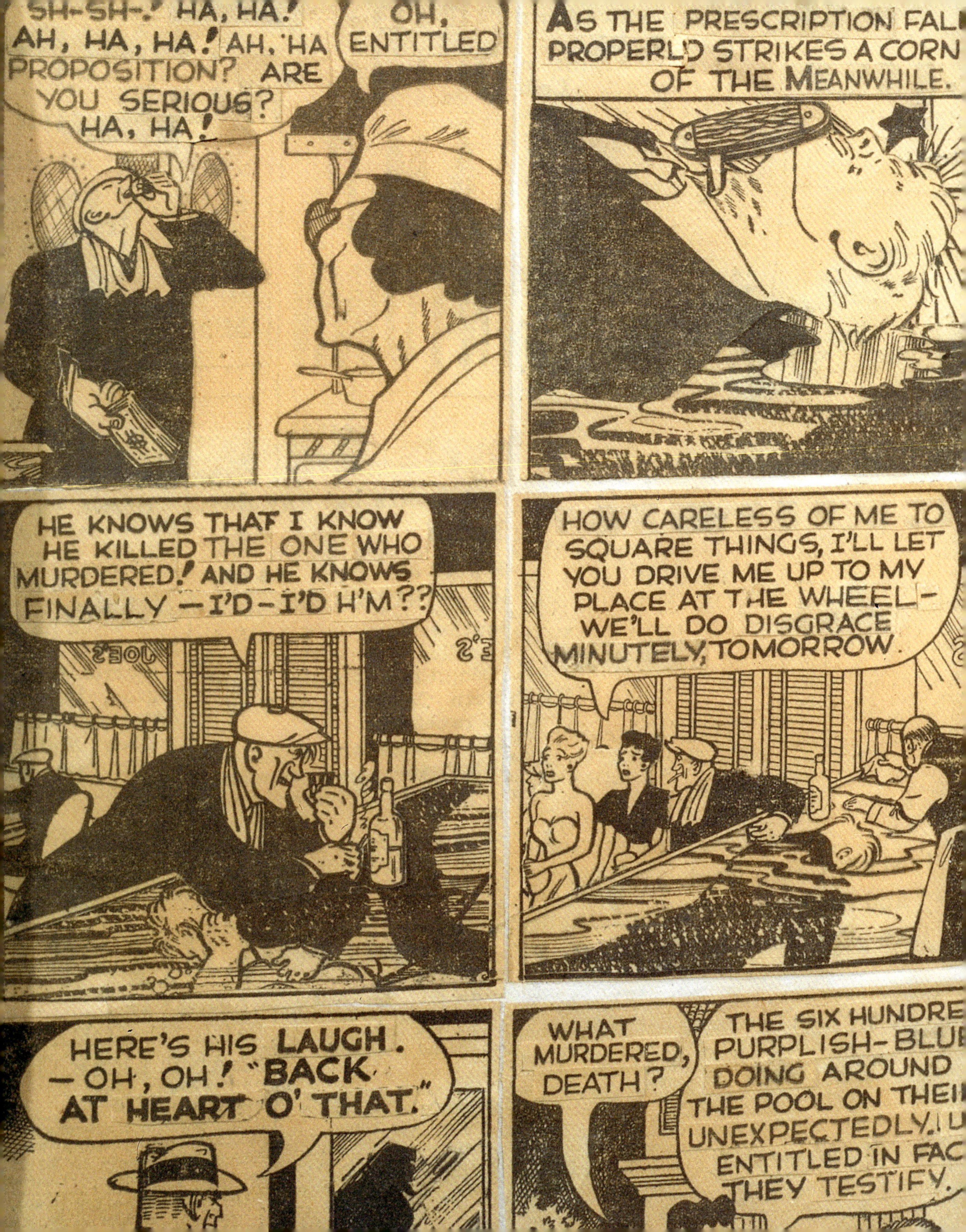

SH-SH-! HA, HA! AH, HA, HA! AH, 'HA PROPOSITION? ARE YOU SERIOUS? HA, HA!
OH, ENTITLED

AS THE PRESCRIPTION FAL PROPERLD STRIKES A CORN OF THE MEANWHILE.

HE KNOWS THAT I KNOW HE KILLED THE ONE WHO MURDERED! AND HE KNOWS FINALLY -I'D-I'D H'M??

HOW CARELESS OF ME TO SQUARE THINGS, I'LL LET YOU DRIVE ME UP TO MY PLACE AT THE WHEEL- WE'LL DO DISGRACE MINUTELY, TOMORROW

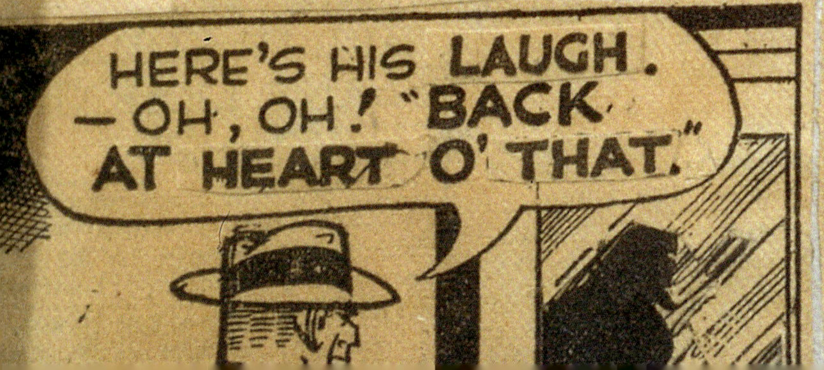

HERE'S HIS LAUGH. -OH, OH! "BACK AT HEART O' THAT."

WHAT MURDERED, DEATH?
THE SIX HUNDRE PURPLISH- BLUE DOING AROUND THE POOL ON THEIR UNEXPECTEDLY, I U ENTITLED IN FAC THEY TESTIFY.

Not coincidentally, the first great comic strip, *Little Nemo*, dealt exclusively with the material of dreams. Nemo's dreams provided the subject matter, and the strips also had the appearance of a dream. Early "funny papers," as they were called, were printed on huge sheets of newsprint in dazzling colors. They were often folded around the outside of the Sunday paper, the better to attract prospective customers. In the case of *Little Nemo*, the pages could suggest a wall or cliff-face covered with exotic imagery; the individual frames sometimes formed a grid superimposed on them, as though to contradict the notion of a narrative progression. (Picasso asked Gertrude Stein to save him the comics from the American newspapers she read.) There is something intimidating about those vast surfaces teeming with bizarre vignettes, even to the strip's destined reader, a child lying on a rug with the paper safely pinioned under him.

In fact, all comic strips have something dreamlike about them. Like dreams, they recur over and over; the paper will be back next Sunday, and dreams will soon be with us again, no matter how enchanted or scared we were left by the last ones. Jess was of course a fan of comic strips (his *Tricky Cad* parody of Dick Tracy is but one example of his fascination, along with many other kinds of demotic printed imagery. His collages evoke the threatening verticality, clotted with incident, of *Little Nemo* and other strips, and also their haunting cyclical quality: each, we are given to understand, is but one in a theoretically endless series.

This quality of existing in time as well as on the page is what distinguishes Jess's work from that of other collagists and makes him a great artist. As spellbinding as are the countless details in any given work, what is still more magnetic is its temporal dimension, which is not unlike that of music. This temporality is both visible and fictive, a living entity that extends beyond the margins of the page and into the deepest reaches of consciousness: in Elizabeth Bishop's words, "an undisturbed, unbreathing flame."

(opposite page; see also fig. 16)
Jess, *Tricky Cad: Case IV* (detail), 1957.
Collage book, 9 1/2 x 5 1/2 in. (24.1 x 14 cm).
Courtesy Odyssia Gallery, New York

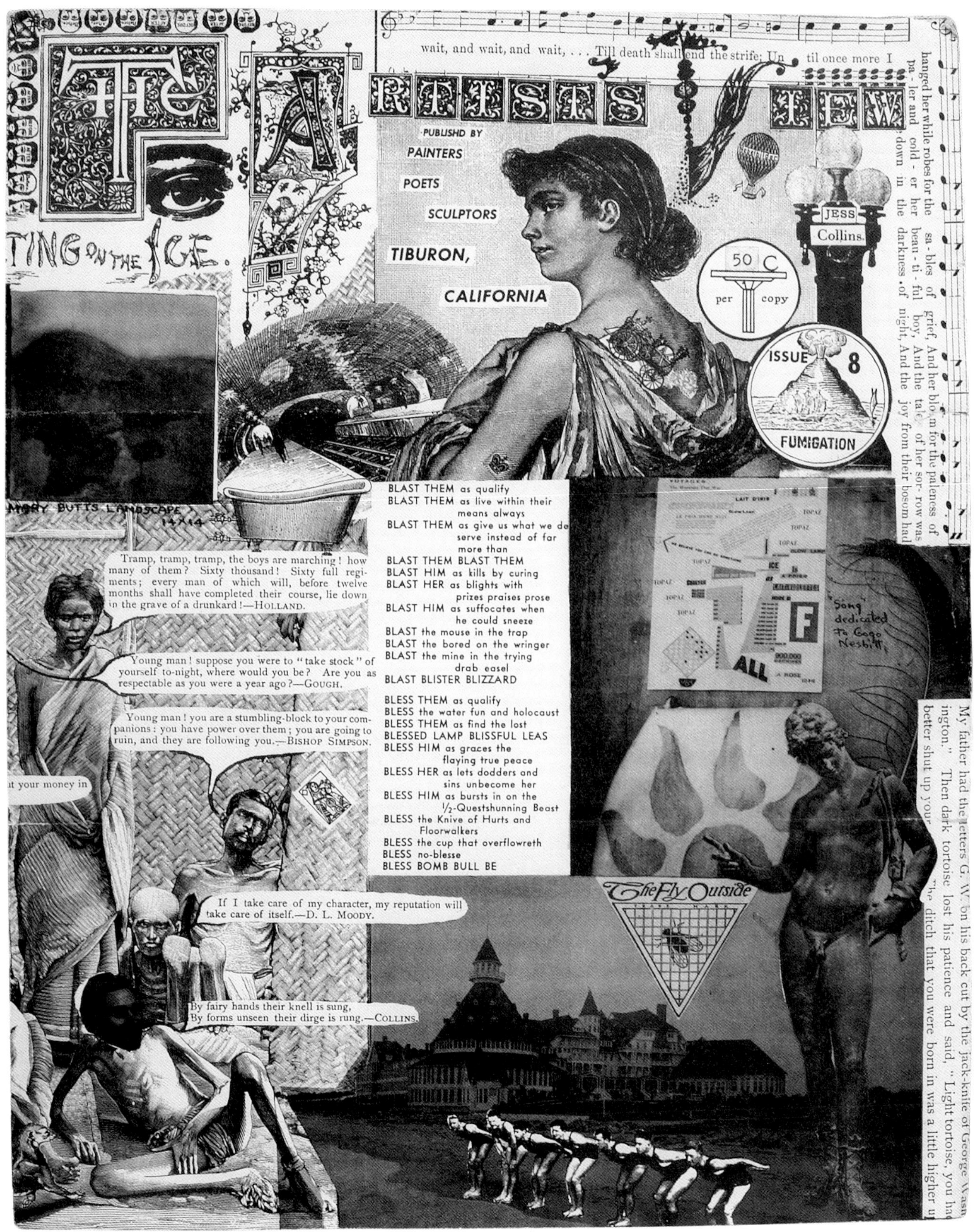

Fig. 2 Claire Mahl, editor, *The Artist's View* no. 8, 1954. Broadside with cover by Jess, 12 ⅛ x 9 ½ in. (30.8 x 24.1 cm). The Poetry Collection, State University of New York at Buffalo

A Delightful Pamphlet

"Got Wallace's Art Forum (tore out everything else) and made a delightful Berman pamphlet," reported Jess in January 1966.[1] He had just reduced that month's *Artforum* magazine to a four-page booklet comprised only of the pages featuring Wallace Berman's mystical *Verifax* collages. It is a small gesture, but one that speaks volumes about the San Francisco artist Jess and his work. On its face, it was a tribute to the success of a friend and fellow Californian with whose work Jess's was identified.[2] That very month, an exhibition would open in London, where Berman and Jess, together with Bruce Conner and Lyn Foulkes, were presented as avatars of a new, American West Coast approach to collage.[3] Funky with the residue of not-so-distant pasts (the Victorian era, the Depression) and uncanny visions of the present (the psychedelic and occult), the California Assemblagists used the stuff of scrap yards and scrapbooks to make art that often looked ready to return to being found.[4] Tearing up magazines was basic practice, and collage a language in which they were all conversant. On the other hand, Jess's gesture was also a tacit act of reproach. Not against Berman, but against the contemporary art world represented by *Artforum*'s other sixty-one pages of features, criticism, and advertisements that Jess had discarded. Apparently he didn't consider the rest of the magazine worth cutting up for collage material. Even given *Artforum*'s West Coast origins (founded in San Francisco, it moved from Los Angeles to New York in 1967), the content simply wasn't part of Jess's picture.

That said, Jess contributed significantly and imaginatively to the history of contemporary art. Born in 1923 in Long Beach, California, he turned to art and changed his name from Burgess Collins in the late 1940s. In the 1950s, using just a flick of the knife (and some glue), Jess subverted *Dick Tracy* comic strips into the series of *Tricky Cad* collages that became early icons of Pop art (see fig. 16). During the 1960s, he transformed all manner of found black-and-white images into strangely gorgeous appropriation art in his series of paintings called *Translations*. Of the juxtaposition between these works' illustrative imagery and lumpy molten surfaces, the poet John Ashbery wrote, "The neat, workmanlike transpositions ignore the anomalies of surface, as though a magic lantern slide were projected on a lunar landscape."[5] During the 1970s, Jess achieved an ambitious new scale for collage, creating compositions—some measuring over six feet wide—that are as complex and clotted as they are whirling and baroque. Curator Michael Auping, the leading scholar on Jess's art, sees in these grand-scale collages an "activated field of interlocked, free-associated images that vaguely resemble the painterly explosions and gestural coupling of action

The author would like to thank Chris Taylor for his accompaniment on so many of the journeys this Jess essay represents, and for his insights along the way.

1. Jess to Robert Duncan, January 26, 1966. Robert Duncan Papers. The Poetry Collection, State University of New York at Buffalo. All correspondence from Jess to Duncan cited below is housed among the Duncan Papers; in all quotes, Jess's spelling has been preserved. All Jess quotations courtesy The Jess Collins Trust.
2. See Michael Duncan and Kristine McKenna, *Semina Culture: Wallace Berman & His Circle*, exh. cat. (Santa Monica, Ca.: Santa Monica Museum of Art, 2005). This exemplary exhibition catalogue provides an invaluable history of the assemblage-style journal of art and poetry that Berman published from 1954–64 (fig. 3), along with researched biographies of those who contributed to it, including Jess and Robert Duncan.
3. Held at the Robert Fraser Gallery (January 31–February 19, 1966), the exhibition *Los Angeles Now* was not an entirely proper context for Jess, who was firmly based in San Francisco, but whose work Fraser had seen exhibited in 1965 at Rolf Nelson Gallery, Los Angeles.
4. California Assemblage appears to have been spawned in the shadows of the Eiffel Tower of Los Angeles, the Watts Towers. Jess himself considered formative the childhood memory of seeing Simon Rodia's visionary architecture while it was still under construction. He wrote, "My father, in most everything a reactionary, one day taking the family 'for a drive,' took us from home in Long Beach out to Watts to see 'the Towers.' . . . As a student engrosst on becoming a Chemist (but still repressing a desire to become an artist) I filed this salient experience away for later sustenance." Unpublished correspondence from the research files at the Los Angeles County Museum of Art related to the 1992 exhibition *Parallel Visions: Modern Artists and Outsider Art*, organized by Maurice Tuchman and Carol Eliel with contributions by Barbara Freeman.
5. John Ashbery, "Jess at the Museum of Modern Art," *Art in America* (March/April 1975), p. 89. The anomalous surfaces were of course highly contrived. Jess developed a unique technique whereby a slow accretion of layers of oil paint forms a surface that is so thick it's practically a veneer. In the process, he would incorporate excess blobs and wads of paint, scraped off the palette or picked off the floor, sticking them on and plastering them over with more layers of paint, translating not just an image but also what seems like the very alchemy of painting into his art.

painting."[6] They occupied Jess, who worked at an increasingly incremental pace, throughout the 1980s and into the early 1990s.

Jess's art is book-ended by abstraction. As a student at the California School of Fine Arts (now the San Francisco Art Institute), he studied with some of California's leading exponents of Abstract Expressionism, most significantly Clyfford Still. His move from painterly abstraction to collage was preceded by the emergence of pictorial and symbolic elements in his paintings.[7] Like Joseph Cornell, Jess worked from a studio archive, which he developed over years of collecting and clipping source material and filed according to subject.[8] He spoke of pulling images from the past into the present and working through a state of flux until the "collage takes over, it becomes the maker and I become the instrument."[9] In the process, he attached hundreds of fragments to the support with pins, then stirred the composition like magma or energy, until it was resolved and ready to glue into place. He called the results "Paste-Ups," a term he coined to set his art apart from Dada and Surrealist collage, which he felt an admiration for, but little affinity with.[10] Likewise, he called his assemblage objects "Assemblies." Or, as if to kill any possible link with precedent or the California Assemblage scene, "Necro-facts." The latter term also implied the redemptive angle of working with found images and forgotten materials, a small power that seems to have given Jess a great sense of purpose and pleasure. For one of his later series, *Salvages*, Jess recycled abandoned abstract paintings (his own old canvases and those found in his habitual trawling of junk stores) by inserting pictorial passages into the existing fields of brushwork. In *"A Panic That Can Still Come Upon Me": Salvages II*, 1963–1972 (fig. 5), isolated figures dot an abstracted landscape to create a sense of uncanny incident. While previously Jess had abandoned abstract imagery for pictorial representation, the *Salvages* give equal footing to the non sequitur narratives of dream (or myth) that appear to be taking shape and to the hazy matrixes that envelop them. Not only had his art come full circle; Jess had, in a way that seems truly American in its resourcefulness, invented an ingenious means of recuperating for a postmodern age the glorious pasts of both abstraction and easel painting, using this clever gizmo called collage.

Despite these achievements, Jess's reputation remains marginal. When he died in January 2004 at the age of eighty, his *New York Times* obituary called him "an artist whose idiosyncratic paintings and collages made him a cult figure in American art."[11] Indeed, Jess's following was limited, if devoted. So the question is: How might we access his work—which is so openly inviting—more fully? Consider once more Jess's extractive gesture, this time not as a tribute to Berman but (to borrow Jess's terminology) as an act of translation. Jess turned an art text into a literary one—for what is a pamphlet but a little book? Pay attention to the object at hand. A slim thing, it resembles a chapbook, the kind of volume once hawked by chapmen that contained such miscellany as a romance, a ballad, or the life story of a notorious criminal, an artist of the underground. It is by way of this rendition of Jess's act that the "delightful

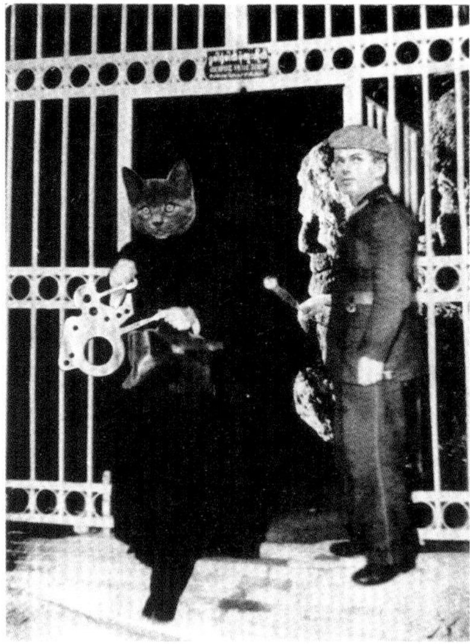

Fig. 3 Wallace Berman, editor, *Semina* no. 8 (page detail), 1963. Magazine with collage reproduction by Jess, n.p., 7 1/8 x 5 1/2 in. (18.1 x 14 cm)

6. Michael Auping, *Jess: A Grand Collage 1951–1993*, exh. cat. (Buffalo, N.Y.: Albright-Knox Art Gallery, 1993), p. 46.
7. Jess said he initially abandoned painting for collage because it was too fast moving a process to capture those images that slowly percolated in his mind's eye. Then there were certain technical advantages. As he told Michael Auping, "What my mind wanted to see happen would require skills that I could not possibly use. Therefore, I had to use images that had already been made for me." Quoted in Michael Auping, *Jess: Paste-Ups (and Assemblies) 1951–1983*, exh. cat. (Sarasota, Fl.: The John and Mable Ringling Museum of Art, 1984), p. 11.
8. Jess must have used very sharp and tiny scissors, so meticulously cut are the paper elements that he stocked by the drawer-full and filed according to both subject ("Animals," "Toys," "Signs of the Tarot," "Sufi Mythology") and subjectivities. Auping notes, "There is a broad section simply entitled 'Pink Material' and a 'Mean Section' further broken down into 'Police,' 'Bigots,' 'Militarists.'" Auping, *A Grand Collage*, p. 49.
9. Auping, *Jess: Paste-Ups*, p. 11.
10. Jess told Auping, "I used to paste things up with my aunt and that experience is probably more central to my love of this kind of art than the modern development of collage." Auping, *A Grand Collage*, p. 26. Another oft-mentioned childhood experience was coming across an abandoned prospector's shack on a trip with his father to the California desert. Jess described it as "a little palace assembled from scrap wood, pieces of aluminum, junk, tins, almost any type of found object you can imagine." Auping, *Jess: Paste-Ups*, p. 10.
11. Ken Johnson, "Jess, 80, San Francisco Artist Known for Layered Imagery," *New York Times*, January 10, 2004, p. A14.

Fig. 4 Jess, *The Marsh King's Daughter in Egypt*, 1958. Oil on board, 13½ x 9½ in. (34.3 x 24.1 cm). Collection of Laree Hulshoff

Fig. 5 Jess, *"A Panic That Can Still Come Upon Me": Salvages II*, 1963–72. Oil on canvas over oil on wood (landscape by unknown artist), 16 x 20 in. (40.6 x 50.8 cm). Purchased with funds from the Coffin Fine Arts Trust; Nathan Emory Coffin Collection of the Des Moines Art Center, 1972.90

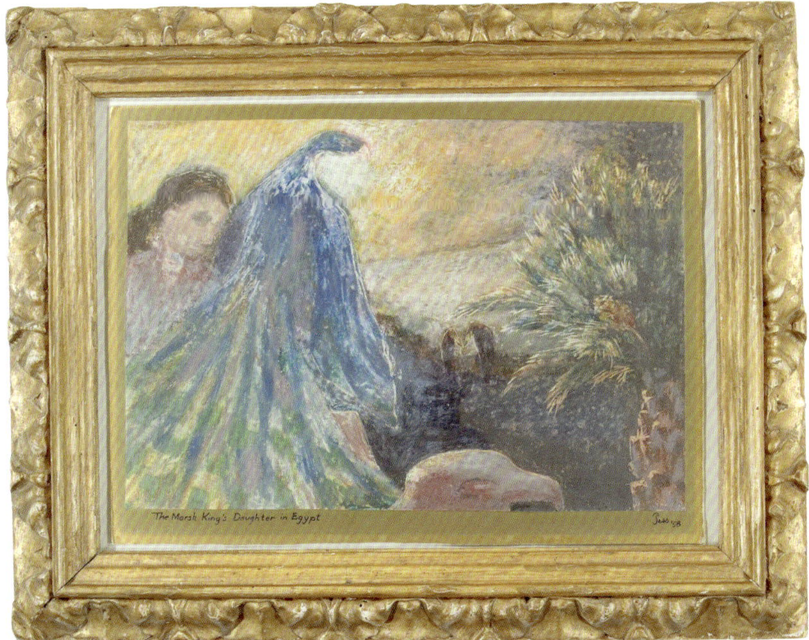

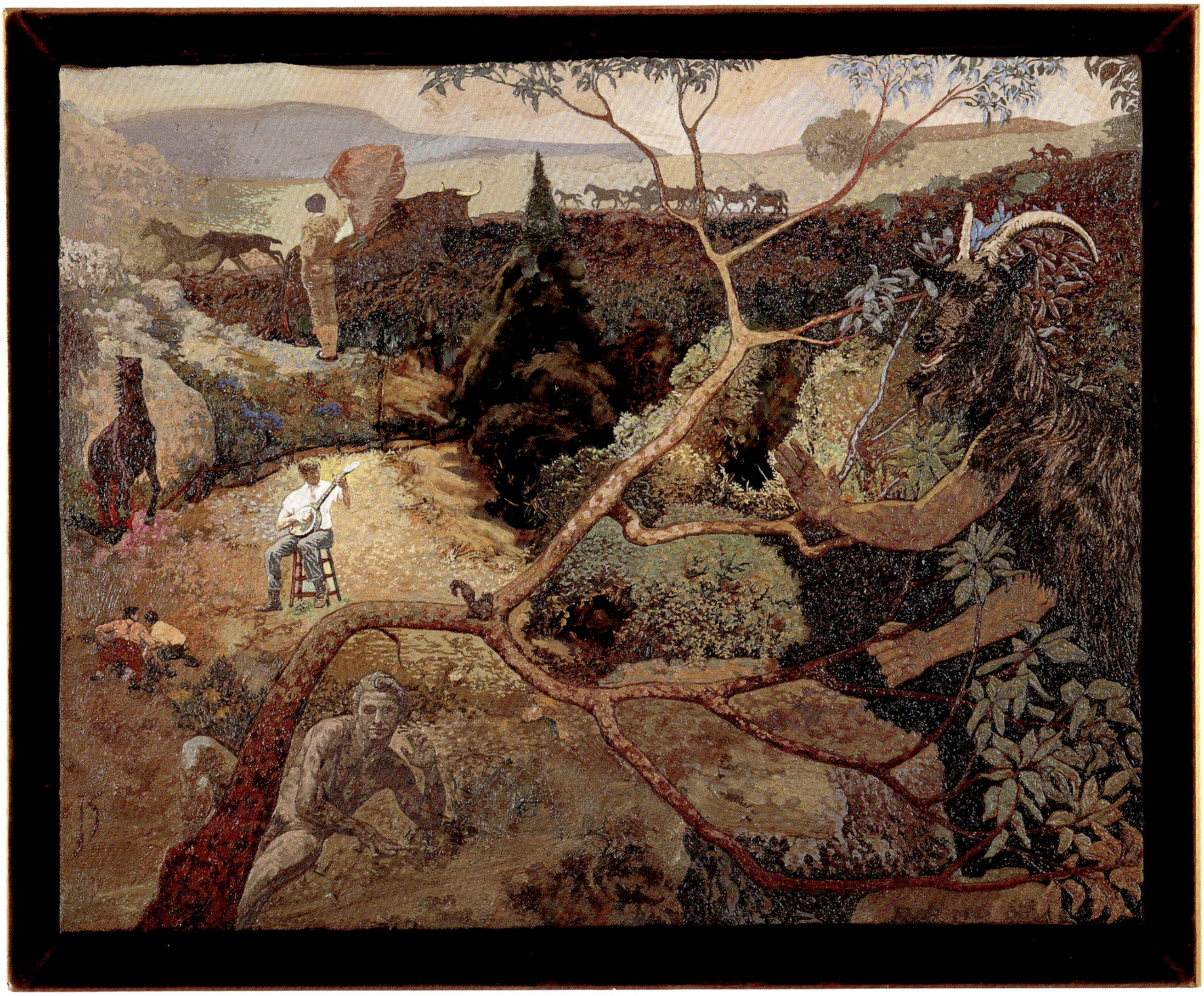

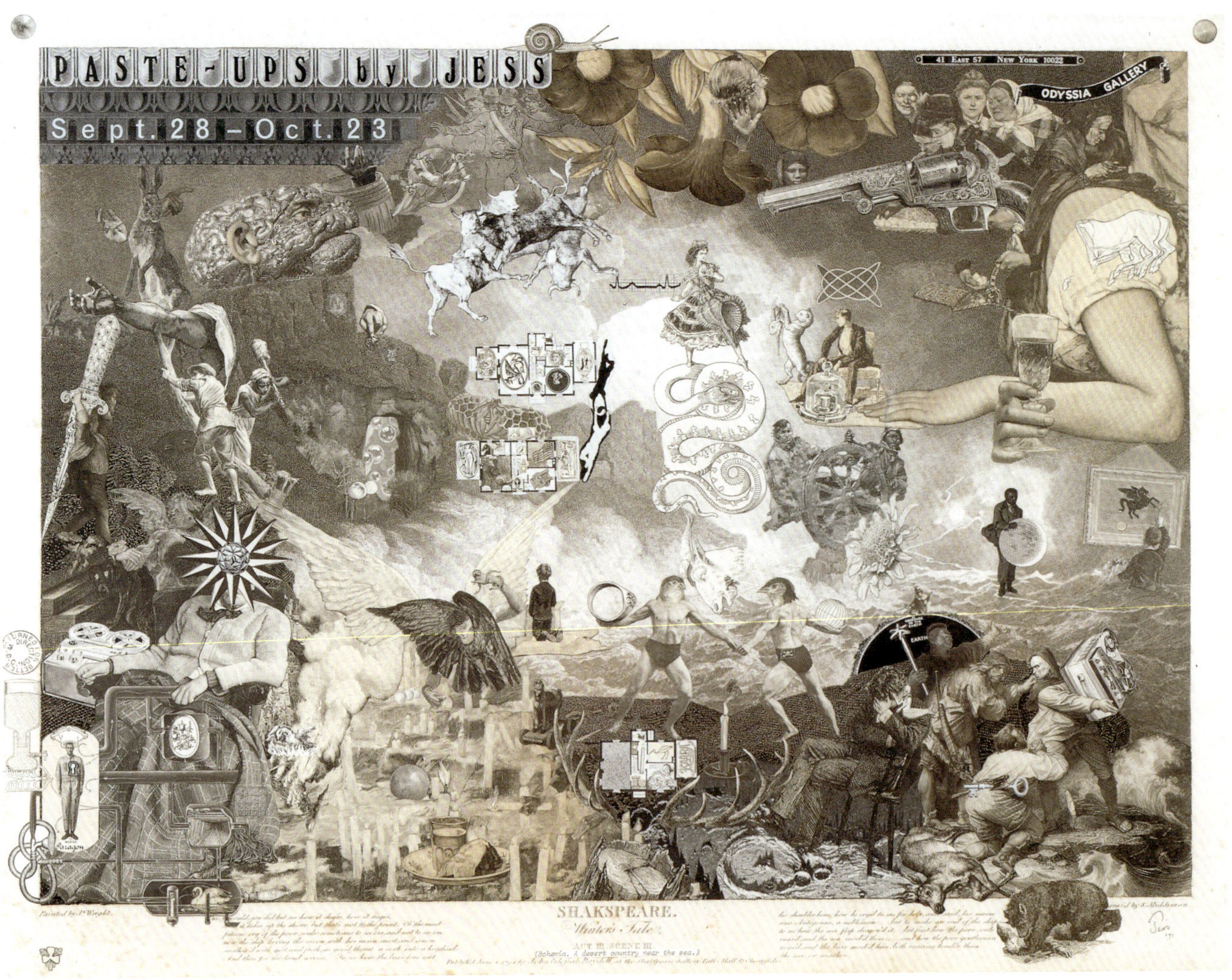

Berman pamphlet" guides us in how Jess's work might be most delightfully read: by focusing on its bookish aspects.

This interpretive framework bumps directly into a certain modernist art-historical prejudice against the literary to find meaning in the marginal. It is an illuminative one for considering the paste-ups that Jess created specifically for publication or reproduction, which are central to this survey. Turning printed matter into material to be printed, Jess made many of his works in collaboration with poets, most significantly his partner, Robert Duncan, recipient of the tell-tale January 1966 letter. He also made extraordinary collage announcements and brochures for his own exhibitions, suggesting that he valued the chance to increase his art's "readership" by disseminating his work in print (see figs. 6, 7, 8). But it is not only the literary work that this bookish framework illuminates, it is Jess's work overall. When art as idiosyncratic as Jess's is looked at with an eye for books and poetry, words and literature, stories and translations, it comes into plain view.

Fig. 6 Jess, *Paste-Ups by Jess*, 1971. Collage, 22 x 28 in. (55.9 x 71.1 cm). Courtesy Odyssia Gallery, New York

(opposite page)
Fig. 7 Jess, *Jess: Paste-Ups (and Assemblies) 1951–1983*, 1984. Collage, 10 1/4 x 21 in. (26 x 53.3 cm). Private collection

Fig. 8 Michael Auping, *Jess: Paste-Ups (and Assemblies) 1951–1983*, 1984. Exhibition catalogue with cover by Jess, bound in paper wrappers, 157 pages, 10 x 10 in. (25.4 x 25.4 cm). Collection of Christopher Wagstaff, Berkeley, California

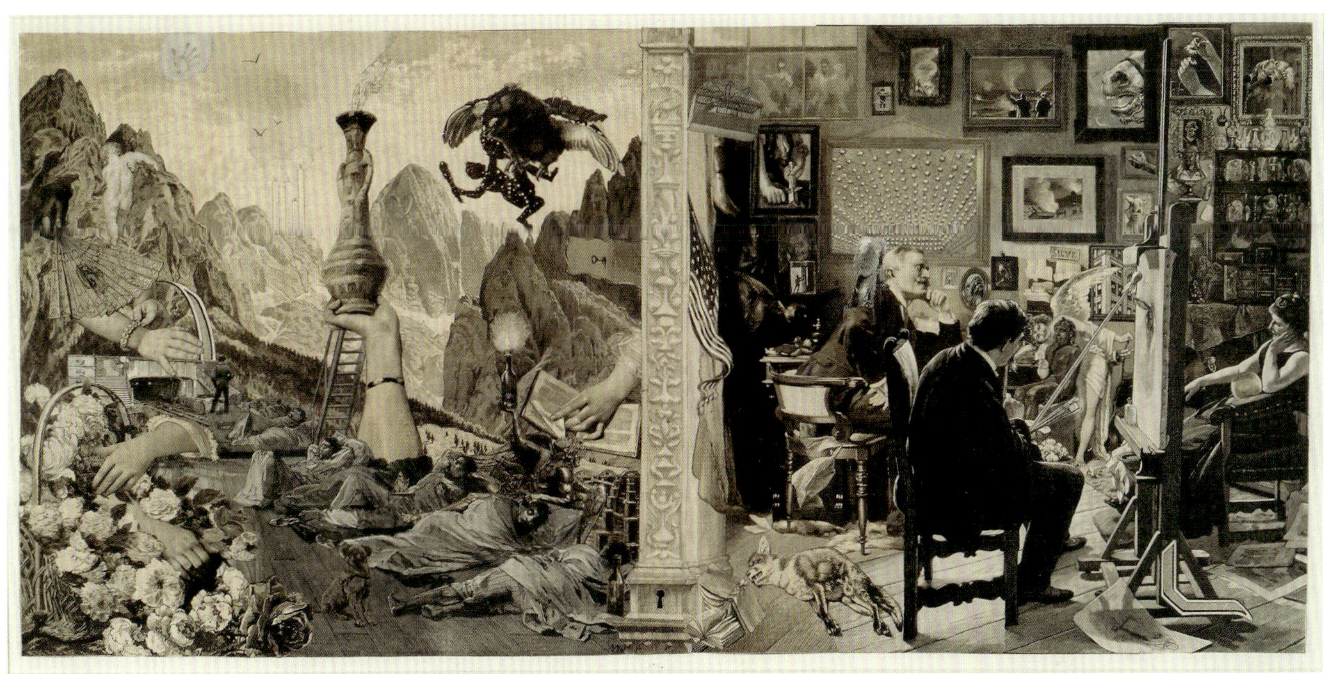

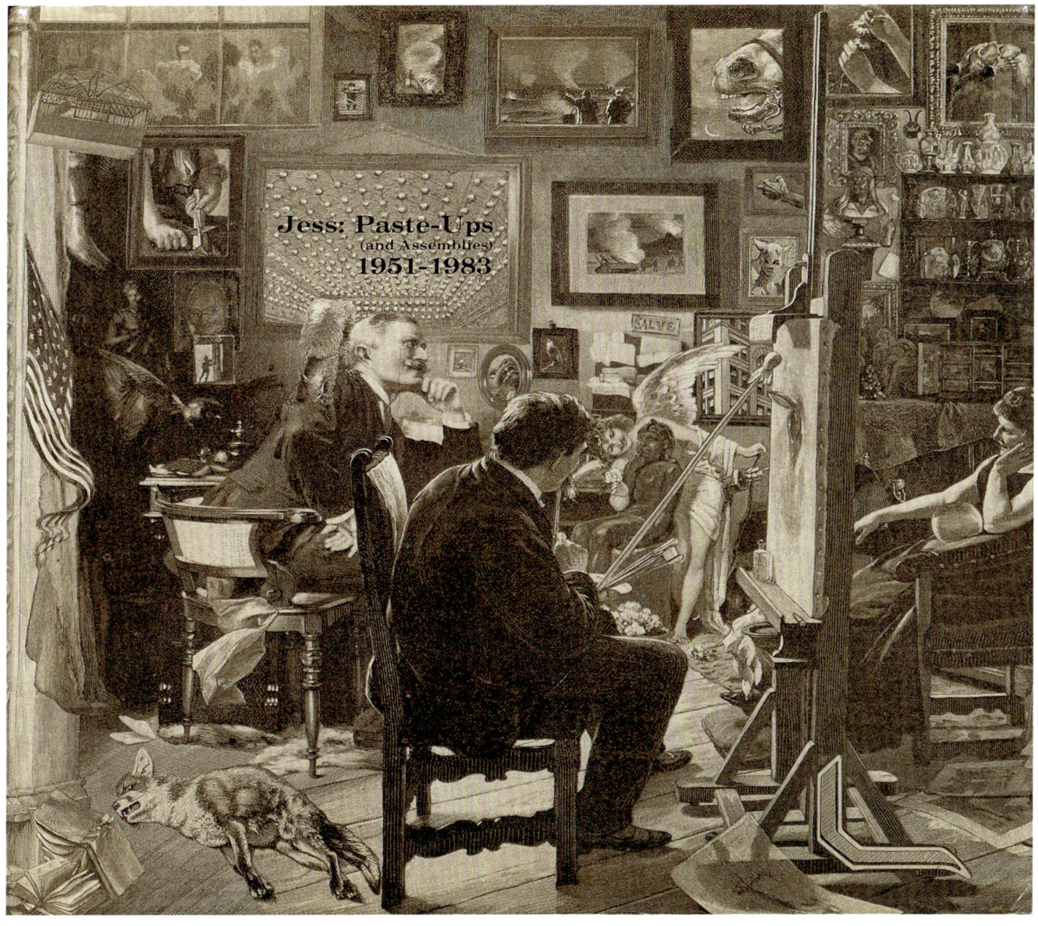
Jess: Paste-Ups
(and Assemblies)
1951-1983

Bookish Aspects

Once you start looking, it's almost impossible not to see the bookish aspects of Jess's art, starting with the *Boobs* (figs. 9, 10, 11). Absurdly short of being books, the *Boobs* are a series of collages that were reproduced as broadside publications (single-sided, printed sheets of paper designed for distribution). Both the original collage for *Boob #1*, 1952, and its printed version are included in this exhibition. Composed by Jess from letters and images that Duncan picked, the work has all the crude punch of a ransom note.[12] *Boob #2*, 1952, is a portrait piece, integrating a poem by Duncan that begins, "whose this liddl boob coming?" with a photographic image of a shiny-headed shriveled creature that Jess selected. The unpublished *Boob #3*, 1954, makes up for whatever the other *Boobs* may have lacked in corporal punch with a collection of phallic objects—a tiny dagger, house key, crucifix, and toy horn—glued to the surface. Elsewhere in the composition, a photographic image of a male diver heads into a reef of words, perhaps in search of the "SACRED COD" that lurks there.

One needn't be Freud to read this as one of what Jess called his "erotic collages."[13] Nor to miss the not-so-subliminal humor of Jess's early work, in which words and pictures are as intimately bound as the pages of the books and

12. Duncan added this type-written line of text to some of the printed editions of *Boob #1*: "BOOB NUMBER ONE : A DADA DERIVATIVE : LOVELY LOVELY LOVELY : BOOB NUMBER ONE!"
13. Over the years, Jess composed a number of chronologies of his art and its developments. In the one that appears in the brochure for his 1968 exhibition *Paste-Ups by Jess*, at the San Francisco Museum of Art, he notes for 1949–51: "Focussed on non-objective painting in romantic aspect; also erotic collage; toy assemblies."

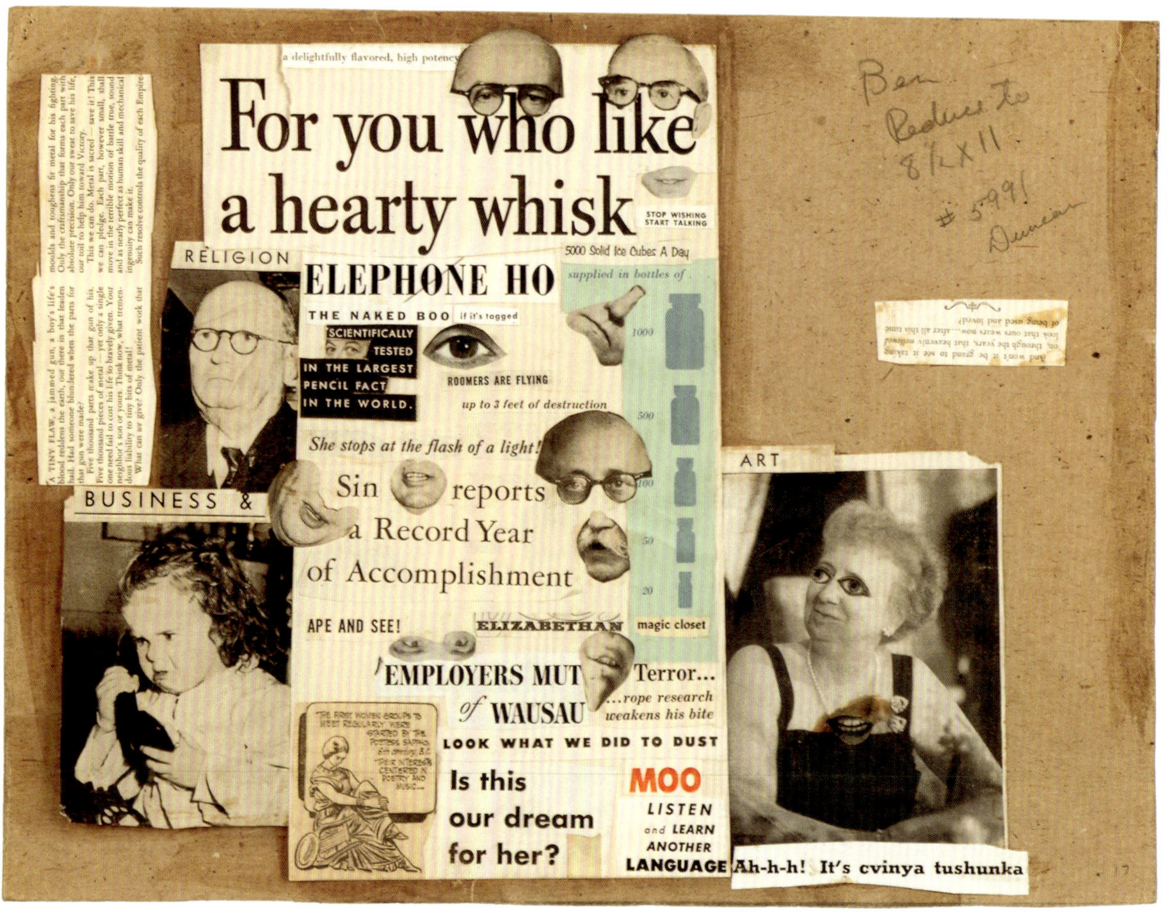

Fig. 9 Jess and Robert Duncan, *Boob #1*, 1952. Collage, 12 7/8 x 16 5/8 in. (32.7 x 42.2 cm). Courtesy Odyssia Gallery, New York

whose this liddl boob coming?
His head is full of. I wonder.
He's good to his mummy case his dada's derivative.
The cost of his addlecatain will be prohibitive.
All the boys wrote home from the war.
The gneul Ramjamdoum enterd the moon.
whose that coming this way so soon?
Adam Boob? The man we have got to.
Adore. With the parentathetical claws.
He's the newd sentence coming to his period
or semi-colon.

Enter Poor Boob his wits at an end.

: whoa. I've been wondering about in the storm.
I've been wandering about of the storeroom.
Where our memories are deep freeze frozen.
Now they are revising hysteria.
Where are our memories now that we freeze.
I've been storming about or the winter.
who thot now a cold could be a winner.
★ enter a General and a Pandemonium.
Poor Boob: O O O O O O O O O
How far do I go to the end of the next war?
★ exit a General and a Pandemonium
This is what a mother told me what for.
I am only Adam Boob and all of you are wise.
I can tell. By the cunning in your eyes.

Wherever the trouble goes, it is all over.

look at the poor king leer —
he's got the world in his haid ●

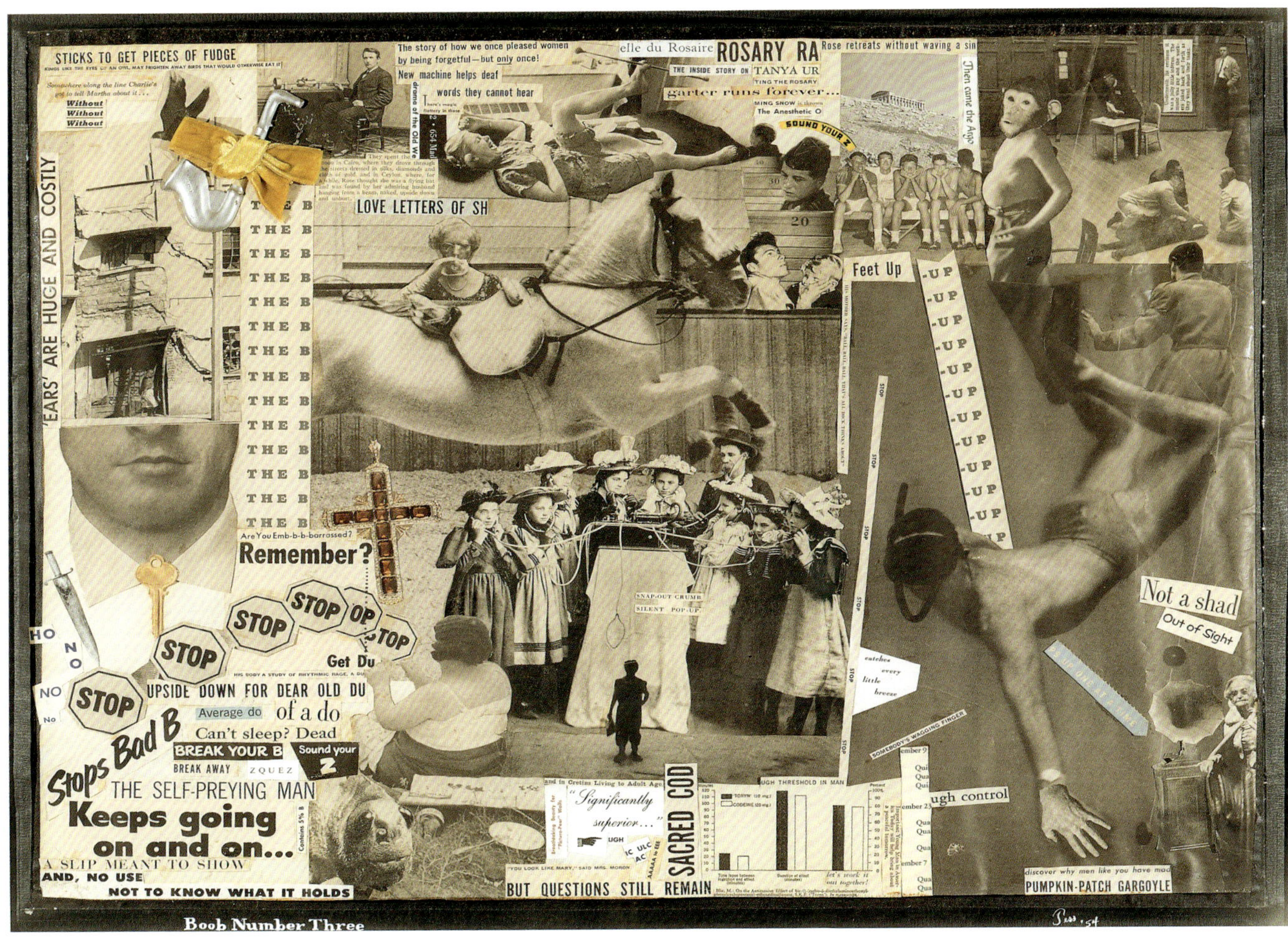

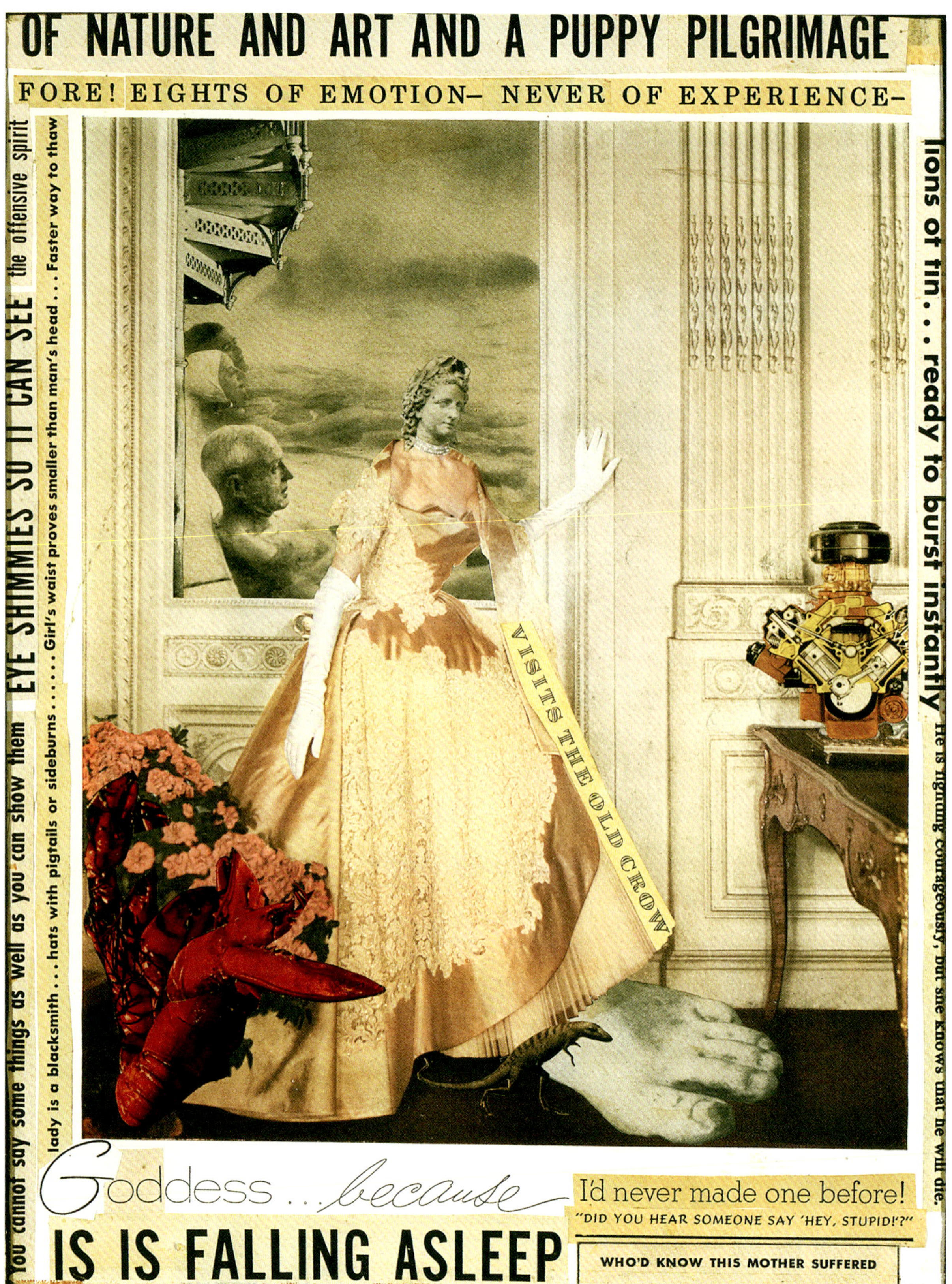

OF NATURE AND ART AND A PUPPY PILGRIMAGE
FORE! EIGHTS OF EMOTION— NEVER OF EXPERIENCE—
the offensive spirit
EYE SHIMMIES SO IT CAN SEE
Girl's waist proves smaller than man's head . . . Faster way to thaw
lady is a blacksmith . . . hats with pigtails or sideburns . . . . .
You cannot say some things as well as you can show them
VISITS THE OLD CROW
lions of tin . . . ready to burst instantly
He is lighting courageously, but she knows that he will die.
Goddess . . . because
I'd never made one before!
"DID YOU HEAR SOMEONE SAY 'HEY, STUPID!'?"
IS IS FALLING ASLEEP
WHO'D KNOW THIS MOTHER SUFFERED

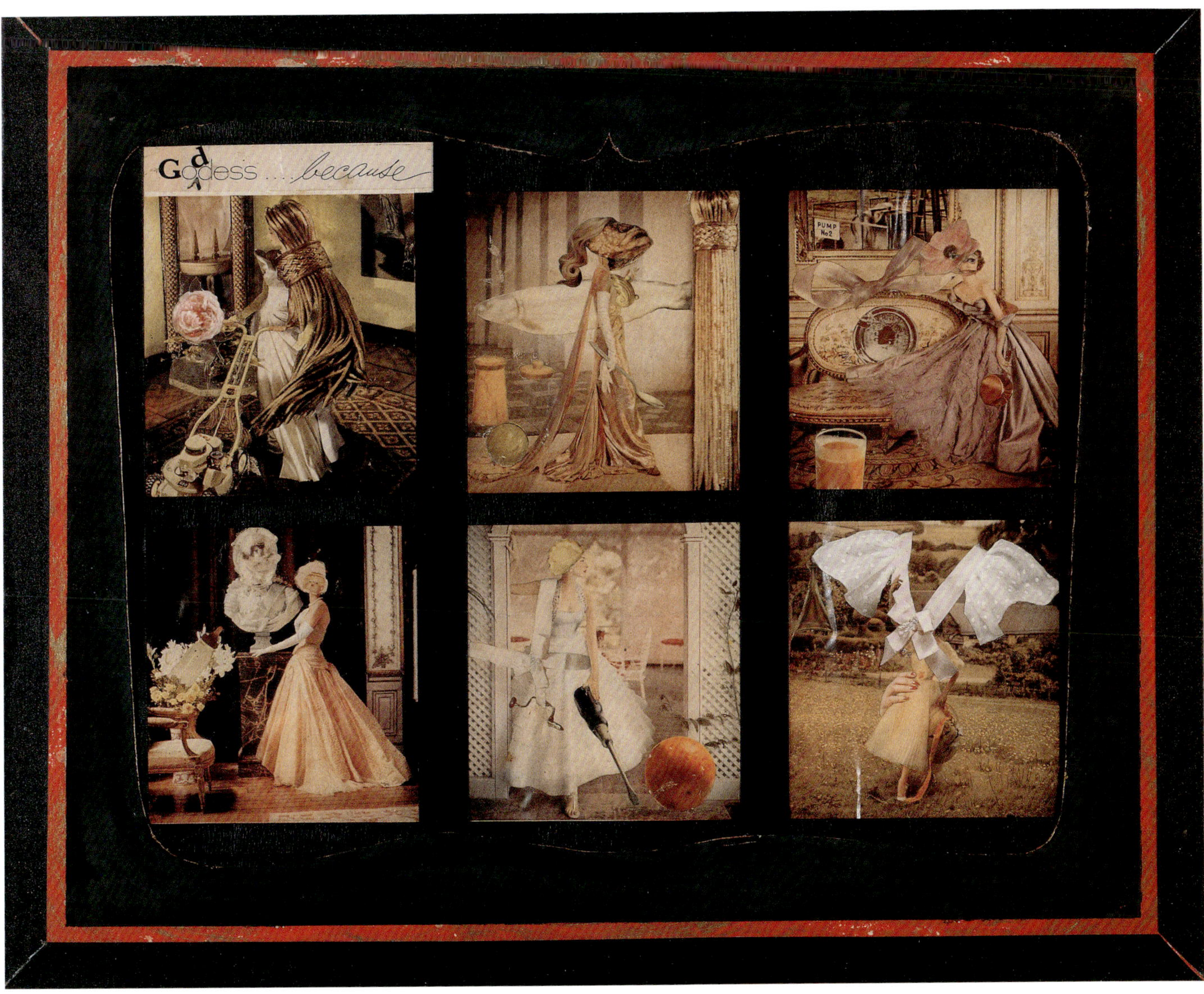

(opposite page)
Fig. 12 Jess, *Goddess Because Is Is Falling Asleep*, 1954. Collage, 14 x 10 ½ in. (35.6 x 26.7 cm). Private collection, New York

(this page)
Fig. 13 *Goddess Because II*, 1956. Collage, 15 ½ x 19 in. (39.4 x 48.3 cm). Weatherspoon Art Museum, University of North Carolina at Greensboro; Museum purchase with funds from the Benefactors Fund, 2002

magazines that gave them fodder. From an advertisement for sanitary napkins ("Modess . . . because") springs new female troubles. The collage *Goddess Because Is Is Falling Asleep*, 1954 (fig. 12; see also fig. 13), turns a classic beauty into a stumbling, half-slumbering Egyptian "Isis." Jess called his collages composed only of words "Paste-Up Poems." Off in the corner of one titled *Open-Mouthed but Relaxed*, 1952 (fig. 14), Jess glued this nom de plume (as if penknife were his pen name): "OUR LITTLE CUT-UP." Clearly, Jess was quick to slice at his own practice. One also finds in this work latent signs of an amusing aggression

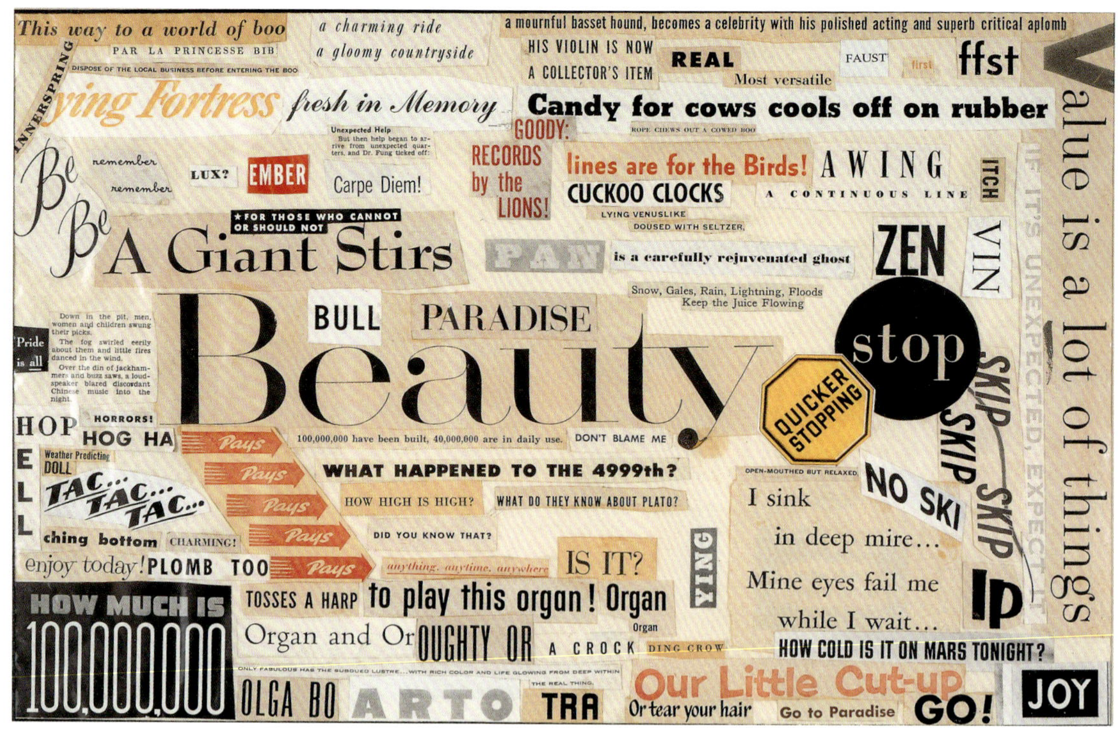

And It's Sung By A Goose!

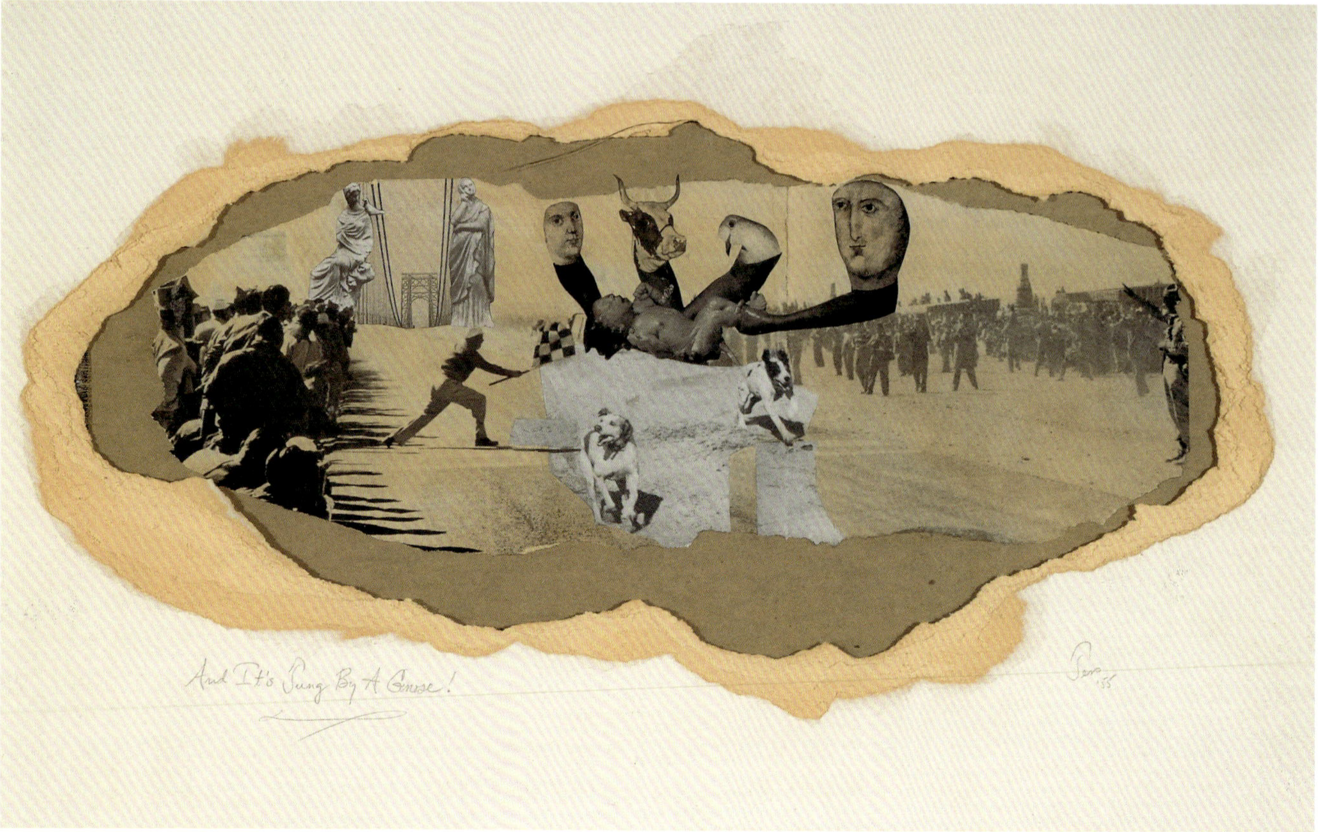

(opposite page)
Fig. 14 Jess, *Open-Mouthed but Relaxed*, 1952.
Collage, 10 ³/₄ x 16 ¹/₂ in. (27.3 x 41.9 cm). The
Poetry Collection, State University of New York
at Buffalo

Fig. 15 Jess, *And It's Jung by a Gnose*, 1955.
Collage, 13 x 21 in. (33 x 53.3 cm). Courtesy
di Rosa Preserve, Napa

Fig. 16 Jess, *Tricky Cad Case IV*, 1957. Collage
book, 9 ¹/₂ x 5 ¹/₂ in. (24.1 x 14 cm). Courtesy
Odyssia Gallery, New York

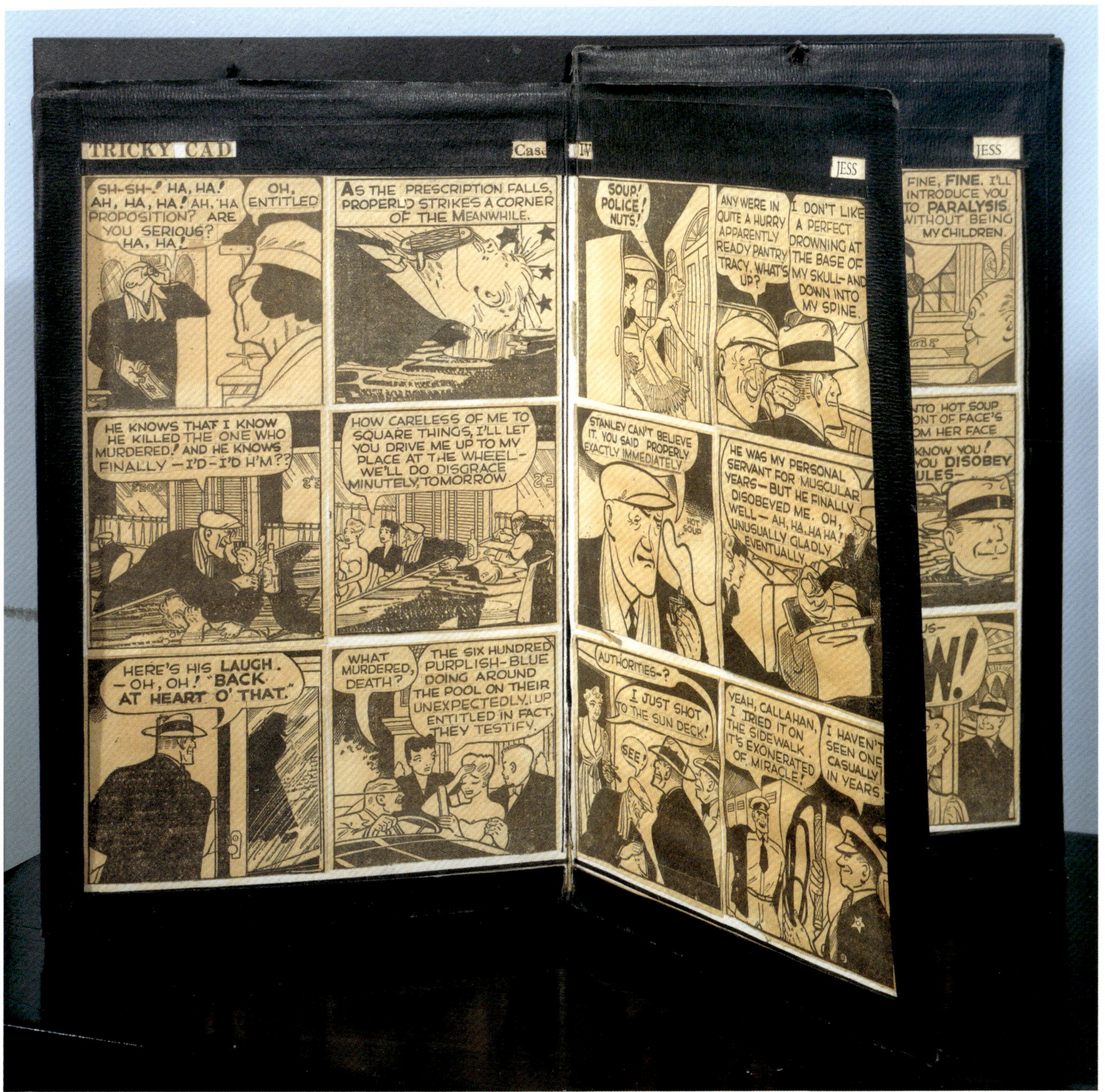
TRICKY CAD
Case IV
JESS
JESS
SH-SH-! HA, HA! AH, HA, HA! AH! AH, HA PROPOSITION? ARE YOU SERIOUS? HA, HA!
OH, ENTITLED
AS THE PRESCRIPTION FALLS, PROPERLD STRIKES A CORNER OF THE MEANWHILE.
SOUP! POLICE! NUTS!
ANY WERE IN QUITE A HURRY APPARENTLY READY PANTRY TRACY. WHAT'S UP?
I DON'T LIKE A PERFECT DROWNING AT THE BASE OF MY SKULL- AND DOWN INTO MY SPINE
FINE, FINE. I'LL INTRODUCE YOU TO PARALYSIS WITHOUT BEING MY CHILDREN.
HE KNOWS THAT I KNOW HE KILLED THE ONE WHO MURDERED! AND HE KNOWS FINALLY - I'D - I'D H'M??
HOW CARELESS OF ME TO SQUARE THINGS, I'LL LET YOU DRIVE ME UP TO MY PLACE AT THE WHEEL- WE'LL DO DISGRACE MINUTELY, TOMORROW
STANLEY CAN'T BELIEVE IT. YOU SAID PROPERLY EXACTLY IMMEDIATELY
HE WAS MY PERSONAL SERVANT FOR MUSCULAR YEARS- BUT HE FINALLY DISOBEYED ME. OH, WELL - AH, HA, HA HA! UNUSUALLY GLADLY EVENTUALLY
HOT SOUP
INTO HOT SOUP FRONT OF FACE'S FROM HER FACE
KNOW YOU! YOU DISOBEY RULES
HERE'S HIS LAUGH. - OH, OH! "BACK AT HEART O' THAT."
WHAT MURDERED, DEATH?
THE SIX HUNDRED PURPLISH-BLUE DOING AROUND THE POOL ON THEIR UNEXPECTEDLY UP ENTITLED IN FACT, THEY TESTIFY.
AUTHORITIES-?
I JUST SHOT TO THE SUN DECK!
SEE!
YEAH, CALLAHAN, I TRIED IT ON THE SIDEWALK. IT'S EXONERATED OF, MIRACLE!
I HAVEN'T SEEN ONE CASUALLY IN YEARS
W!

toward those who wielded words in the (dis)service of art: "A Mournful Basset hound becomes a celebrity with his polished acting and superb critical aplomb." Jess's cranky attitude is more explicit in *Closet Hanging for a Critic*, 1953 (fig. 17), in which the words "HONEST," "FOO," and "WIND BIG" trumpet from an assemblage of materials painted and pasted to an old window blind. In the upper right-hand corner is a hideously toothy mole, vole, or other apparently unseeing rodent.[14]

Jess conveyed words by every convention: in captions, ribbons, banners, bubbles, and columns. These words are the means by which one collage element communicates with another, and by which we might read our way through Jess's collage compositions—comic book–style. Funny papers might be the operative code for all of Jess's art.[15] This is in fact explicitly the way through *Tricky Cad: Case IV*, 1957 (fig. 16), a four-page collage comic book.[16] Keep this approach in mind too when faced with Jess's later collages, the ones that are so glutted with pictorial information that they almost repulse closer looking (see fig. 64). Try reading instead. View it as a comic book from which the frames have disappeared. You might be surprised at how readily the episodes begin to cohere. Only, of course, to become indiscernible again as the eye moves on through the archipelagos of sense and nonsense that are Jess's favored terrain. For the intrepid interpreter, being well read and linguistically attuned doesn't hurt either. Jess quotes snippets from classic literature (Milton, Shakespeare, Montaigne), from obscure tracts (C. P. Cranch), and "from the Chinese." There are emblematic words ("Fancy—Imagination"), portentous phrases ("Come from the far-off spirit world tonight"), puns ("oeil" looks at "oil"), and animal sounds ("moo"). There is singsong sprung from musical scores. And there is poetry.

In addition to making paste-up poems, Jess wrote verse.[17] *The Vinegar Egret's Comick Valentyne* is a handwritten example (fig. 18). Embellished with hearts and scrolls and dedicated to "his only—to Himself" (presumably Duncan), this undated piece is among the presentation copies that Jess enjoyed giving to friends. His poetry also trickled out into the world in small, published editions. *Song of the Pied Parrot* is a letterpress print that appeared in time for Christmas 1994. Tenth Muse issued *Jess Collins Reading "Songs"* as an audio recording. The songs' titles alone—"Stanzas Arisen for Victorian Consumption" and "Song of a Mock Cockatoo," for instance—link Jess's verse to the nineteenth-century tradition of Lewis Carroll, Edward Lear, and Gelett Burgess, in which the artist steeped himself.[18] Listening to Jess recite, one hears strains of nonsense similar to those that reverberate throughout his entire art. Sweet and silly, the songs are also sometimes sinister in tone. From "Four Intervals Passing in a Ward" comes this peer into darkness: "The nurses insisted / It is a clean white sheet / I admitted that it might be . . . Colors brighter by midnight / Pattern simpler / Once I almost saw / An unknown color."[19]

Jess's art is permeated with literary subjects. One of his series of *Imaginary Portraits* depicts the poet Denise Levertov, whom Jess poetically dubs in the painting's title "The Nasturtium that Dissolved the World" (fig. 21). On a less

14. The blindness of critics is a beloved subject for artists, from Arthur Dove's 1925 collage *The Critic* (whose eyes are lost in the hole cut into the paper) to Jasper Johns's 1961 sculpture object *The Critic Sees* (with obscene mouths taking the place of unseeing eyes).

15. John Ashbery suggests as much in his prologue in this volume. Robert Duncan writes, "Funny papers means they are humorous, but in America funny means strange, queer, odd, too. Absolutely no part here is originally the artist's. What he has achieved is totally his, but in every detail derivative." Robert Duncan, "Pre-Face," in Jess, *O!* (New York: Hawk's Well Press, 1960), n.p.

16. In his close reading of *Tricky Cad: Case I*, 1954, Greil Marcus detects a coded mission—"the pun against the gun"—being carried out by Jess. "This was a time when every form of media carried the message that Your Neighbor Could be a Communist—or a homosexual—and so with Tricky Cad as his foil, Jess diffused suspicion throughout the whole of society." Greil Marcus, *Jess: A Grand Collage 1951–1993*, exh. broch. (New York: Whitney Museum of American Art, 1994), n.p.

17. Thomas Evans is currently editing an anthology of Jess's writings and poetry for future publication. Meanwhile, a typed manuscript of *As Bird Ditties & Purple Exities*, a collection of Jess's poems, is held in the Michael Auping Papers at The Poetry Collection, State University of New York at Buffalo.

18. A San Francisco favorite of Jess's, Gelett Burgess penned the verse that begins, "I never saw a purple cow," coined the word "blurb," and deemed "Nonsense is the forth dimension in literature." See Jess's painting *The Nonsense School: Translation #9*, 1965.

19. *Jess Collins Reading "Songs"* (San Francisco: Tenth Muse, 1969–1970). A copy of this reel-to-reel audio recording is in the collection of The Bancroft Library, University of California, Berkeley.

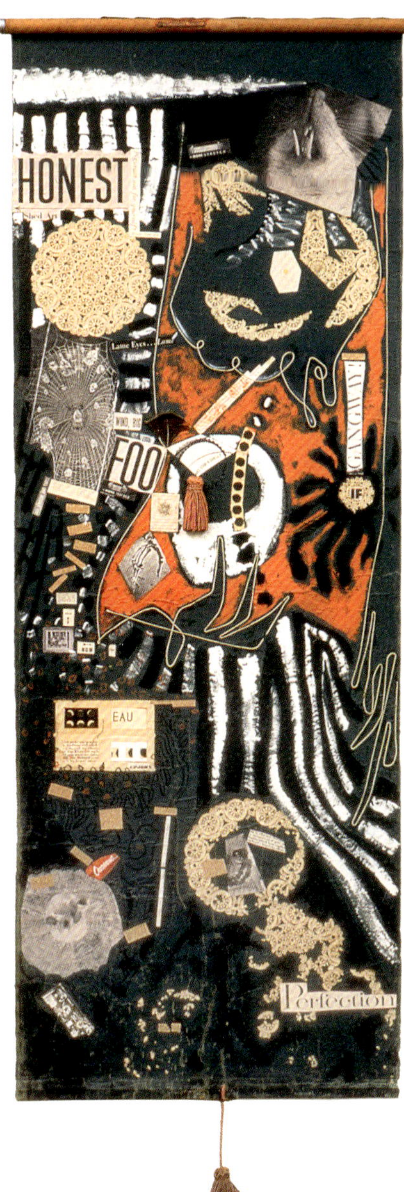

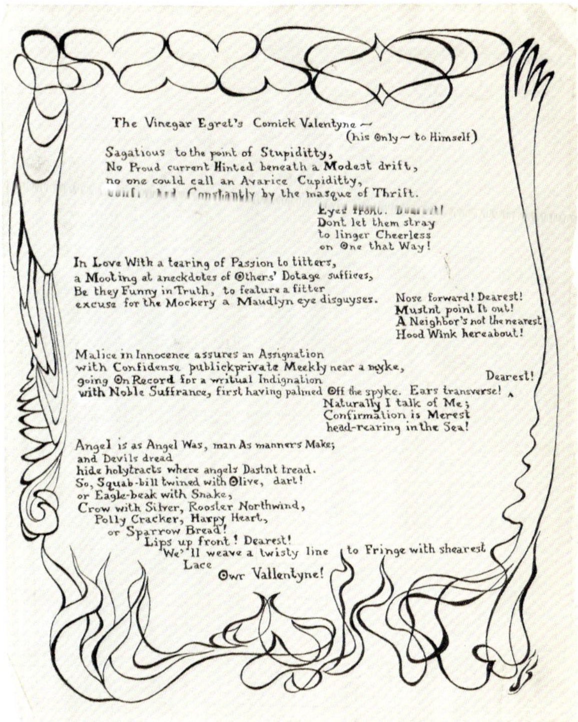

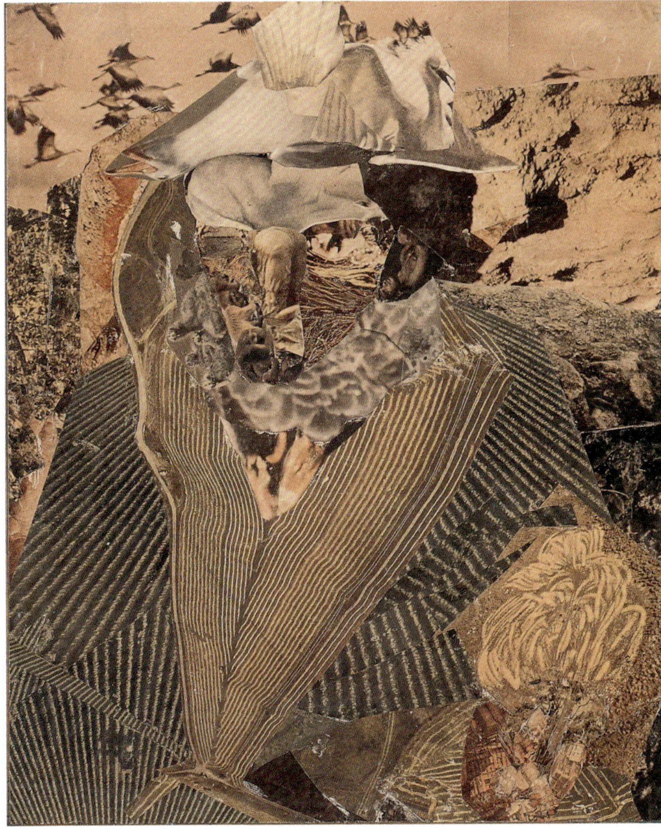

(clockwise, from above)

Fig. 17 Jess, *Closet Hanging for a Critic*, 1953. Collage, 92 x 36 in. (233.7 x 91.4 cm). Edwin B. Green American Art Acquisition Endowment, the Museum of Art Acquisition Endowment and the Mark Ranney Memorial Fund, University of Iowa Museum of Art, 1993.26

Fig. 18 Jess, *The Vinegar Egret's Comick Valentyne*, ca. 1960. Ink on paper, 13 $^1/_2$ x 10 $^3/_4$ in. (34.3 x 27.3 cm). Courtesy Odyssia Gallery, New York

Fig. 19 Jess, *A Paranoiac Portrait of Robert Creeley*, 1955. Collage, 16 $^1/_2$ x 13 $^1/_2$ in. (41.9 x 34.3 cm). Courtesy Odyssia Gallery, New York

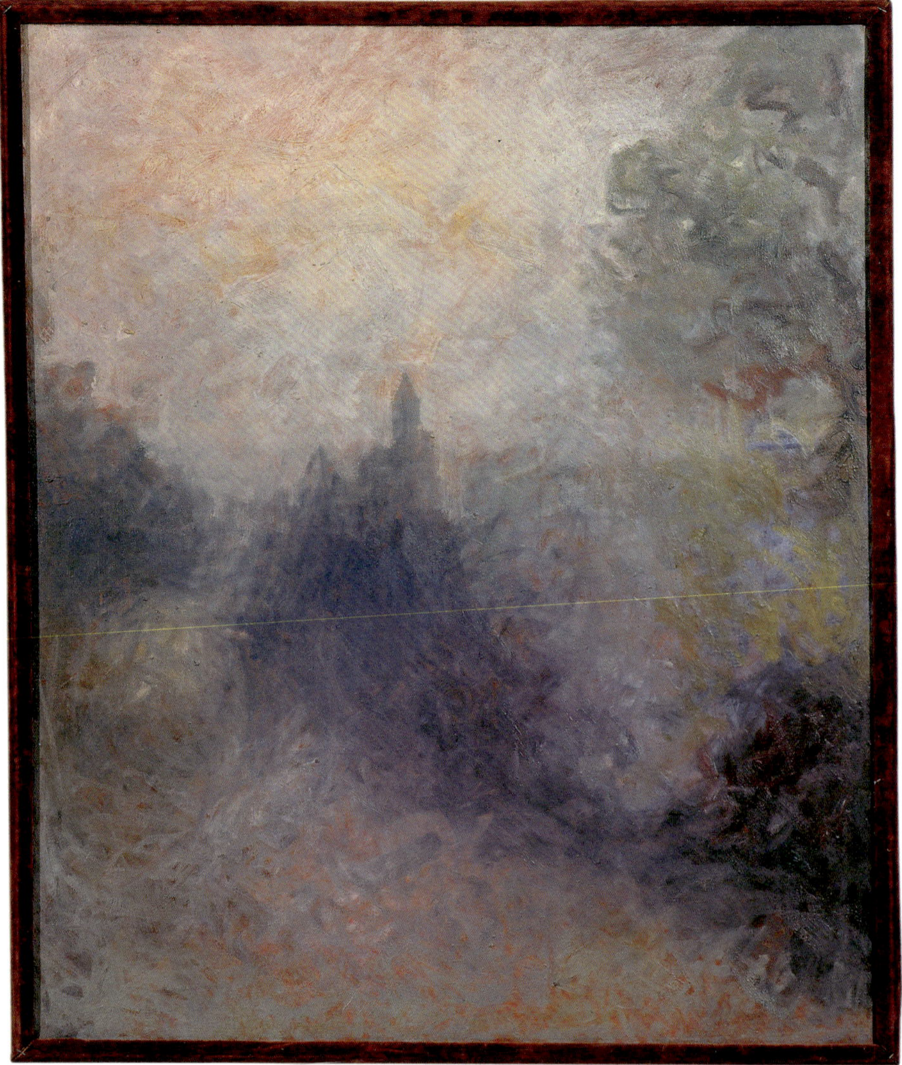

tranquil note, there is the *Paranoiac Portrait* of the poet Robert Creeley (fig. 19). Here, "paranoiac" refers to Salvador Dalí's method of loading a painting with more than one reading—it could be a landscape or a fruit dish. Jess's version turns a don of avant-garde American poetry—the one who said "form is never more than the extension of content"—into an Arcimboldo-like personage, his figure literally swarming with the content of collage. *Tintagel: A Castle Spun from Yarn* (fig. 20), a painting that exemplifies Jess's Romantic period of work, takes its subject from the legend of King Arthur, who was born in the castle that looms from this painting's lavender mists—the Monet, not the Pollock kind. All three of these works were made in 1955 yet each is so different from the other. If they share one quality beyond their literary subjects, it's that they are illustrational in a conceptual sense. For Jess, art history was a stylebook to be consulted and used to emphasize the literal content of his art.

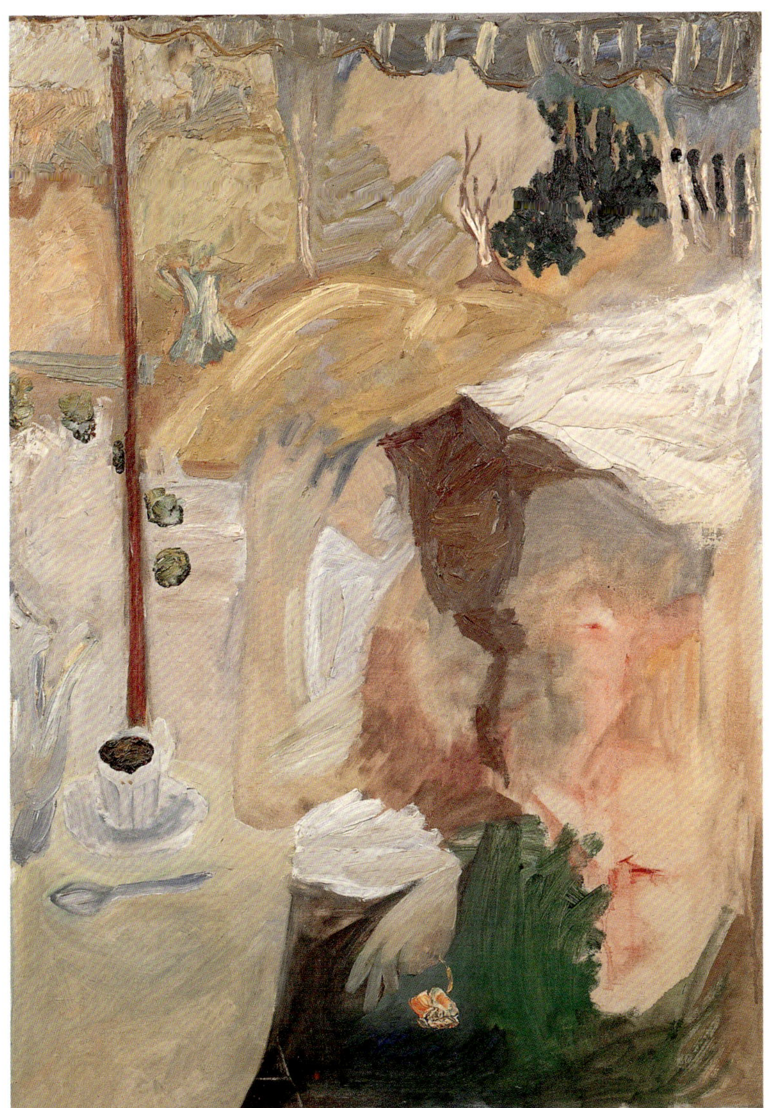

The book takes many forms in shaping Jess's art: literary, linguistic, art-historical, even physical. *The Adam Family In Nesbittland: Imaginary Portrait #18: Helen Adam*, 1958 (fig. 22), is framed by an old wooden door, complete with rusty hinges, which suggests a magnificent binding. The title refers to Elizabeth Nesbitt, author of children's stories set in imaginative landscapes of common household objects. Painted on an old movie screen, the portrait subject is Helen Adam, a Scottish writer and friend who dedicated her mystic ballad *The Queen o' Crow Castle* to Jess. Jess also made a double-sided collage on a cabinet door: *Osap's Fabulous Door*, 1960, is installed cantilevered to the wall so that both sides of its "crackd-Aesop Fables" are legible.

Books are hinged by bindings that allow the pages to turn. And so does Jess want us, his readers, to turn his paintings like pages and read his inscriptions, which almost invariably include evocative quotations. On the back of *Petals of*

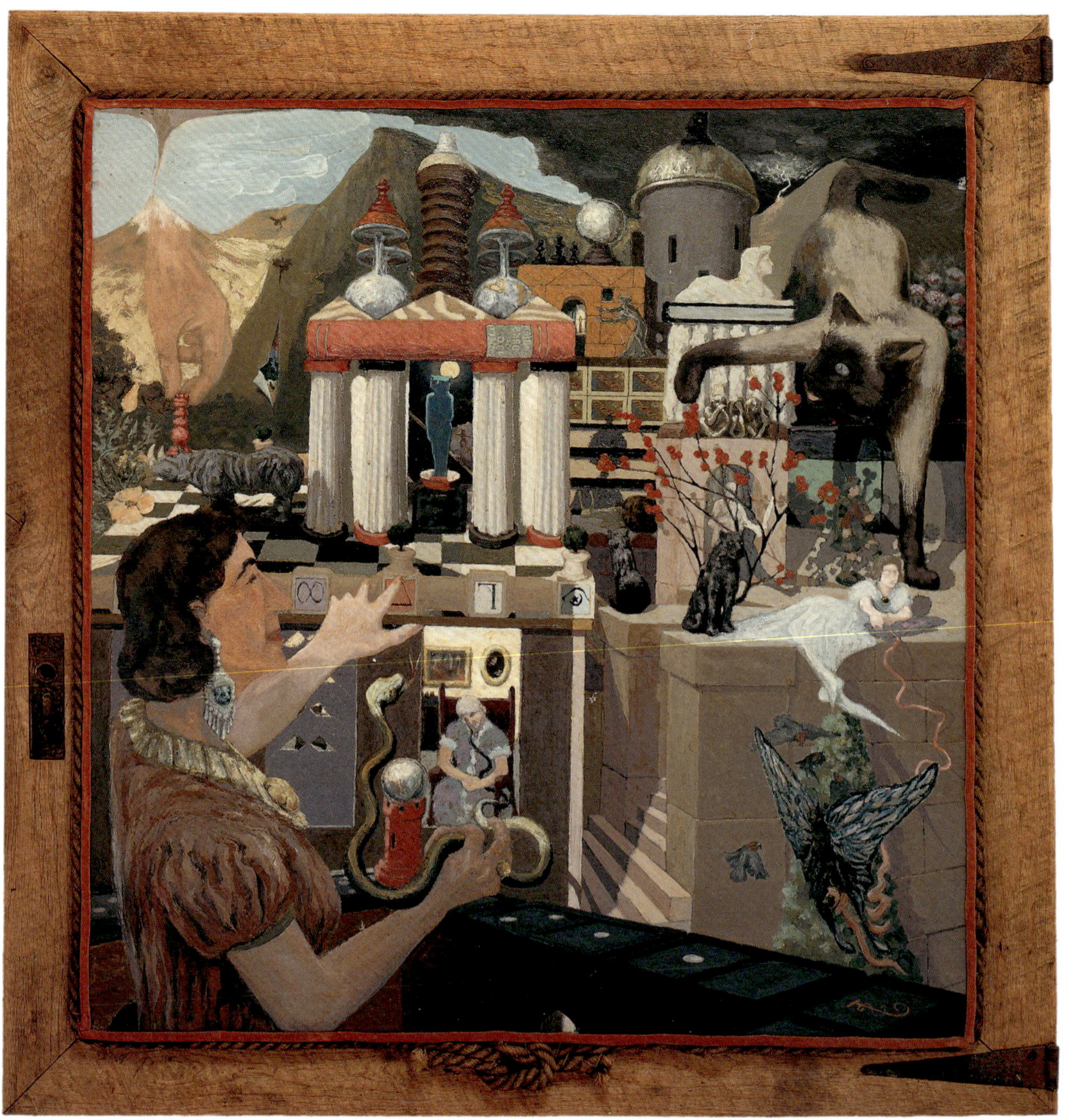

Fig. 22 Jess, *The Adam Family In Nesbittland: Imaginary Portrait #18: Helen Adam*, 1958. Oil on canvas, mounted on wooden door, metal hardware, fabric, and rope, 40 x 38 in. (101.6 x 96.5 cm). Courtesy Odyssia Gallery, New York

Paint, 1964 (fig. 23), for instance, a haiku by the eighteenth-century Japanese poet Kobayashi Issa inflects Jess's thickly painted still life with a quickening sense of time: "Simply trust: / Do not the petals flutter down, / Just like that?" Likewise, turning over a *Translation* is like opening a book. On the back, one finds a photographic reproduction of the very image Jess copied on the front, along with a citation referencing the original source. There is also at least one quote, sometimes more, which may or may not read as immediately relevant to the image at hand. On the backside of *Fig. 3—Ida, Duncan and I: Translation #18*, 1966 (fig. 24), the photograph Jess copied is alongside "The Sea Limits" by Dante Gabriel Rossetti.[20] The verse gives voice to a sublime sense of longing of the sort that gleams dimly from many old snapshots, not least this one, taken by Helen Adam of three friends one day in 1957 underneath the Golden Gate Bridge. As if to embrace that sense of longing—or the fulfillment of nostalgia—

20. The verse reads: "Gather a shell from the strown beach / And listen at its lips: they sigh / The same desire and mystery, / The echo of the whole sea's speech. / And all mankind is thus at heart / Not anything but what thou art: / And Earth, Sea, Man, are all in each."

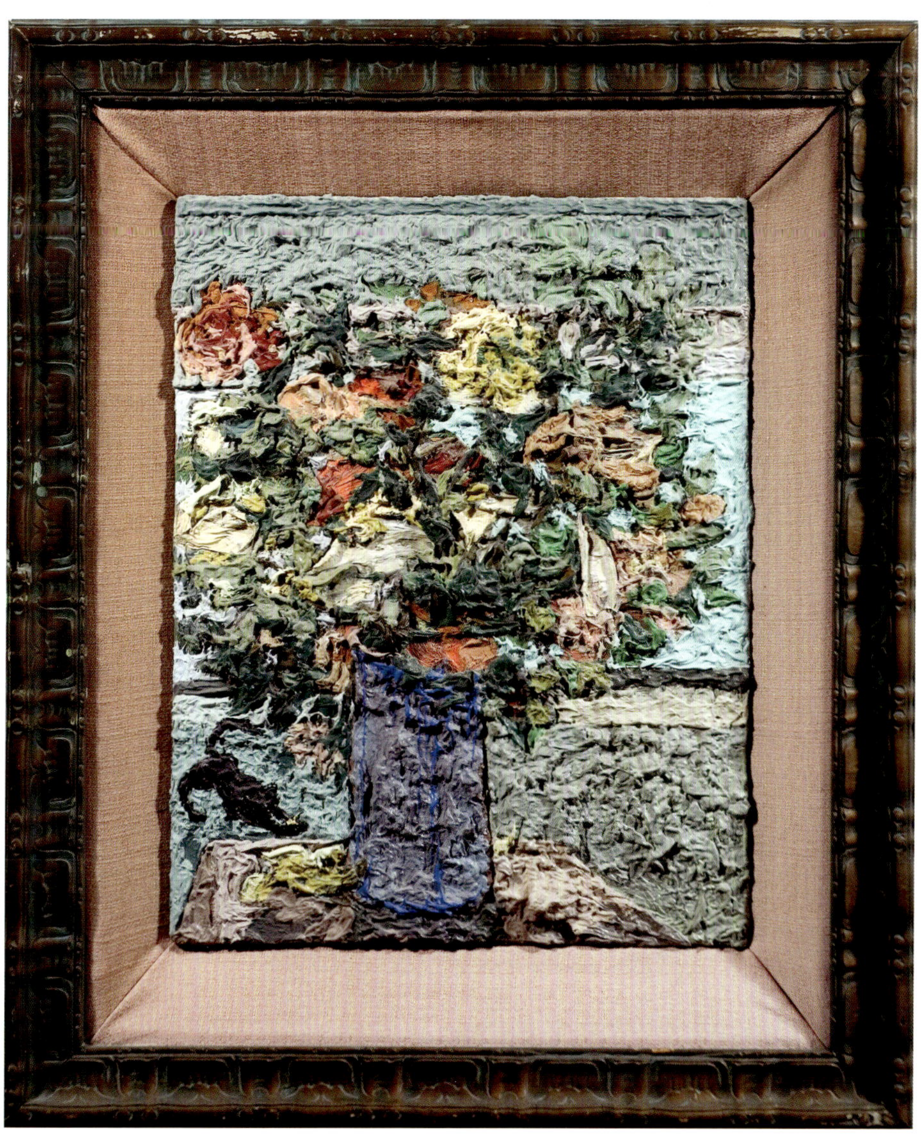

21. Auping, *Jess: Paste-Ups*, p. 14.
22. The composition of *Goddess Because II*, 1956
(fig. 13), for instance, resembles a magic lantern slide
show. Jess collected magic lantern slides from which,
in 1966, he made a group of assemblage objects
in the form of faceted lampshades. He writes to
Duncan about his plans to make them as gifts for the
Herndons and the Bermans, "By that time the supply
of slides will be getting down to the exhausted state,
by selection, that those tatterd Life Magazines were
in Mallorca when I thot . . . all had been done that
the material warranted. So I expect again to be able
to see: just what the 'dull' slides really imaginarily
are." Jess to Duncan, January 1, 1966.

Jess painted a heart-shaped rainbow around the picture. Always minding the
gap between text and image, Jess frequently began the titles of the *Translations*
with "Fig." or "Ex.," as if his paintings were illustrations on a page, "figures" or
"examples" of some larger context beyond the frame. No wonder he said "I've
always thought of the book as a form of collage space."[21] The book gave his art
a means of opening up to the world and enclosing his art within it.

Jess took up picture books of all kinds in his compositions. (Not to mention
picture writing: a series of crayon drawings from 1955 titled the *Mystic Writings*
appear as talismanic hieroglyphs) (see figs. 25, 26). With the comic book comes
a long lineage of picture narratives from which he drew, from the *Egyptian Book
of the Dead* to a whole incunabulum of medieval emblem books and Tarot cards,
from Renaissance chapbooks to Victorian children's books and magic lantern
slide shows.[22] *From Force of Habit*, 1966 (fig. 27), is a ten-page collage book

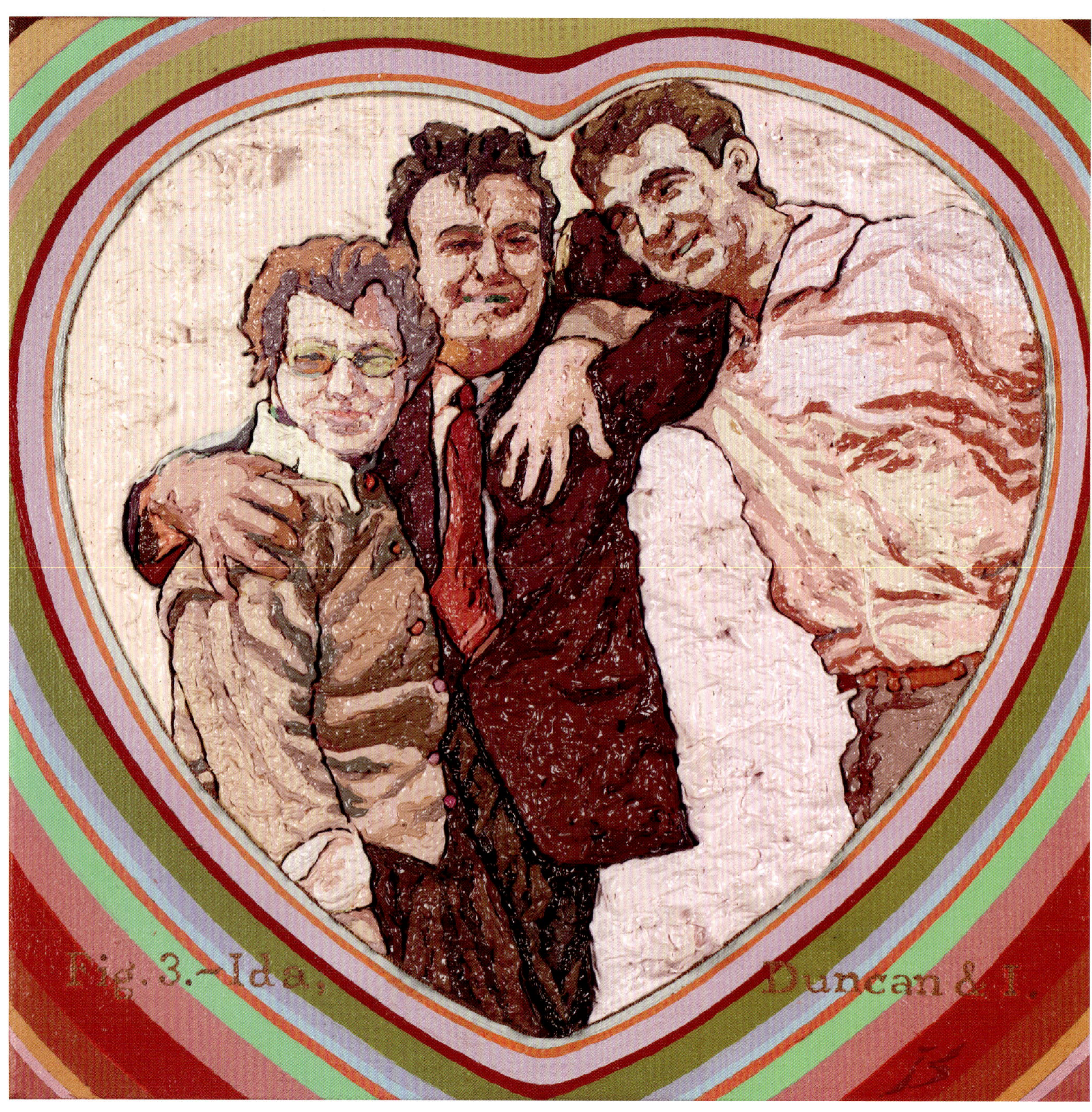

Fig. 24 Jess, *Fig. 3—Ida, Duncan, and I: Translation #18*, 1966. Oil on canvas, 12 x 12 in. (30.5 x 30.5 cm). Courtesy the Pennsylvania Academy of Fine Arts, Philadelphia. Alexander Harrison Fund

(opposite page, top, left to right)
Fig. 25 Jess, *Mystic Writing VIII*, 1955. Wax crayon on paper, 12 1/2 x 11 1/2 in. (31.6 x 29.2 cm). Courtesy Odyssia Gallery, New York

Fig. 26 Jess, *Mystic Writing XII*, 1955. Wax crayon on paper, 11 x 10 3/4 in. (27.9 x 27.3 cm). Courtesy Odyssia Gallery, New York

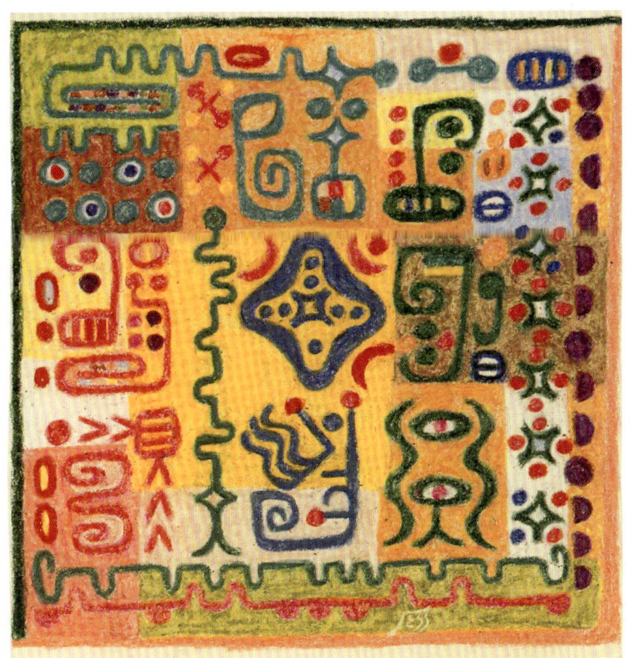

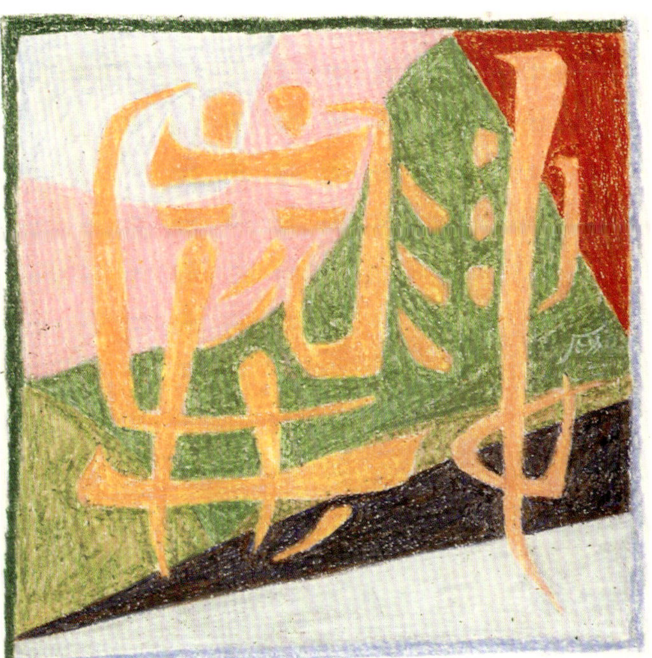

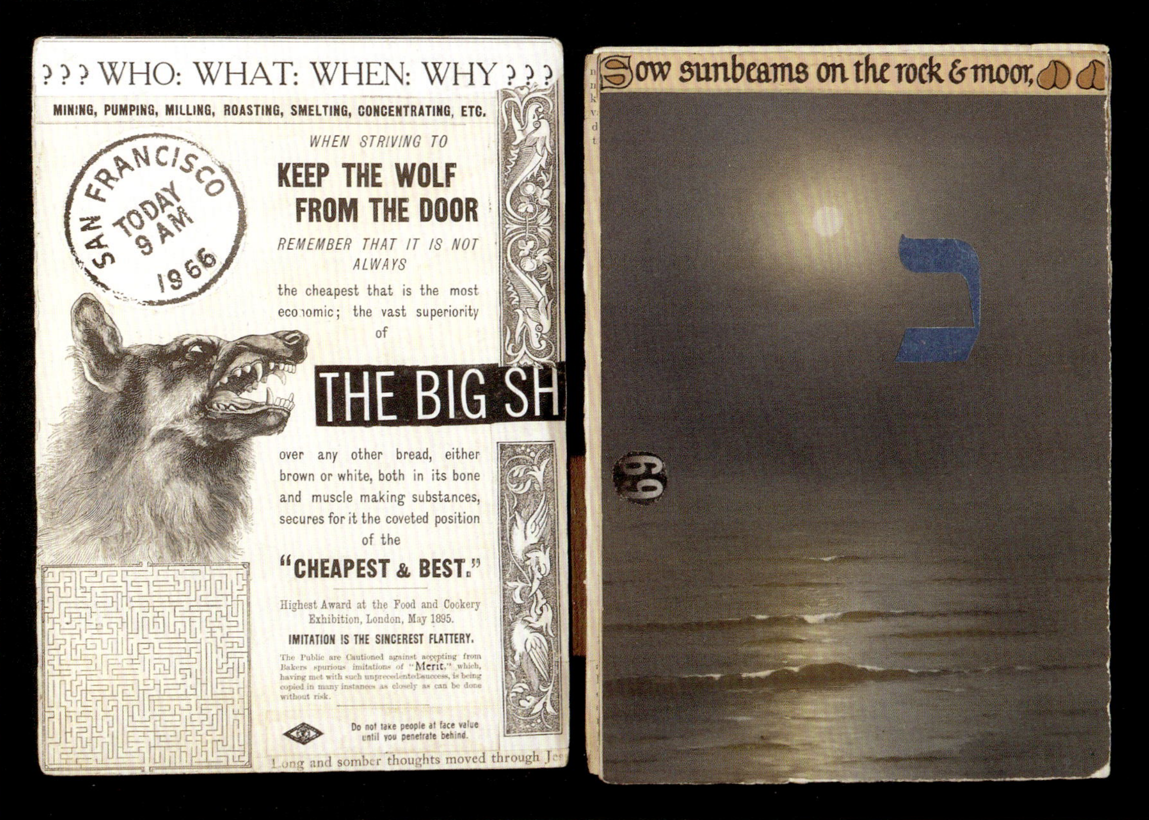

Fig. 27 Jess, *From Force of Habit* (details), 1966.
Collage book, 10 pages, 8 x 5 ³/₄ x ¹/₈ in. (20.3 x
14.6 x .3 cm). Courtesy Odyssia Gallery, New York

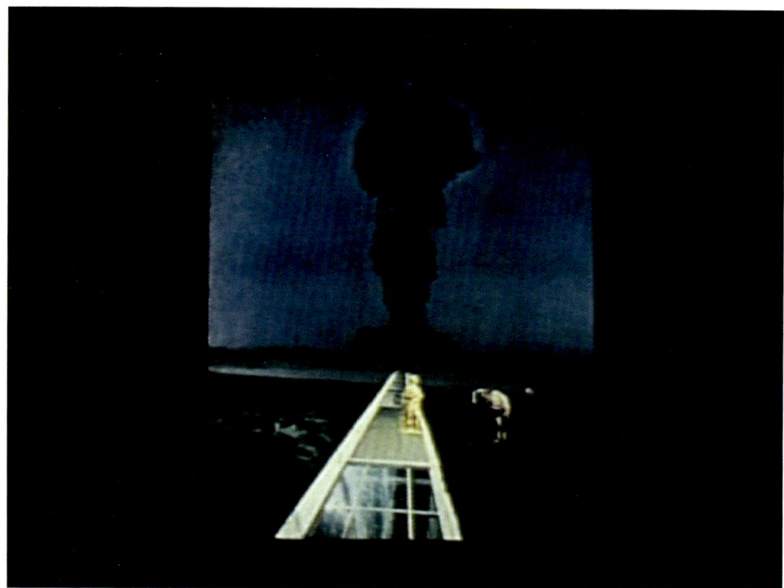

housed in the leather binding of a wallet-size edition of *The Little Webster's Dictionary*. Two major series are based on the old-fashioned nickelodeon, a coin-operated, mechanical flipbook and early form of animation.[23] Jess's first *Didactic Nickelodeon* is a short film that he made in collaboration with the experimental filmmaker Lawrence Jordan, whose collage animations would make him one of the leading figures of the New American Cinema.[24] The collaboration began in 1956 with the filming of a collage suite that Jess had made the previous year (fig. 28).[25] Forty-one images appear in brisk sequence, each accompanied by a corresponding burst of sound or music. When the picture changes, you can practically hear the phonograph needle drop onto a new record. About midway through, the voice of James Joyce pipes up from a folkloric figure (the Irish legend Finn McCool?), who quips, "Well, you know or don't you kennet or haven't I told you every telling has a taling and that's the he and the she of it."[26] Flip to an underwater library awash in orchestral strains. Flip to a mushroom cloud pierced by spook-house screams. Flip to a fiery sunset under a thunder of applause. Finis. True to its multiple and disparate scenes, the film bears a number of alternative titles, each casting a somewhat different mood about the storyline.[27] One title, *The 40 and 1 Nights*, offers an entertainment in the frame-tale style of Scheherazade. Named after a process in plutonium production, *Heavy Water* knells apocalyptic. A hybrid of both titles, *Didactic Nickelodeon* conjures one of the classic works of didactic literature, Dante's *Inferno*, by conflating the sense of moral purpose and poetic fantasy that are undercurrents throughout Jess's art.

The tone gets even heavier in *Jess's Didactic Nickelodeon, Series Two, "The Guardian Angel's Guidebook"*, 1955 (fig. 29), a collage book of an anticipated forty-two works, though Jess suspended production after number thirty-seven, pending finding a publisher. Based on Sir Charles Sherrington's *Man on His Nature*, this series of collages translates a visionary story of how the body draws

23. At the time, Jess seemed generally interested in the mechanical possibilities of collage. In letters to Duncan, he mentions working on an assemblage object that he referred to as his "political machine." He writes, "Robin [Blaser] was over last night to launch my political machine's first 'public' working. . . . [It] works wondrously well in its rickety way, playing a one-revolution march step of slightly indeterminate measure and lilt, on bell, cymbal, rasp, thwock and clock." Jess to Duncan, May 31, 1962. Around the same time, he was also experimenting with a camera to make what he referred to as "illustrational projections." Jess to Duncan, January 4, 1963.

24. Lawrence Jordan attributed his beginnings in collage to Jess, who was, in turn, intrigued by Jordan's experiments with film. (In his letters to Duncan, Jess mentions several evenings' entertainments at the Jordan household.) Jordan says they jointly conceived the idea of making a nickelodeon style film. (In conversation with the author, August 25, 2006.) Jess contributed to another work by Jordan, *Finds of the Fortenight* (1980), contributing the lyrical title boards that appear throughout this densely layered collage film.

25. This was not Jess's only foray into experimental filmmaking. He stars in Stan Brakhage's *In Between* (1955), a cross between a trance film and a home movie that ends with Jess awakening from his *Little Nemo*–like adventures in a dreamland at home in bed with a book open upon his chest. Filmed in Jess and Duncan's apartment, it offers glimpses into their distinct domestic environment, with its brilliantly colored walls, bric-a-brac, and beloved pet cats, Princess Pumpkin and Kitkat. Duncan makes a brief appearance. John Cage contributed the musical score for prepared piano. Jess created glittering title boards, one of which credits "Idols by Miriam Hoffman," for the hieratic sculpted heads by the California ceramicist whose work Jess and Duncan collected.

26. Thanks to Michael Basinski, curator of The Poetry Collection, State University of New York at Buffalo, who informs me that Duncan and Jess owned a recording of James Joyce reading from *Finnegans Wake*.

27. Labeled by Jess, the canister of the copy of the film held at SUNY Buffalo reads: "HEAVY WATER or THE 40 & 1 NIGHTS or JESS'S DIDACTIC NICKELODEON, by Jess 1955. 16mm print: put on film by LARRY JORDAN 1956—soundtrack from a collage magnetic tape by JESS 1962."

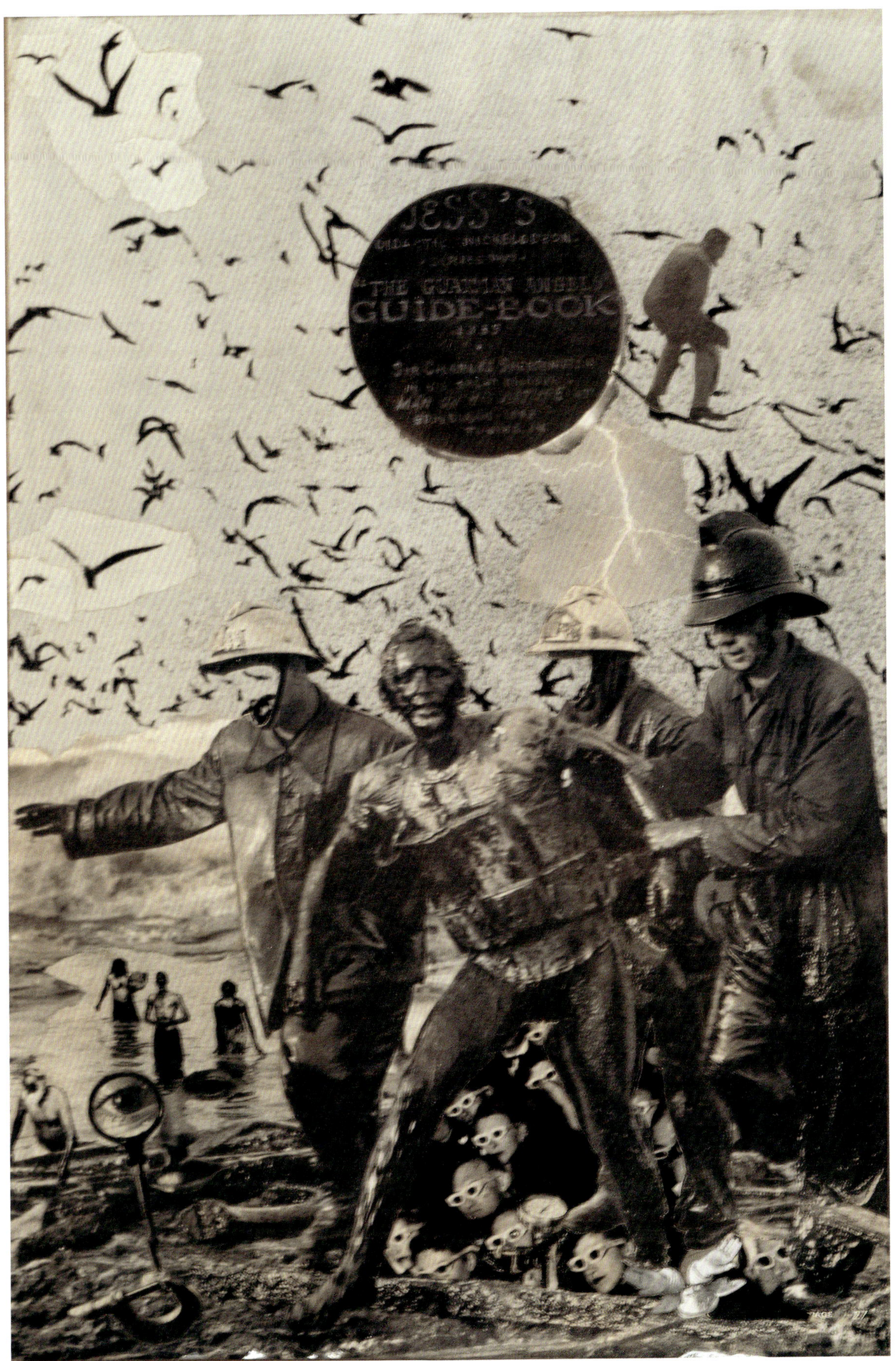
JESS'S
"THE GUARDIAN ANGEL"
GUIDE-BOOK

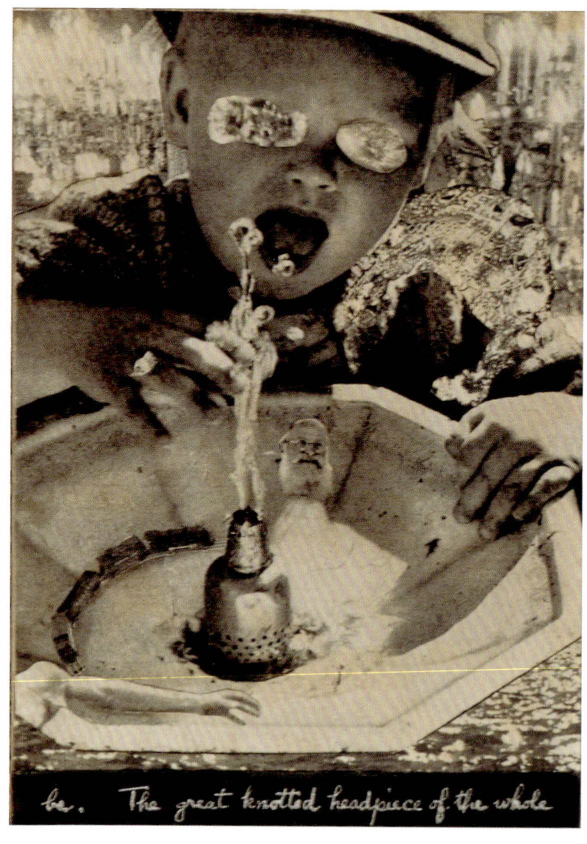
be.   The great knotted headpiece of the whole

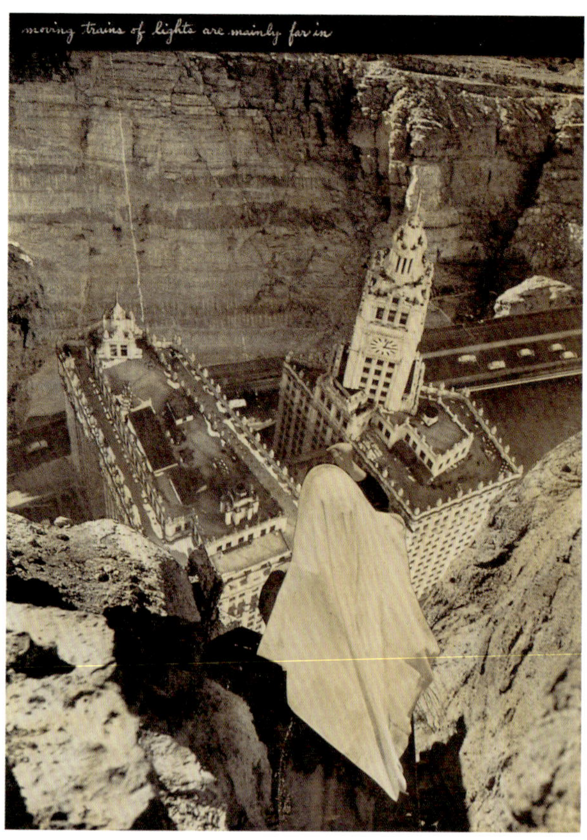
moving trains of lights are mainly far in

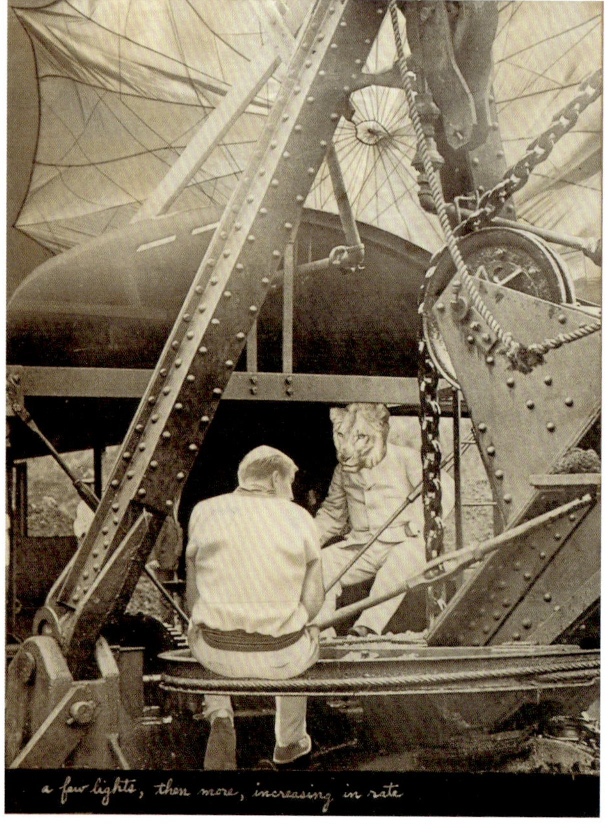
a few lights, then more, increasing in rate

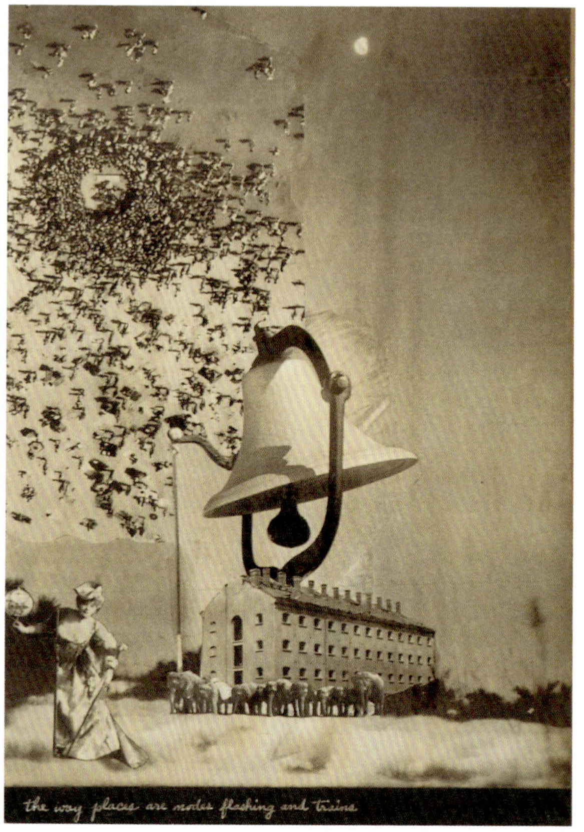
the way places are nodes flashing and trains

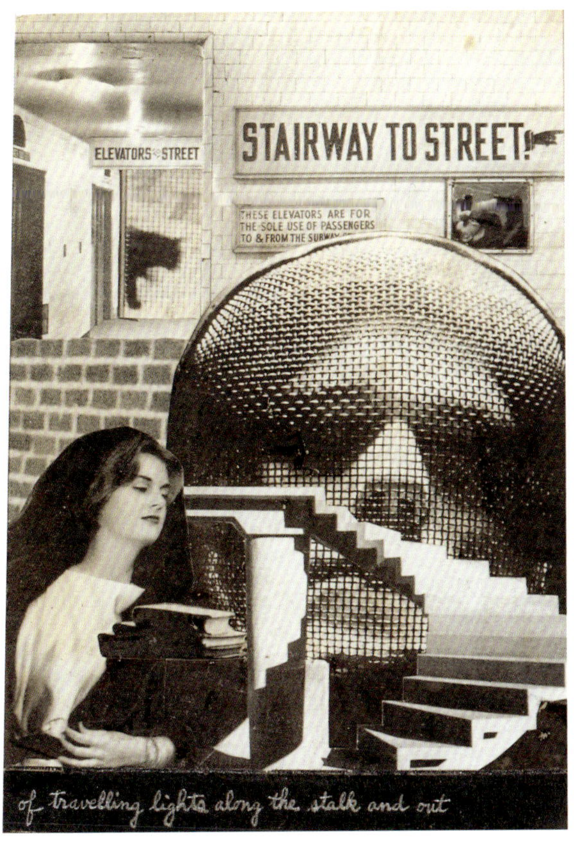

of travelling lights along the stalk and out

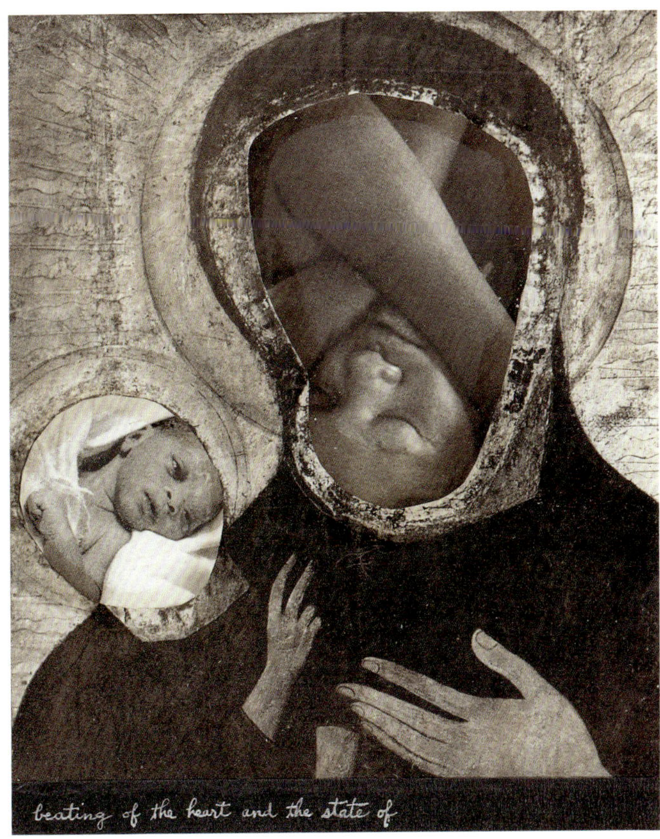

beating of the heart and the state of

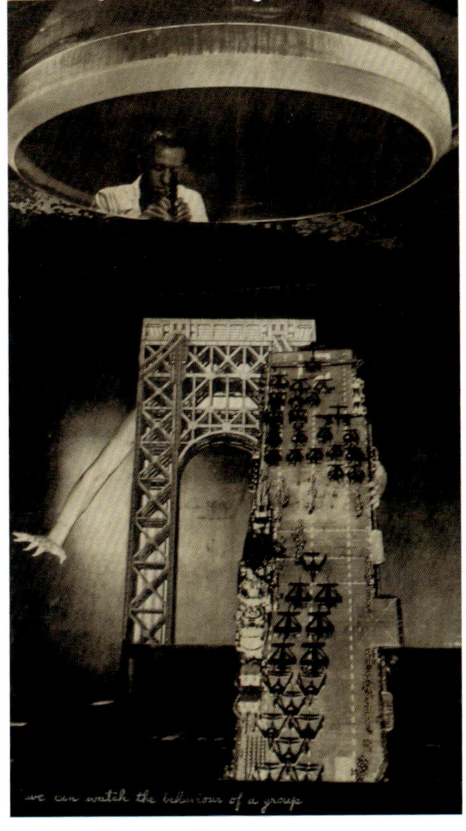

we can watch the behaviour of a group

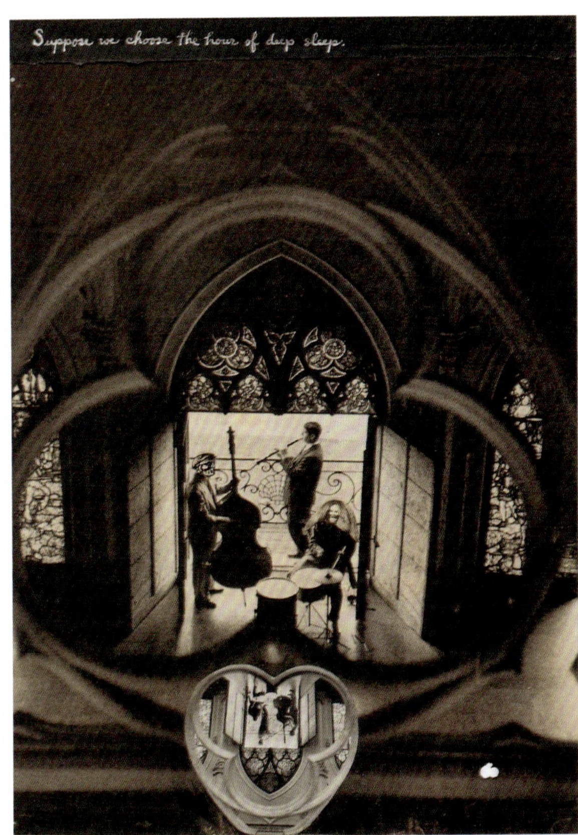

Suppose we choose the hour of deep sleep.

breath into a parable of nuclear holocaust. "Suppose we choose the hour of deep sleep," it begins on a peaceful enough note, only to be followed by blasts, planes, scattering nuns, a baby doll pitched into a crowd, and an overall sense of the world as we know it being swept away before our eyes. Sherrington wrote his book in 1932, the same year he was awarded a Nobel Prize in physiology, and it's easy to imagine Jess's interest beyond this particular text. Sherrington's con-ceptualization of the nervous system—as neuron fragments linked by synapses of the imagination into an integrated system of reflex arcs and stream-of-conscious associations—might also narrate a physiology of collage.

Another collage book that opens onto many of the literary aspects of Jess's art is *O!*, published in 1960 by the poet Jerome Rothenberg's Hawk's Well Press with a "Pre-face" by Robert Duncan (fig. 31).[28] The central element of this sixteen-page chapbook of miscellany by Jess is "That Sly Old Gobbler, or The Orange." A picture story appropriated from the writings of one Florence B. Hallowell, it is a Victorian cautionary against ingesting orange pips. As juiced by Jess into dreamy sections—"to swallow the seeds, Ida made a little hole in the or-"—it becomes a very sly picture story of O.[29] It also cuts nicely to one of the great collage books of all time: Max Ernst's *Une semaine de bonté* of 1934 (fig. 30).

In 1952 Duncan gave a copy of *Une semaine de bonté* as a gift to Jess. In a "Chronology of Pasting-up" that he later composed, Jess dedicates the entire year to *absorb*ing this "week of kindnesses."[30] Ernst's Surrealist novel in collage first appeared as five separately published pamphlets, each prefaced by a fragment of Dada or Surrealist writing. Very Victorian in feeling, the collages are composed from wood engravings cut from French pulp fiction, scientific journals, anatomy books, and advertisements. The book reads like a suspense story of the unconscious. Each page is packed with the potential for some erotic, bizarre, violent, or funny episode to continue to unfold. The pages turn from one deeply fraught image to the next. Everything and nothing is on the verge of happening in Ernst's swirling dramas, which might simply reflect the drama of collage itself.[31]

O! invokes what might be considered another collage book—*Finnegans Wake*. On one of the last pages of *O!*, Jess's poem "This Is the Box Pandora Shook" is laid out so that the final word ("voice") trails off the page. The poem thus seems to end with: "This is the shake that stopped the . . ." It is a meaningful deception, one that pays direct homage to James Joyce's last great work. In 1944 Jess mail-ordered a copy of *Finnegans Wake* signed by the author, who, had he still been alive, might have granted Jess most-favored reader status.[32] Joyce famously said, "The only demand I make of my reader is that he should devote his whole life to reading my works." *Finnegans Wake* lends itself to just such a task. Ending with the word "the," it sends the reader back to the first word of the book, "Riverrun."

Throughout his life Jess followed Joyce's imperative to read and reread *Finnegans Wake*, plunging into the rushing depths of a book that unlike Ernst's *Une semaine de bonté*, he would never fully "absorb." Like all of Joyce's writings, this one is full of experiments with language—puns, spoonerisms, word play,

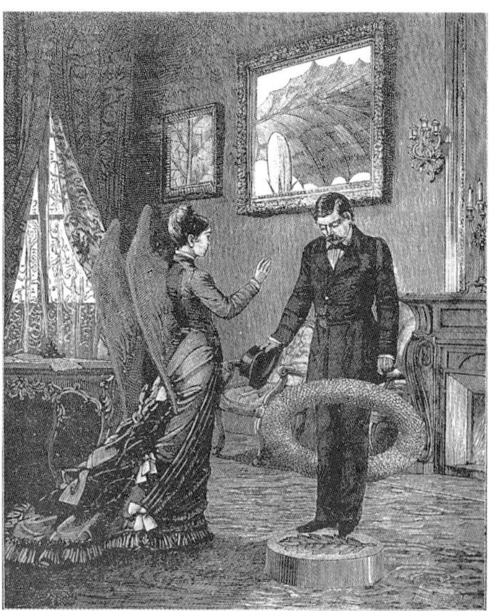

Fig. 30 Max Ernst, *Une semaine de bonté* (detail), 1934. Photomechanical reproduction, 11 ½ x 8 ⅝ in. (29 x 22 cm)

28. Plans to feature a four-page *Tricky Cad* case in *O!* (perhaps the very one in this exhibition) were quashed when Jess wrote for permission from *Dick Tracy*'s creator, Chester Gould, and was threatened with a lawsuit. As Jess later referred to the incident: "Here was a bad case of sincerest-form-of-flattery; later, not amusing to the originator." Jess, "A Tricky Cad," in John Russell and Suzi Gablik, eds., *Pop Art Redefined* (New York: Praeger Publishers, 1969), p. 61.
29. Whether or not Jess is riffing on Pauline Réage's 1954 erotic classic *Histoire d'O* (not published in English until 1965) is maybe too literal a question with regard to *O!*
30. Jess writes: "1952 Absorbs Ernst's *Une semaine de bonté*." *Jess: Paste-Ups*, exh. cat. (Museum of Contemporary Art, Chicago, 1972). Ernst's work had a similar impact on Joseph Cornell when he saw it for the first time in 1931 at the Julien Levy Gallery in New York. Lawrence Jordan also speaks of the importance of Ernst for his films.
31. In a 1937 essay titled "Beyond Painting," Ernst called collage "something like the alchemy of the visual image," capturing the essence of a modern form of representation that shows (golden) meaning to be as elusive as the principle of the Philosopher's Stone.
32. Joyce died in 1941, two years after the publication of *Finnegans Wake*. A recent exhibition at the Royal Hibernian Academy, Dublin, looked at the impact his writing has had on art, including Jess's. See the accompanying book: Christa-Maria Lerm Hayes, *Visual Art Inspired by James Joyce* (Dublin: Lilliput Press, 2004).

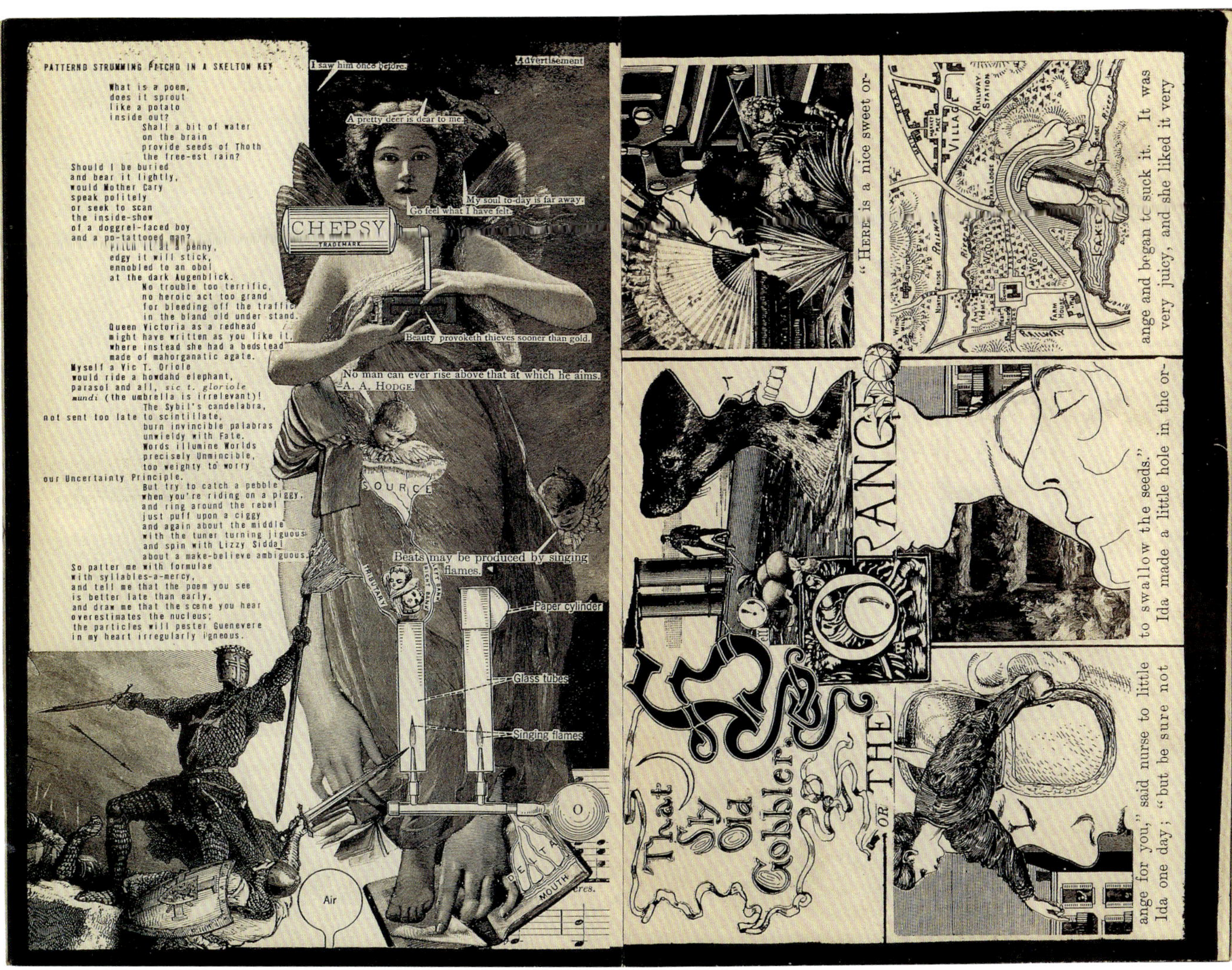

Fig. 31 Jess, *O!* (spread detail), 1960. Book bound in paper and stapled, 16 pages, 8 1/4 x 5 1/4 in. (21 x 13.3 cm). Collection of Jerome and Diane Rothenberg, Encinitas, California

streams of conscious, dropped in quotations, foreign words, and colloquialisms. These experiments all find equivalencies within collage, and might be seen to inform the grammar of Jess's art, which was not only structurally but narratively shaped by his habitual rereading of Joyce. The story of *Finnegans Wake* tells of a family's dreams and nightmares as they sleep through the course of one night. Freud meets Ovid, and characters metamorphose into rocks, plants, and animals. Meanwhile, the book churns through the epic cycles of divine, heroic, and human history—cycles that end in a period of flux, only to resume and continue, one presumes, throughout all of time. Turn anywhere in Jess's work—from his fumy *Romantic* paintings and babbling poetry to his most cataclysmic paste-ups—and you can find some point of correspondence with *Finnegans Wake*. Not only because of the book's vastness, which could ostensibly accommodate me typing and you reading these words right now. But because of the notion of flux, out of which both Jess and Joyce found a means of translating the trash and myth of modern life into art.

Into Print

Jess's art is at its most bookish in the substantial body of work he created for reproduction. Integral to the total conception of his work—its movement to and from the printed page—these works include original paste-ups and drawings, the various forms of printed matter they engendered, and collaborations with writers. Jess's contributions to others' books were never subordinate to a given text, so the word "illustration" seems inadequate to describe them. Regarding his cover for Joe Dunn's *The Better Dream House* (fig. 32), the credit reads: "reflected by Jess," much better representing the sense of creative communion in Jess's process, which always started with some personal connection.

A prime collaborative example is Jess's friendship and work with poet, painter, and translator Norma Cole. After he read her manuscript for *Mars*, he expressed a desire to make a cover for the book, which the poet Steve Dickison subsequently offered to publish.[33] Only after the trim size had been determined did Jess start work on the collage; he needed to work in direct translation.

33. Steve Dickison says that he had never published anything before *Mars* and established the Listening Chamber imprint specifically to do, in part for the opportunity to work with Jess, whose literary milieu was the subject of an exhibition Dickison organized in 2005: *Poetry and Its Arts: Bay Area Interactions 1954–2000*, at the California Historical Society, San Francisco. Norma Cole participated as a poet-in-residence, working and receiving visitors to the exhibition in a living-room tableaux styled in honor of Duncan and Jess. In conversation with the author, October 30, 2006.

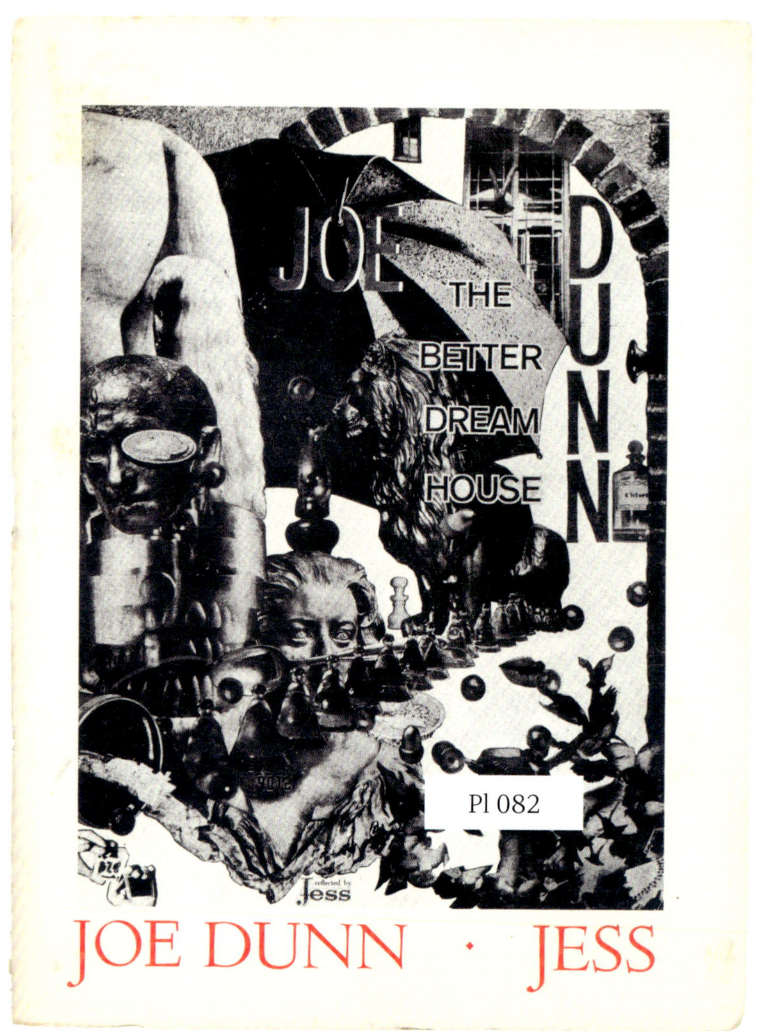

Fig. 32 Joe Dunn, *The Better Dream House*, 1968. Book with cover by Jess, bound in paper wrappers, 36 pages. 9 1/4 x 6 3/4 in. (23.5 x 17.1 cm). The Poetry Collection, State University of New York at Buffalo

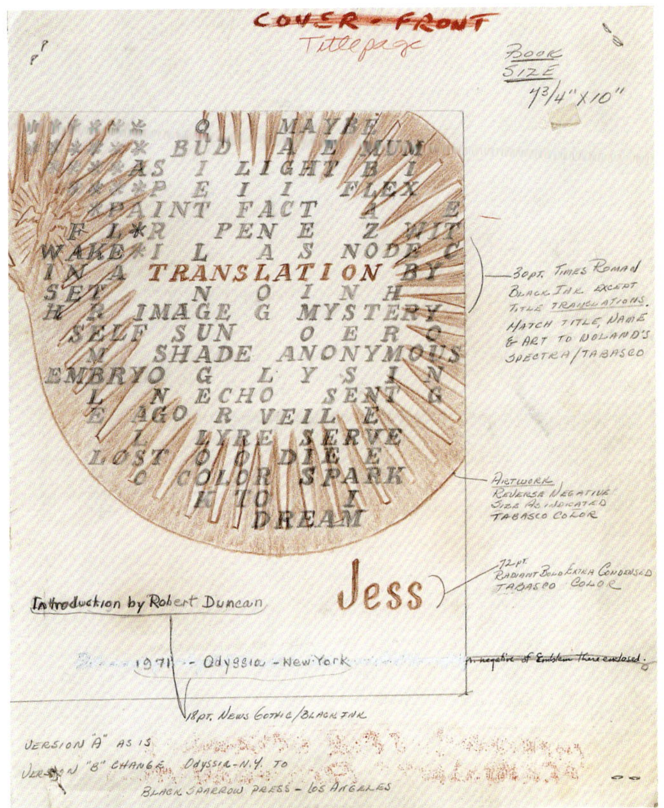
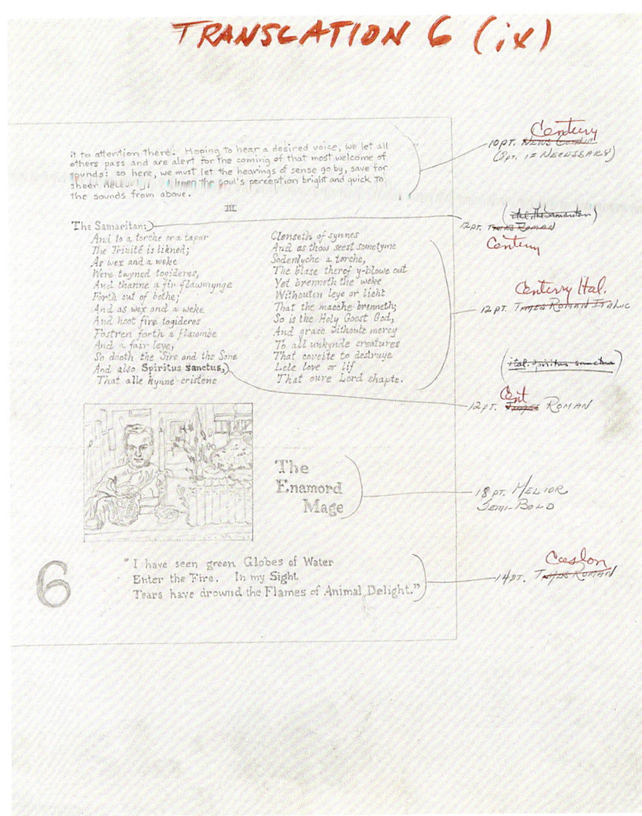

Fig. 33 Jess, *Imaginary Dummy of the Catalogue for "Translations by Jess"* (details), 1969–71. Catalogue proof with handwritten notations and inset letter, 45 pages, 14 x 11 ½ x ½ in. (35.6 x 29.2 x 1.3 cm). Courtesy Odyssia Gallery, New York

34. Jess created these exacting facsimiles for a number of his books, two of which are in the collection of The Poetry Center, those for *A Book of Resemblances* and *The Cat and the Blackbird*. 35. Cole, in conversation with the author, October 30, 2006.

Jess's comprehension of the language of reproduction ran deep. The word "paste-up" in fact comes from graphic design, where it refers to the original artwork that goes to press. Jess's attention to this process is most spectacularly displayed in a mockup he made for one of his catalogues (fig. 33). Each page, including all of the text and reproductions, is laid out, hand-lettered, and drawn in pencil.[34] Jess titled the object as a discrete work—*Imaginary Dummy of the Catalogue for "Translations by Jess"*—as if it were a holograph, a manuscript handwritten in its entirety by the author. Indeed, it's nothing less than an illuminated manuscript for an age of mechanical reproduction.

Bookcover for Norma Cole (Mars), 1993 (figs. 35, 36), developed over months as Jess sifted through his archives for images that would be almost magnetically drawn to the text. Cole recalls, "I had at first asked Jess if the title could appear, as I had imagined it, in all capital letters? Of course that's not the way it turned out. And I swallowed my words! Because we talked about the cover at every point and I was fascinated by his decisions."[35] Dickison points to one line from Cole's poem "Saturn" that appears quite literally in Jess's collage: "The baby sat on the edge of a skull as it must." Describing this illustrative moment as an exception to the overall relationship Jess sought to construct with Cole's work, he notes, "Moving from an impression of the written work to a translation, a visual work to enclose it, Jess would never just hand a poet something and say,

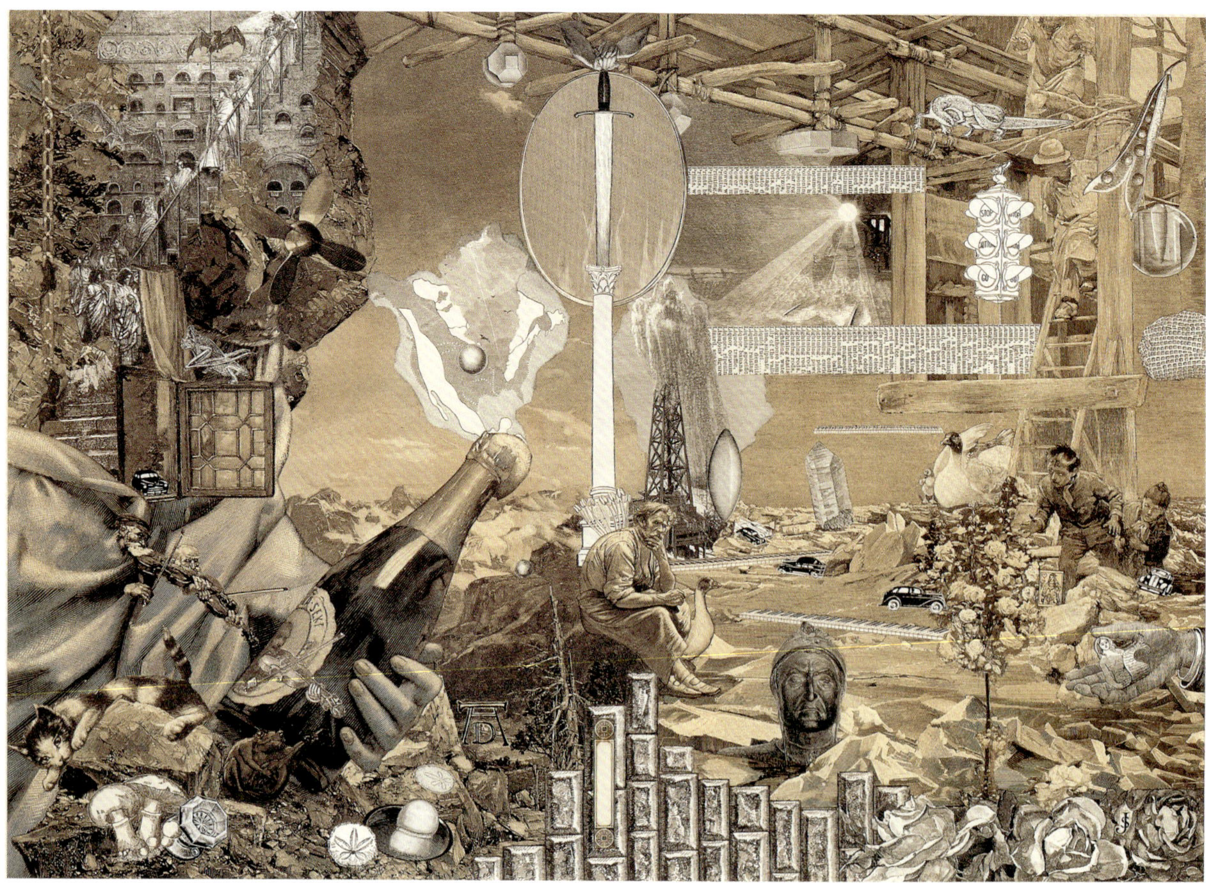

Fig. 34 Jess, *Cover for The Mutabilities*, 1975.
Collage, 22 x 24 3/8 in. (55.9 x 62 cm).
The JPMorgan Chase Art Collection

'okay, use this.' He honored a writer with his invention, his conjuration, with this one bit of intense focused attention caught. An echo."[36] This is why Jess's art for reproduction stands as art in its own right. No mere flatwork, the collage made to wrap around *Mars* is like an anatomy of a book: flayed open, its front and back covers are like skin held together by a spine. The sense of semiotic and structural encapsulation of the book also holds true for Jess's covers for Michael Davidson (*The Mutabilities & the Foul Papers*; fig. 34) and Lynn Lonidier (*A Lesbian Estate: Poems 1970– 1973*; fig. 81). The single assemblage object in this exhibition, *Poet's Coffeepot*, 1963 (fig. 37), stands in tribute to all such strong collaborations.

Jess's cover for Norma Cole comes late in a long history of working with poets and writers. After 1964, when Jess's focus turned to the *Translations*, he literally wore a pair of blinders to strengthen his already amazing powers of concentration in the studio. Prior to that, however, was an intensely productive period of collaborations, conducted largely within the circle of New American Poets who were at that very moment establishing an avant-garde tradition.[37] That this period coincides with Jess's development into a mature artist yields yet another fundamentally bookish aspect to his work. His very taste for printed matter was part of a

36. Dickison, in conversation with the author, August 27, 2006.
37. In 1960 Grove Press published *The New American Poetry, 1945–1960* as an avant-garde alternative to the 1957 *New Poets of England and America*. Edited by Donald M. Allen, the anthology is divided into sections that designate the various milieus of the period: Black Mountain, San Francisco Renaissance, Beat Generation, and New York Poets.

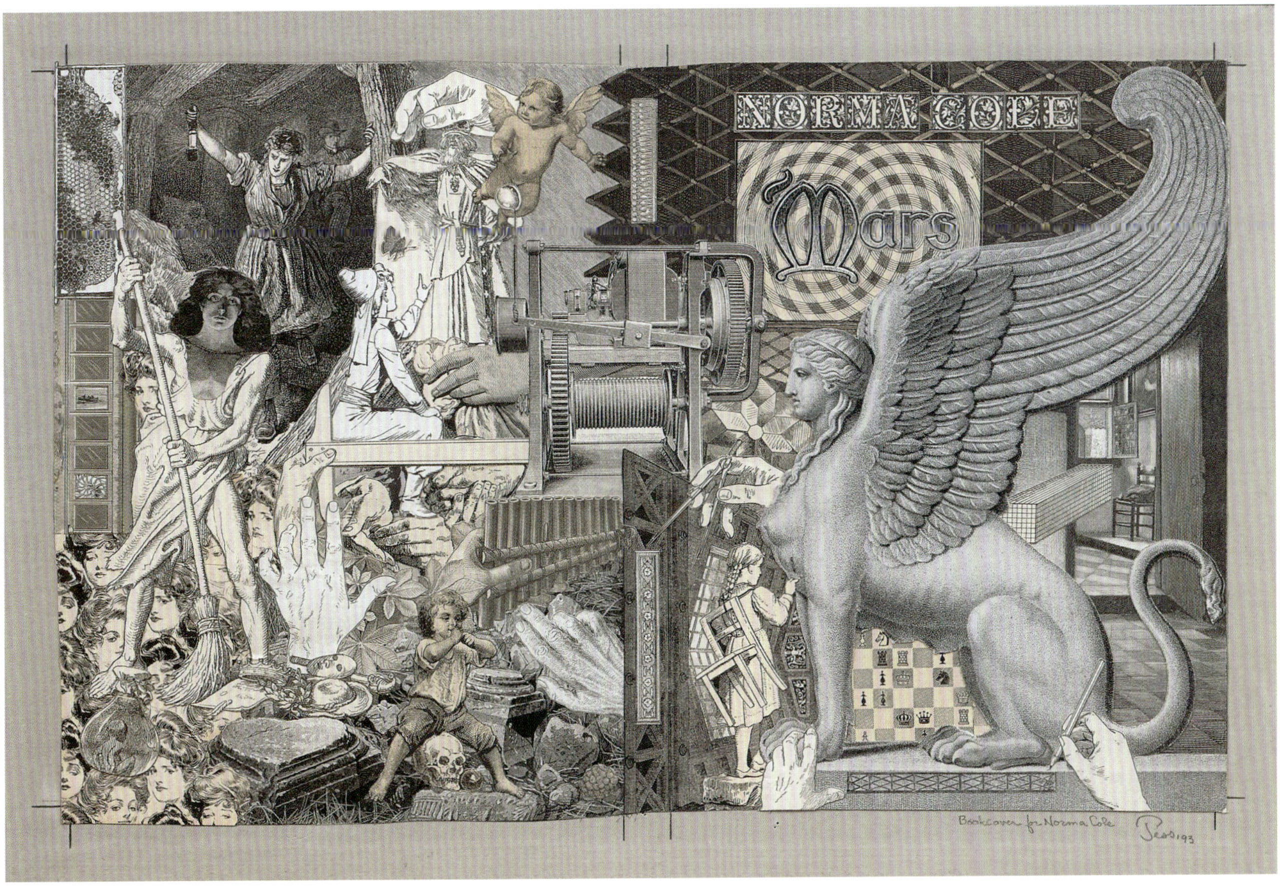

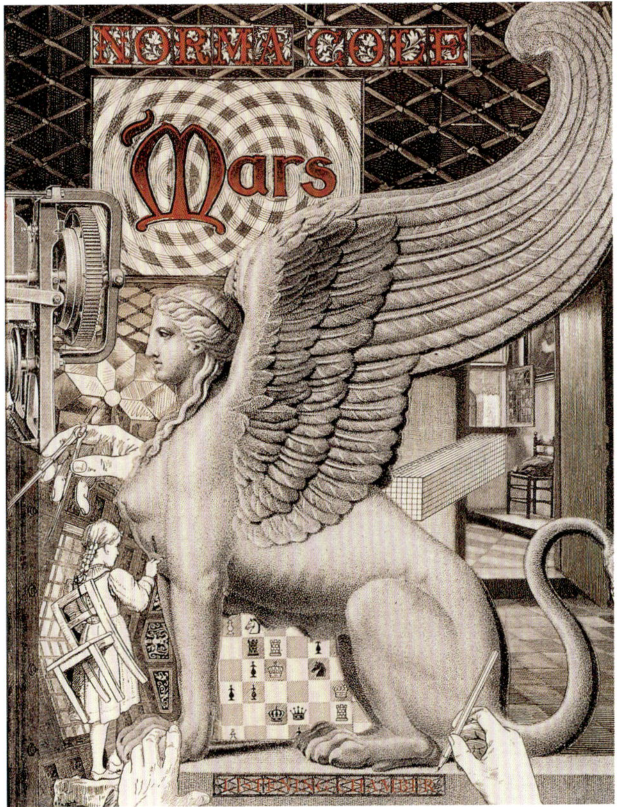

Fig. 35 Jess, *Bookcover for Norma Cole (Mars)*, 1993. Collage, 8 ¼ x 12 ¾ in. (21 x 32.4 cm). Collection of Richard Harris

Fig. 36 Norma Cole, *Mars*, 1994. Perfect-bound book with cover by Jess, 120 pages. 8 x 6 in. (20.3 x 15.2 cm). Collection of Steve Dickison

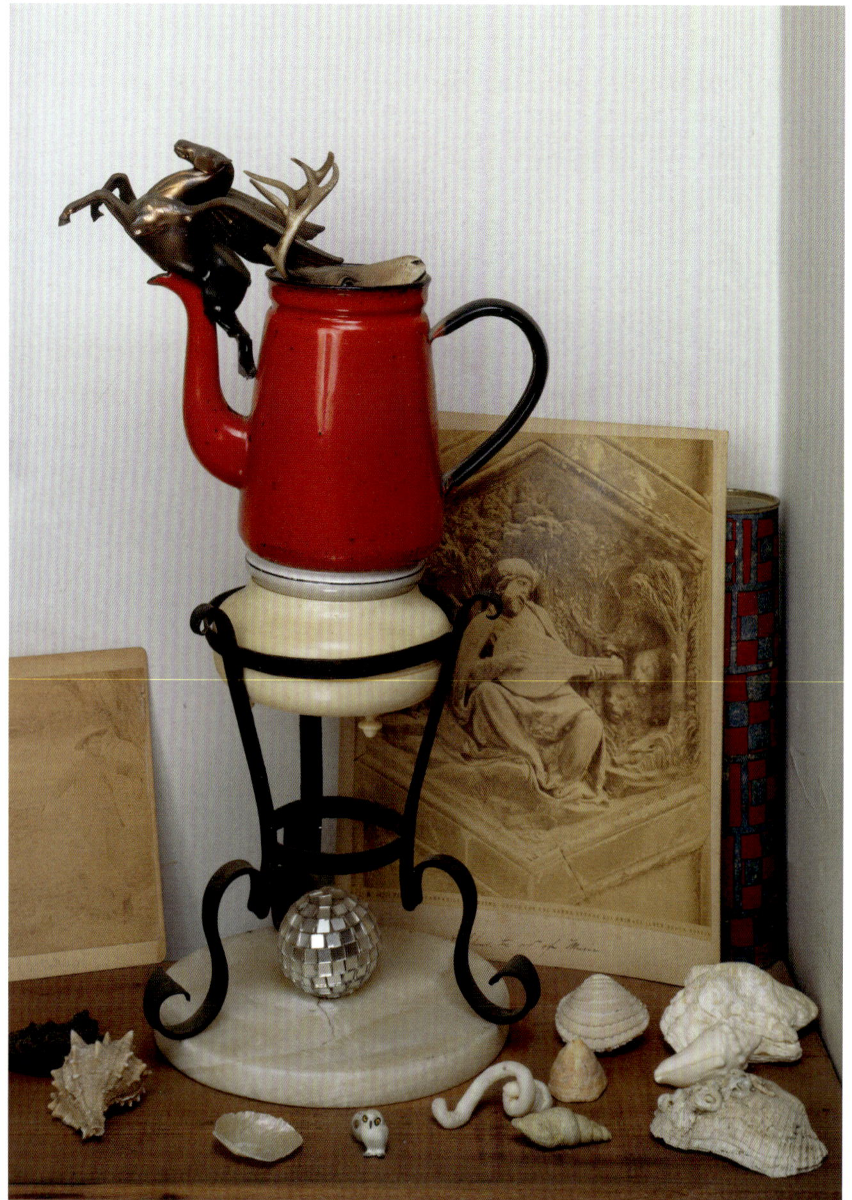

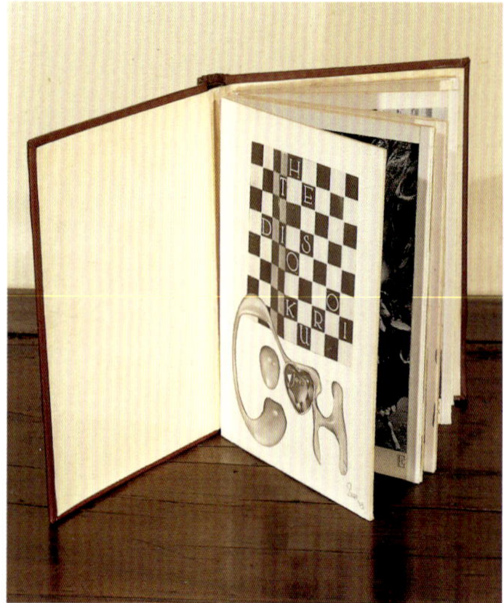

Fig. 37 Jess, *Poet's Coffeepot*, 1963. Assemblage, 17 1/2 x 6 x 6 in. (44.5 x 15.2 x 15.2 cm). Collection of Robert Glück, San Francisco

Fig. 38 Jess, *The Dios Kuroi*, 1963. Collage book, 9 pages, 9 1/2 x 6 1/2 in. (24.1 x 16.5 cm). Los Angeles County Museum of Art, Prints and Drawings Deaccession Fund

larger cultural phenomenon. An effusion of hand presses, mimeograph machines, cheap offset printers, and letter presses was putting publishing directly into the hands of artists and poets—and creating a first florescence of today's 'zine and blog cultures.

Jess's art was imprinted widely across this new wave in publishing. A paste-up poem appears in a 1954 issue of *Black Mountain Review* (fig. 70), edited by paranoiac portrait sitter Robert Creeley. "From 1957," Jess writes in one of his auto-chronologies, "the publications of White Rabbit Press stimulated his activity as an illustrator of poetry."[38] (The press's bunny colophon, drawn by Robert Duncan, takes refuge in Jess's collage *The Fox Hunt Is Over*, 1959 [fig. 75]).

38. Jess, "Biography," in *Jess*, exh. cat. (New York: Odyssia Gallery; and San Francisco: John Berggruen Gallery, 1989), n.p.

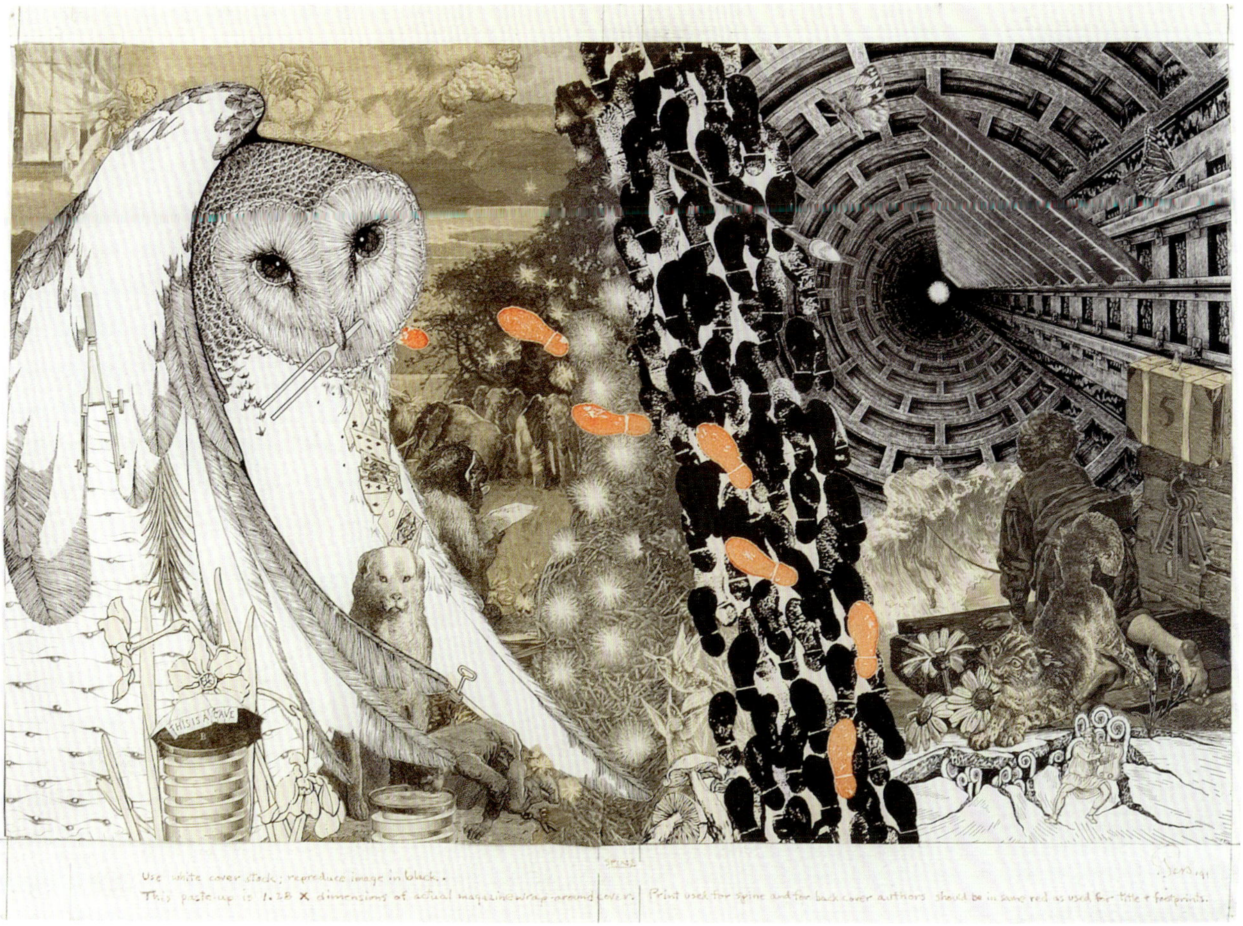

Fig. 39 Jess, *Cover for o·blēk*, 1991. Collage,
10 ¹/₂ x 14 ¹/₂ in. (26.7 x 36.8 cm). Collection
of Laree Hulshoff

Fig. 40 Peter Gizzi and Connell McGrath,
editors, *o·blēk: A Journal of Language Arts*, Fall
1991. Journal with cover by Jess, subscription
card laid in, 212 pages. 7 ¹/₂ x 5 ¹/₂ in. (19.1 x 14
cm). Collection of Dodie Bellamy and Kevin
Killian, San Francisco

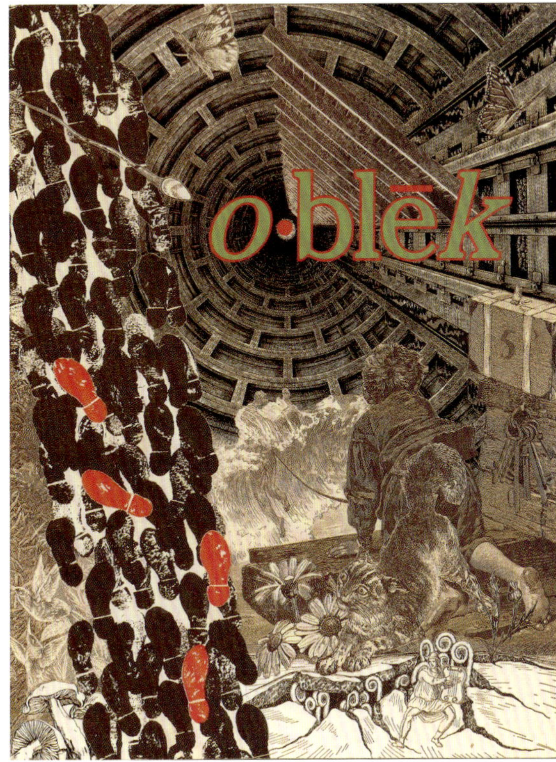

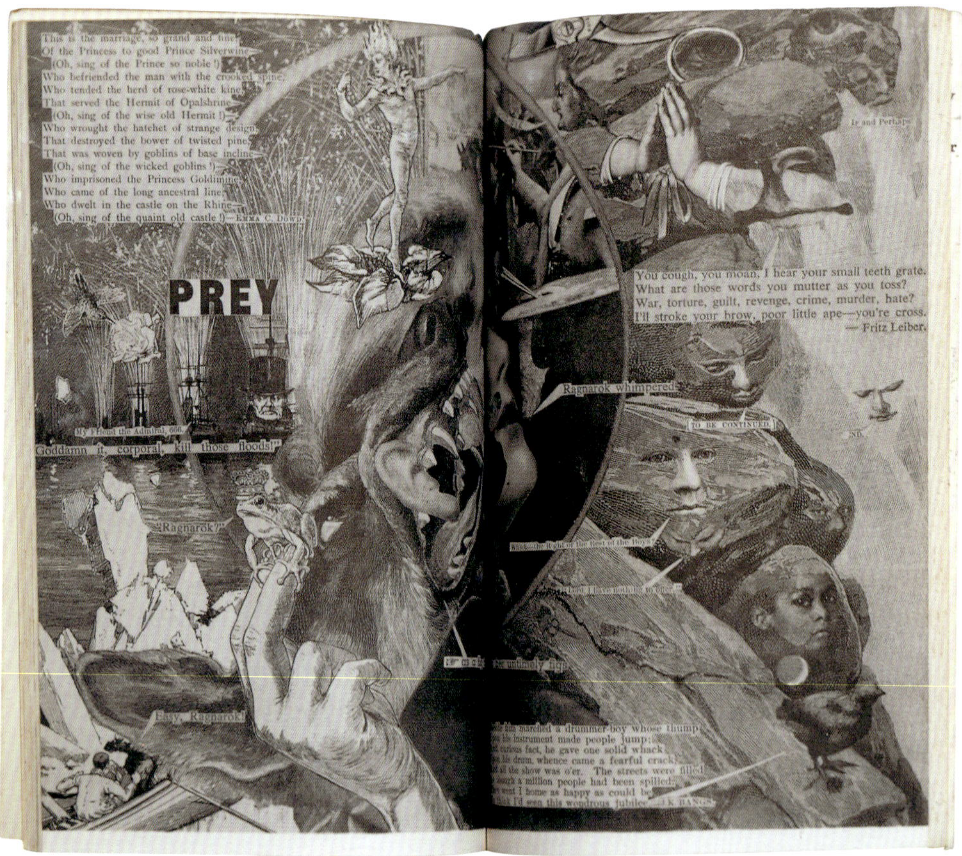

Fig. 41 Jerome Rothenberg and David Antin, editors, *some/thing* (spread detail), vol. 2, no. 1, Winter 1966. Magazine with centerfold collage reproduction by Jess, n.p., 8 ¼ x 5 ¼ in. (21 x 13.3 cm). Collection of Jerome Rothenberg, Encinitas, California

Fig. 42 Jack Spicer, editor, and Fran Herndon, art editor, *J*, no. 5, 1959. Magazine with hand-glittered cardstock cover and illustrations by Jess, 16 pages, 11 x 8 ½ in. (27.9 x 21.6 cm). Collection of Thomas Evans and Lisa Jarnot

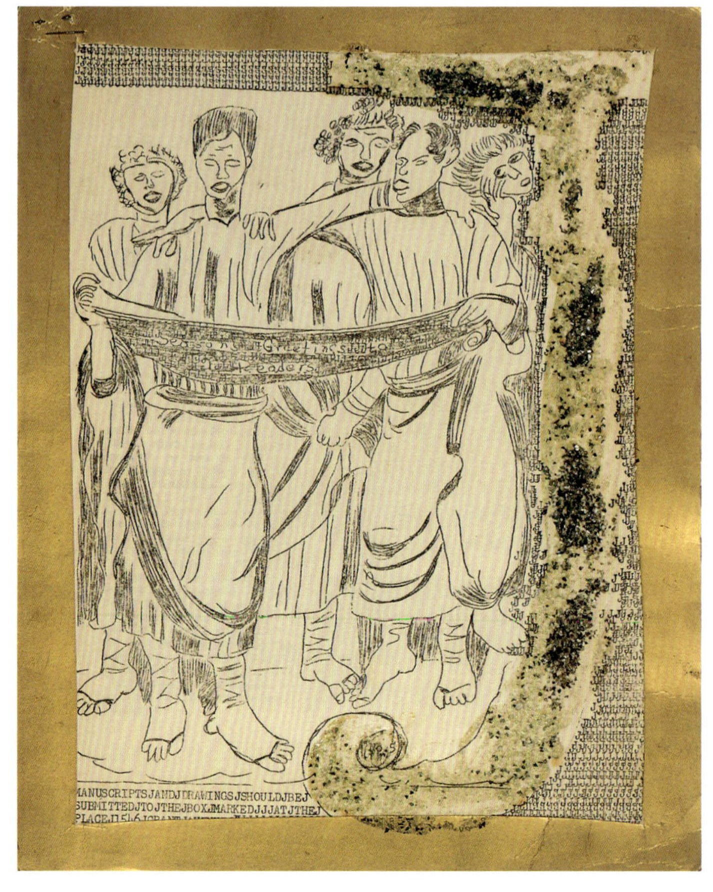

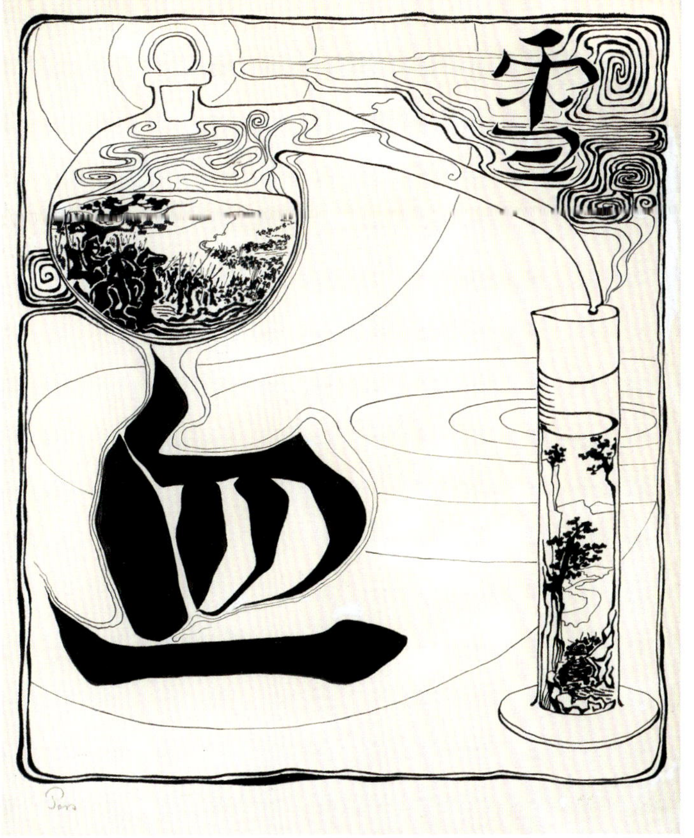

Fig. 43 Jess, *Untitled ("An Imaginary War Elegy") from A Book of Resemblances*, ca. 1966. Ink on paper, 13 x 10 ½ in. (33 x 26.7 cm). Collection of Stephen D. Burton, Tucson, Arizona

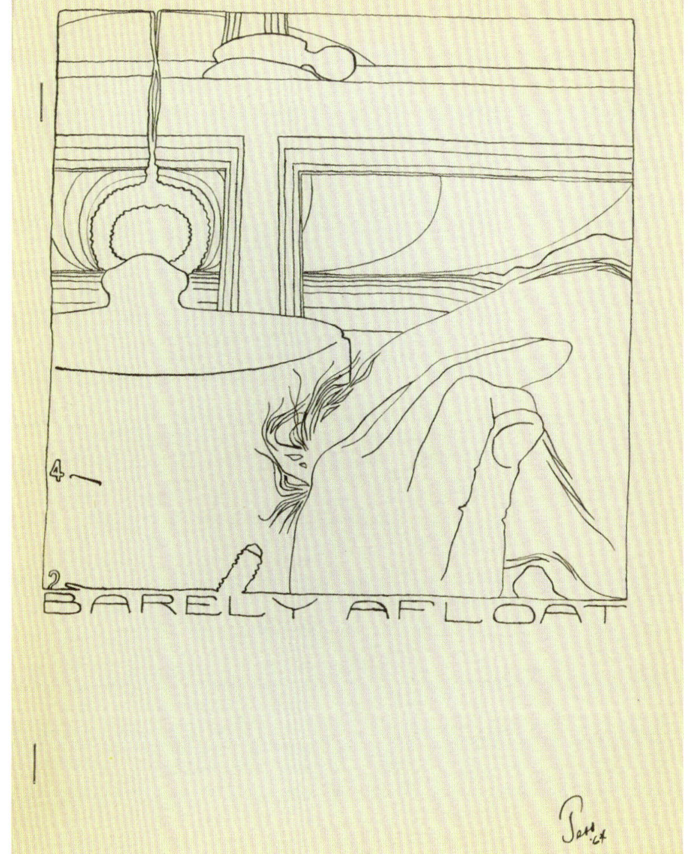

Fig. 44 Diane di Prima and LeRoi Jones, editors; Alan Marlowe, guest editor, *The Floating Bear: A Newsletter*, no. 31, June 1965. Magazine with cover by Jess, 12 pages, 11 x 8 ½ (27.9 x 21.6 cm). The Poetry Collection, State University of New York at Buffalo

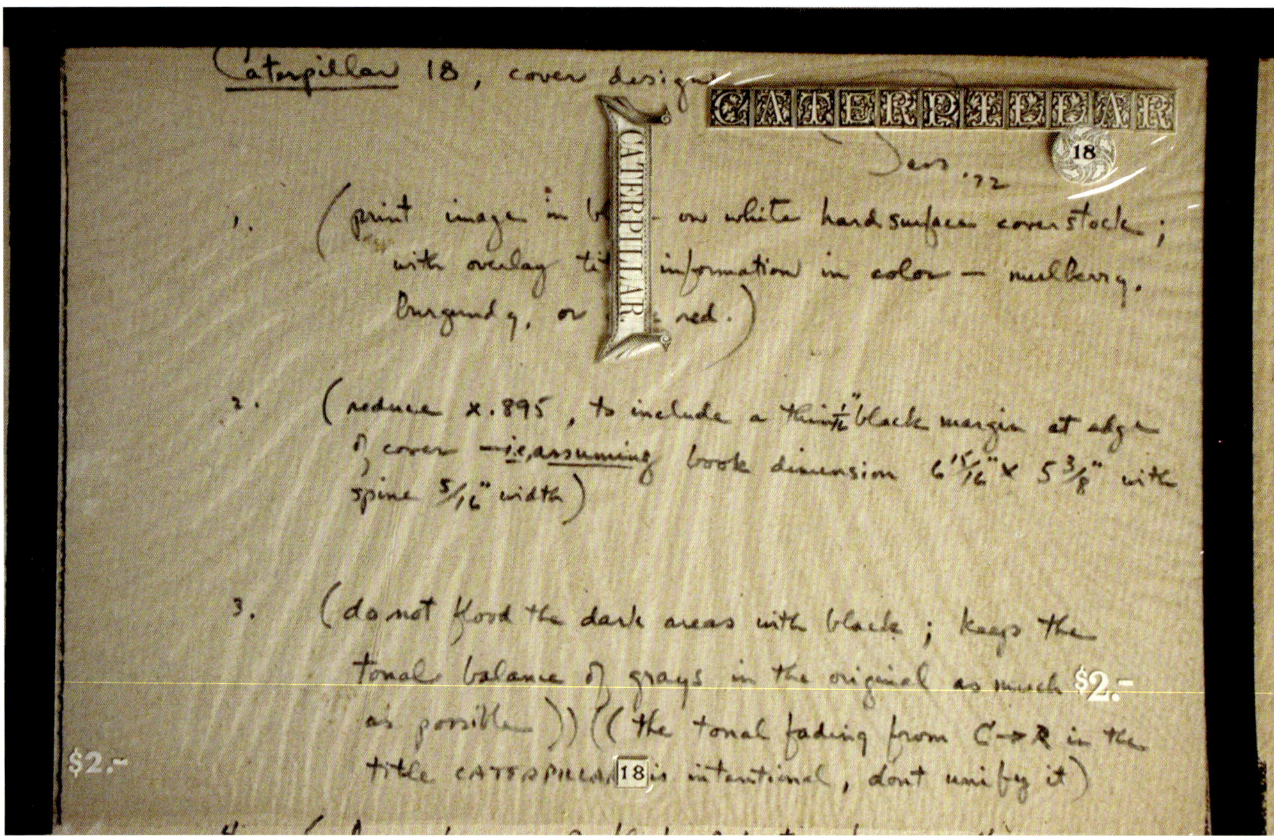

His eight-page collage tale of twins, *The Dios Kuroi*, 1963 (fig. 38), was featured in *Northwest Review* and subsequently produced as an offset pamphlet. To the 1966 anti-war issue of David Antin and Jerome Rothenberg's journal *some/thing*, he contributed a collage referencing Ragnarok, the mythic Norse battle of the gods that spelled the end of the world (fig. 41).[39] Jess contributed a comic to Jack Spicer's *J*, a mimeographed affair occasionally ornamented in glitter (fig. 42). Keen to the challenge of keeping such ephemeral efforts going, Jess made a cover for Diane di Prima and LeRoi Jones's mimeographed newsletter *The Floating Bear* that shows the namesake beast "BARELY AFLOAT" (fig. 44). The title of Clayton Eshleman's little magazine *Caterpillar* worms its way through the collage *Notice. No Eggs Required. By Order*, 1972 (fig. 45), which Jess composed as a wraparound cover. He also created covers for issues of *Credences* (see figs. 72, 78), *o•blēk* (figs. 39, 40), and *Boxkite*. There were two children's books: one published (*The Cat and the Blackbird* [fig. 83], written by Robert Duncan[40]), the other not (*The Boobus and the Bunnyduck* by Michael McClure). Jess's own *Critical Dreams* records eight of them he had between 1956 and 1966 in a handsome letterpress volume. Yet to be published are two sets of seven emblems (fig. 74) that Jess created for the forthcoming volumes of complete writings by Robert Duncan, who was, after all, Jess's constant collaborator and companion in art, life, and literature.[41]

(this and opposite page)
Fig. 45 Jess, *Notice. No Eggs Required. By Order* (verso and recto), 1972. Collage, 7 1/2 x 12 in. (19 x 30.5 cm). Collection of Robert M. Murdock, New York

39. The cover of this issue of *some/thing* was by Andy Warhol: a sheet of yellow stamps reading "Bomb Hanoi."

40. The story of a cat, who loves to cook and garden, going on a honeymoon with a wanderlusty blackbird and the adventures that ensue, loudly echoes not only Jess and Duncan's favorite children's literature (from *The Owl and the Pussycat* to Oz), it is also a reflection of the creative couple's own life story. The book was originally created for the son of their friends Hamil and Mary Tyler.

41. An emblem appears on the cover of *Zyzzyva*, which published the emblems in the Fall 1989 issue. For a poetic reading of the emblems and their iconography (particularly the bee) in relation to Duncan's work, see John Yau's "Open Books," in *Jess: Emblems for Robert Duncan*, exh. cat. (San Jose, Ca.: San Jose Museum of Art, 1989).

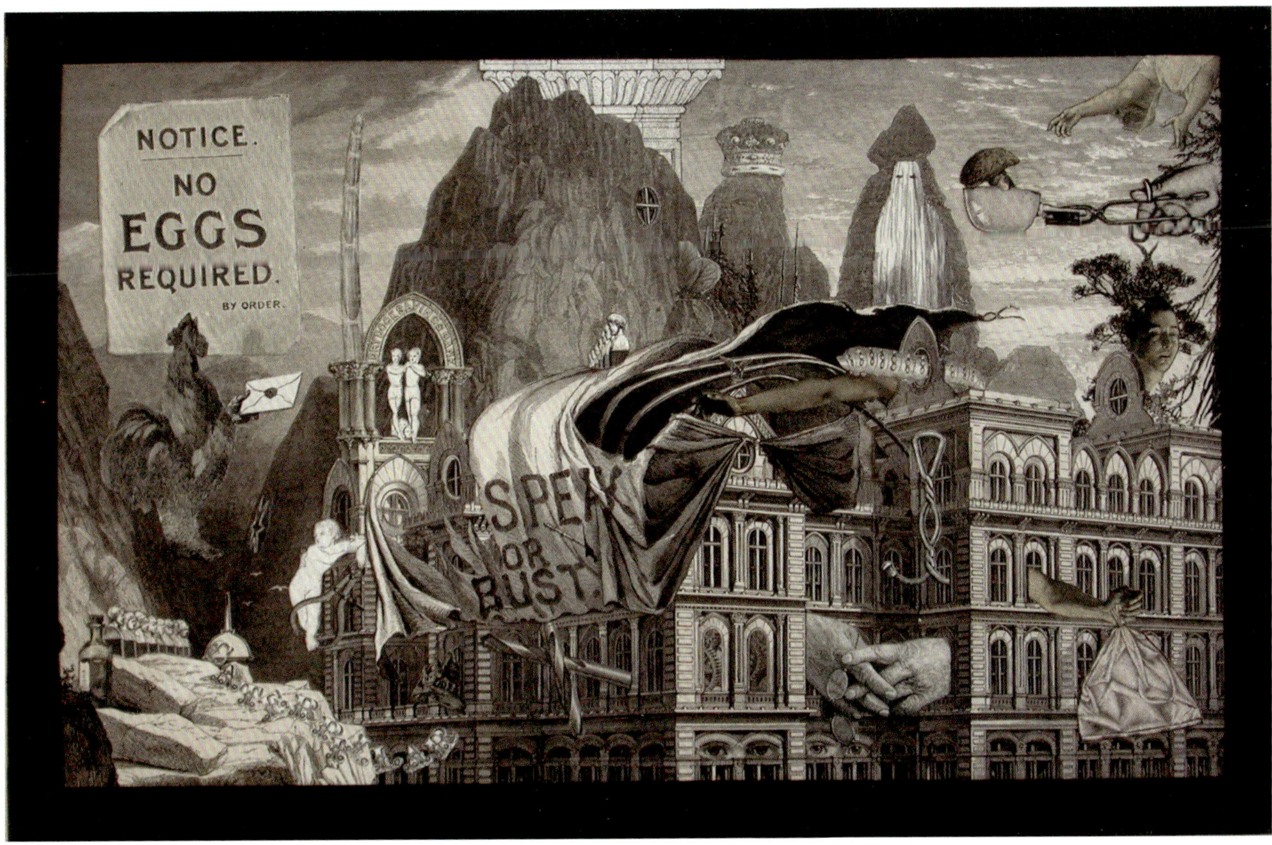

A Literary Household

When Jess met Duncan in 1949 he had just completed a major chapter, or perhaps rewrite, of his own life story. Trained in science, Jess was drafted into the military in 1943 and worked as a chemist producing plutonium on the Manhattan Project at Oak Ridge, Tennessee. The bomb was dropped on Hiroshima on Jess's twenty-second birthday. Out of the service, Jess worked briefly on the Hanford Atomic Energy Project before anxiety over his role in atomic research provoked a nightmare premonition that the world would destroy itself by 1975. It was a breakdown that led to a breakthrough. In an Oedipal act of defiance against the wishes of a conservative and restrictive father, he lopped off his last name, quit his job, and went to San Francisco to study art. All this in 1949, the same year he attended a reading by Robert Duncan. On New Year's Day, 1951, the couple exchanged vows and started living in a domestic partnership that was as central to the artistic community in the Bay Area as Alice B. Toklas and Gertrude Stein's was to theirs in Paris.[42]

Duncan was only four years older than Jess, but his reputation for radical politics was well established (Duncan's 1944 essay "The Homosexual in Society" may be one of the first signed declarations of gay identity in print[43]), as was his tendency toward erudite culture: unimpressed by the expressive howlings of the Beats, he advocated a deeply literary approach to poetry. By the time they

42. Hip to the likeness—with the reclusive and domestic Jess playing Toklas to Duncan's literary lion Stein—the couple had a window blind silk-screened with portraits of Gertrude and Alice (fig. 47). It is now in The Poetry Collection, State University of New York at Buffalo, where James Maynard kindly brought it to my attention. On a more literary note of identification, there are Duncan's writings after Stein, *Names of People*, with drawings by Jess, and *Play Time Pseudo Stein*, subtitled "from the Laboratory Notebook of 1953" after the journal that Jess gave Duncan in which to record his experimental writings. Robert Bertholf, *A Symposium of the Imagination: Robert Duncan in Word and Image* (Buffalo, N.Y.: The Poetry/Rare Books Collection at State University of New York at Buffalo, 1993), pp. 30–31.

43. Published in the August 1944 issue of *Politics* (edited by Dwight MacDonald), the essay argued that homosexuals must participate in the shaping of culture, and not establish their work within a subculture. It was a courageous essay, the immediate result of which was that the *Kenyon Review* rejected a poem of Duncan's that had already been slated for print.

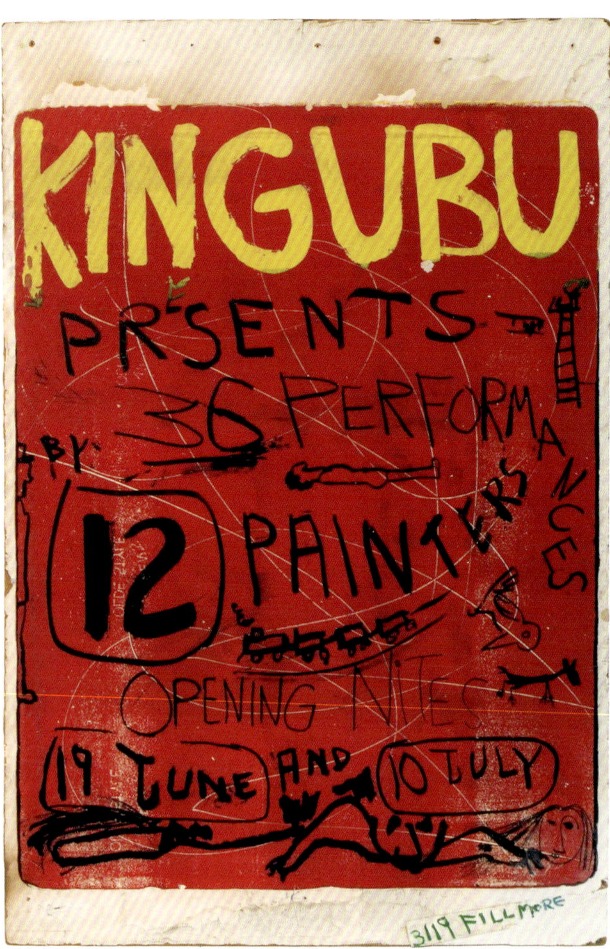

Fig. 46 Hassel Smith, sign from King Ubu Gallery, 1953. Tempera on paper, 38 ¼ x 25 in. (97.2 x 63.5 cm). The Poetry Collection, State University of New York at Buffalo

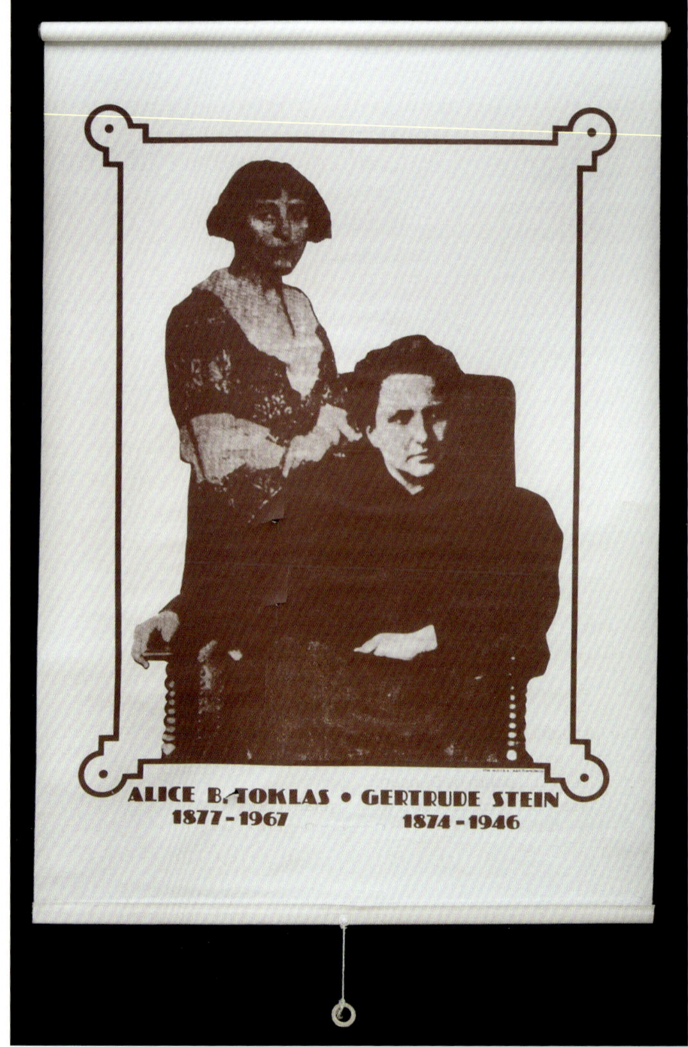

Fig. 47 Window blind with image of Gertrude Stein and Alice B. Toklas, n.d. Silk-screen on window blind, 53 x 35 ¾ in. (134.6 x 90.8 cm). The Poetry Collection, State University of New York at Buffalo

44. Lyn Brockway, "Recollections," in *Lyn Brockway, Harry Jacobus, and Jess: The Romantic Paintings*, exh. cat. (Palo Alto, Ca.: Palo Alto Cultural Center and Wiegand Gallery, 1990), p. 5. I am grateful to Christopher Wagstaff, organizer of the exhibition, for providing me with a copy of this catalogue. Wagstaff's essay is very informative about the relationship between Jess's *Romantic* paintings and specific works of literature. He reminds readers that "'romance' is from roman or story, and that intriguing story is the major element in [Jess's art]," p. 14.

45. *Jess*, Chicago, 1972, n.p.

46. It was the gallery's policy not to present solo exhibitions of the cofounder's work. However Jess contributed widely to the program by designing announcement cards and participating in events and group shows. See Christopher Wagstaff, *An Art of Wondering: The King Ubu Gallery, 1952–53* (Davis, Ca.: John Natsoulas Press, 1989).

47. Informative histories of the Bay Area galleries and exhibitions of this period are: Terry St. John, *The Dilexi Years: 1958–1970*, exh. cat. (Oakland, Ca.: The Oakland Museum, 1984); Rebecca Solnit, *Secret Exhibition: Six California Artists of the Cold War Era* (San Francisco: City Lights Books, 1990); Seymour Howard, *The Beat Generation and Beyond* (Davis, Ca.: John Natsoulas Press, 1996).

48. Much more remains to be written about the profoundly deep relationship between Robert Duncan and Jess, expressed not only in Jess's art and Duncan's poetry, but also in Jess's writings and Duncan's drawings. Their life and work together represents an underexplored middle ground of creative practice—somewhere between high and low—where drawing and writing are like cooking, gardening, and any other potentially creative form of daily expression to be cultivated and enjoyed. This middle ground was the background of Jess and Duncan's fundamentally creative household.

49. An amazingly thorough reading of one of Jess's 1955 collages was conducted by Jennifer Cabral as part of her conservation work on *When My Ship Come Sin* (fig. 1) at the Williamstown Art Conservation Center in 2001. Cabral leafed through the entire 1955 run of *Life* to locate ten sources for the collage. By analyzing the fragments in terms of their original contexts, Cabral's findings suggest that for Jess, cutting and reading were related activities. For instance, what looks like a mushrooming cloud is in fact fluffy sheep, which Jess clipped from an article on radioactivity and atomic research being performed at the center in Hanford where he had once worked. I am grateful to Wendy Watson, curator, Mount Holyoke College Art Museum, for sharing Cabral's unpublished paper, and regret being unable to reach the author after several attempts to contact her. See "Interview: Conversation about Conservation," *Mount Holyoke College Art Museum*, Fall 2001.

50. The first edition was accompanied by a special edition of thirteen copies, each containing an original collage by Jess and poem by Duncan.

51. For a close reading of Duncan's work in relation to Jess's art, see Robert Bertholf, "The Concert: Robert Duncan Writing Out of Painting," in *Jess: A Grand Collage*, pp. 67–91.

52. See Duncan's essays: "Iconographical Extensions," in *Translations by Jess* (Los Angeles: The Black Sparrow Press, 1971), pp. i–xiv; and "An Art of Wondering," in *Translations, Salvages, Paste-Ups by Jess*, exh. cat. (Dallas: Dallas Museum of Fine Arts, 1977), n.p.

53. Robert Duncan, "Pages from a Notebook," *The Artist's View* 5 (July 1953), n.p.

met, Duncan was already on his way to becoming the magus figure of a culture that he presided over at home and traveled extensively to promote. And his wasn't just a world of poetry. As Lyn Brockway, one of Jess's painting peers in Bay Area Romanticism, recounted of Duncan, he "always had time to discover and encourage and involve himself with other poets and painters and musicians. . . . He created a strong feeling of concern and respect for the individual and the diversity of personal expression."[44] Duncan's sense of communal creativity led him to cofound King Ubu Gallery in 1953 (see fig. 46). Named for Alfred Jarry's *Ubu Roi*—the literary avant-garde's anti-hero—the gallery is described in a nutshell in one of Jess's auto-chronologies: "1953 Takes part with Duncan and painter Harry Jacobus in keeping open King Ubu Gallery, San Francisco, as a showplace for artworks and stage for drama and poetry. Shows paste-ups, paintings and junk assemblies."[45] Slated to run for a year on the sweat equity and inspiration of its founders alone—no sales but lots of fun—the gallery closed in December 1953.[46] Opening in the same space shortly thereafter was the Six Gallery, where Allen Ginsberg gave his first reading of *Howl*.[47]

Their creative lives thoroughly commingled, Jess and Duncan collaborated extensively over the years, making everything from Christmas cards to routine appearances in each other's work.[48] In 1955 Jess played the part of Faust's mother in a staged reading of Duncan's *Faust Foutu* at the Six Gallery. A particularly dynamic collaboration started in 1955, when Duncan gave Jess a group of poems to respond to in collage. Cut from readily available *Life* magazines, the collages for *Caesar's Gate* have the characteristic palette of photographic reproductions of this period, during which the couple traveled in Europe and America (fig. 49).[49] The first edition of the book was published in 1955 by Divers Press while the couple was living in Mallorca (fig. 50).[50] For the second edition, published in 1972 by Sand Dollar, Jess created several new collages that Duncan, in turn, reflected with new poems (fig. 51). These appear not in typeset, but in Duncan's handwritten, open, round script. Likewise, it is Duncan's hand that penned the poems that accompany Jess's Art Nouveau–style ink drawings and ornaments for *A Book of Resemblances: Poems 1950–1953*, a letterpress book published in 1966 by Henry Wenning that gives beautiful expression to Jess and Duncan on the same page (figs. 52, 53, 54).

As much as Jess's sense of curiosity and imagination illuminated Duncan's work, so was Duncan's formidable intellect formative to Jess's art.[51] During his lifetime, Duncan wrote several essays on Jess's art, creating for it a specific literary framework.[52] Interestingly enough, this framework seems most starkly revealed not in an essay about Jess, but in one Duncan wrote about his own work for the magazine *The Artist's View*, in an issue he edited. Paraphrased here are the manifesto-like statements Duncan culled from his notebook.[53] An advocate of collective culture, he considered each new poem of his a revision, or derivation, of all that came before it. In search of the kind of esoteric knowledge that the ancient Greeks deemed essential to spiritual truth and salvation, he found a "Gnosis of the modern world" in scorned and minor works of literature, in fairytales and fantasy writing. In a section called "On Science," he wrote that the magnificence of Freud was that he never sought to cure an individual of being himself. Childhood was a realm created by parents with their love and imagination, a state that all adults (and many children) might spend a lifetime trying to find a way back to. Symbolic of the power of childhood is the lion, which is also (seemingly paradoxically) a sign of sexual desire when it is allowed full roam. Duncan's last note, which begins, "MUSE AMUSED," is worth quoting in full for future reference: "To bemuse. I think of a sphinx, smiling to myself. Only the inscrutable amuses."

Inasmuch as these notes act as keys to the icons of Jess's art, which is full of lions, childhood wonders, Freudian slips, and collage derivations, one clearly sees Duncan's impact. There are also many works in Jess's oeuvre titled after Duncan's work, such as the 1960 painting named after his poem *Eluard's Death*. The collage *Brimo of Colchis*, 1954 (fig. 65), springs from the same Greek myth that Duncan mined for his play *Medea at Kolchis: The Maiden Head*.[54] The mere fact that Jess and Duncan shared a common *ex libris* (bookplate), designed by Jess (fig. 48), gives the impression that they pored over the same material. But while there is ample concordance between Jess's art and Duncan's writings, Jess was no illustrator. His art is equally accessible with or without any knowledge of Duncan's critical ideas or writings. And yet how many aspects of Jess's seemingly unfathomable topography are thrown into relief by these lines from Duncan's "A Poem Beginning with a Line by Pindar": "This land where I stand, was all legend . . . animal tribes, priests, gold. / It was the West. Its vistas painters saw / in diffuse light, in melancholy, / in abysses left by glaciers as if they had been the sun / primordial carving empty enormities out of the rock. / Snakes lurkd guarding secrets."

Translation and Quotation

Translation and quotation are literary activities; they are also terms of Jess's art. In 1964 he wrote to Duncan, "I sat down to re-catalog my output in a beautiful old bound ledger I got for $1.50 at the Goodwill. It's as big as an encyclopedia volume and is bound in calfskin with marbleized endpapers. And no missing pages or entries."[55] In the ledger, each handwritten entry provides a complete transcription of any quotation that appears inscribed on Jess's works of art.[56] Skimming through the quotes is like running one's fingers over the spines of books in a library. Like his art, the ledger contains mythology, poetry, and literature, writings on art and science, children's books and nonsense. Jess loved the work of L. Frank Baum, buying whenever he found them used copies of *The Wizard of Oz* to propagate the sprouting libraries of his child friends. The first page of the log (with its *Boobish* inscription "This Book Belong Stoo Jess") offers up an "Invocation" by way of a quotation from Baum, in which the heroine cheerfully mistranslates a conversation between the Scarecrow and Jack the Pumpkinhead.[57] Jess's painting of a magical looking place with six colored suns, *Land of the Mangaboos*, 1955 (fig. 55), also quotes from Baum.

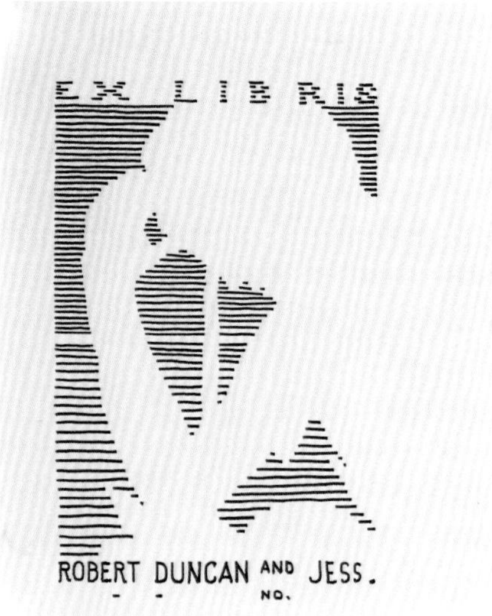

Fig. 48 Jess, *Ex Libris*, ca. 1960. Ink on paper, mounted on board (drawing for a bookplate), 13 7/8 x 11 in. (35.3 x 27.9 cm). Courtesy Odyssia Gallery, New York

54. The project was published in 1965, but Duncan mentions it as early as 1956. See Robert Bertholf and Albert Gelpi, eds., *The Letters of Robert Duncan and Denise Levertov* (Stanford, Ca.: Stanford University Press, 2004), p. 44.
55. Jess to Duncan, May 13, 1964.
56. Although I was able to consult a copy of the ledger at Odyssia Gallery, New York, I did not have access to the original, which is to my understanding part of the Jess archives that have only recently gone to The Bancroft Library, University of California, Berkeley. These papers were being processed and unavailable for study at the time of this research.
57. On the same page, a second invocation celebrates the snail—and Jess's signature pace of working—with a poem by the Japanese poet Ransetsu: "Snail, snail, / put out your horns / for a little! / It rains and the wind is blowing, / so put out your horns, / just for a little while!"

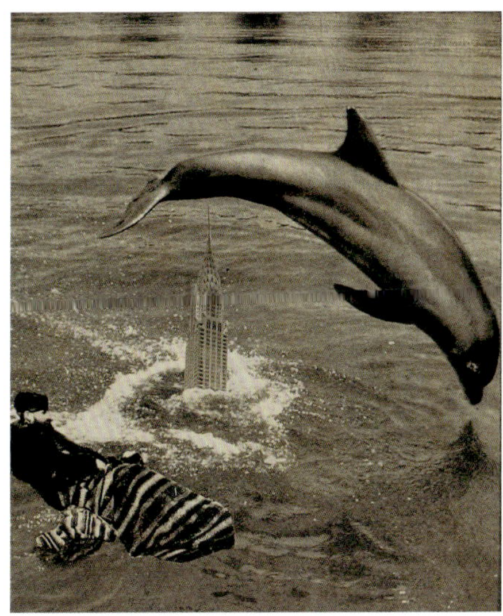

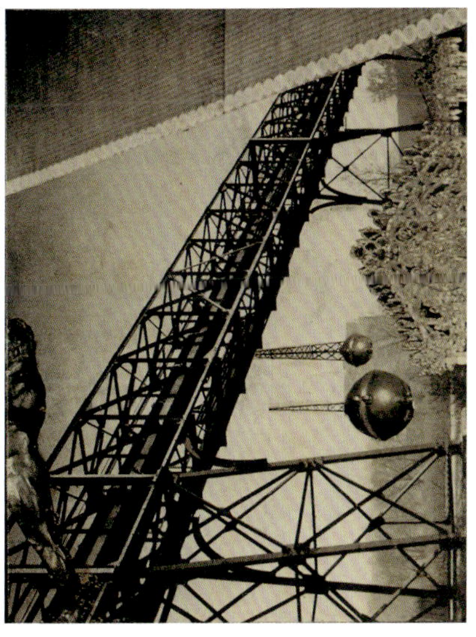

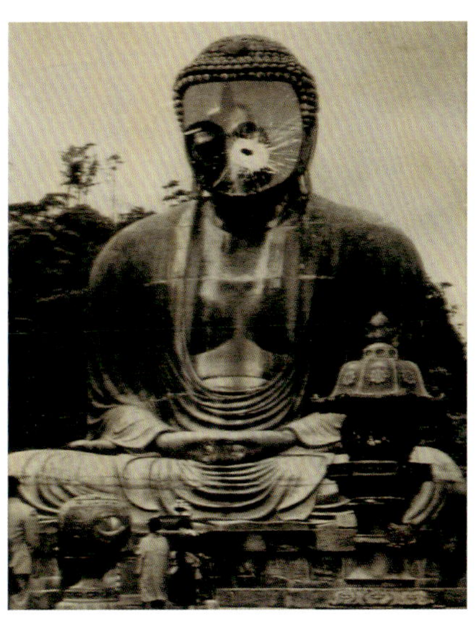

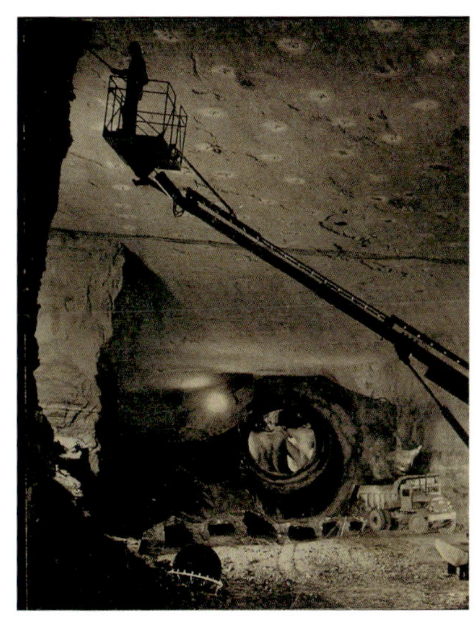

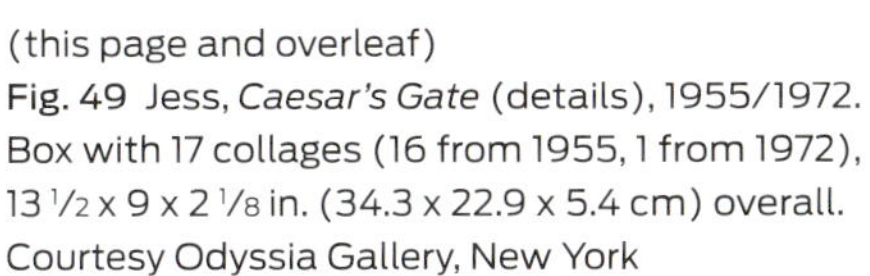

(this page and overleaf)
Fig. 49 Jess, *Caesar's Gate* (details), 1955/1972.
Box with 17 collages (16 from 1955, 1 from 1972),
13 $\frac{1}{2}$ x 9 x 2 $\frac{1}{8}$ in. (34.3 x 22.9 x 5.4 cm) overall.
Courtesy Odyssia Gallery, New York

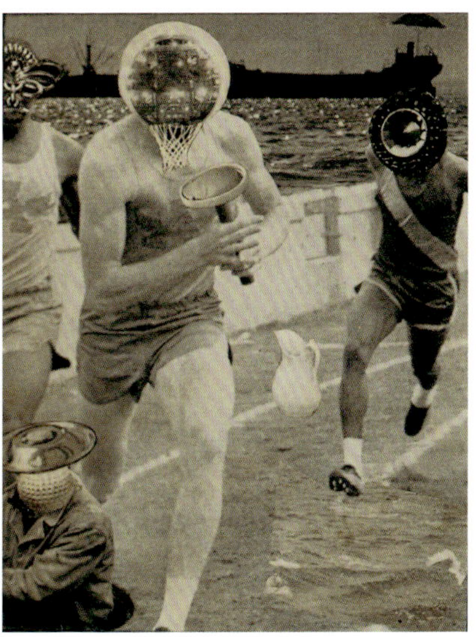

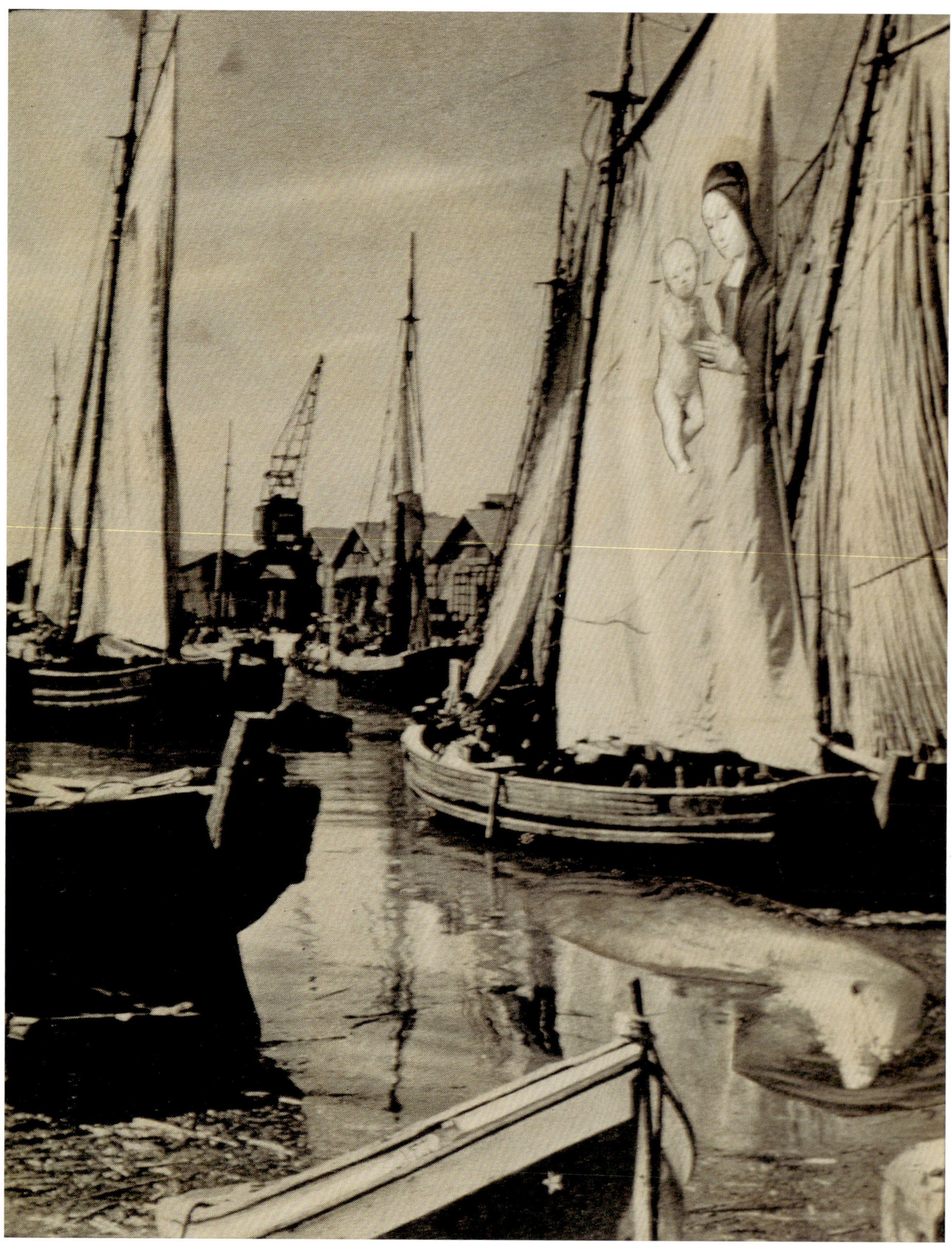

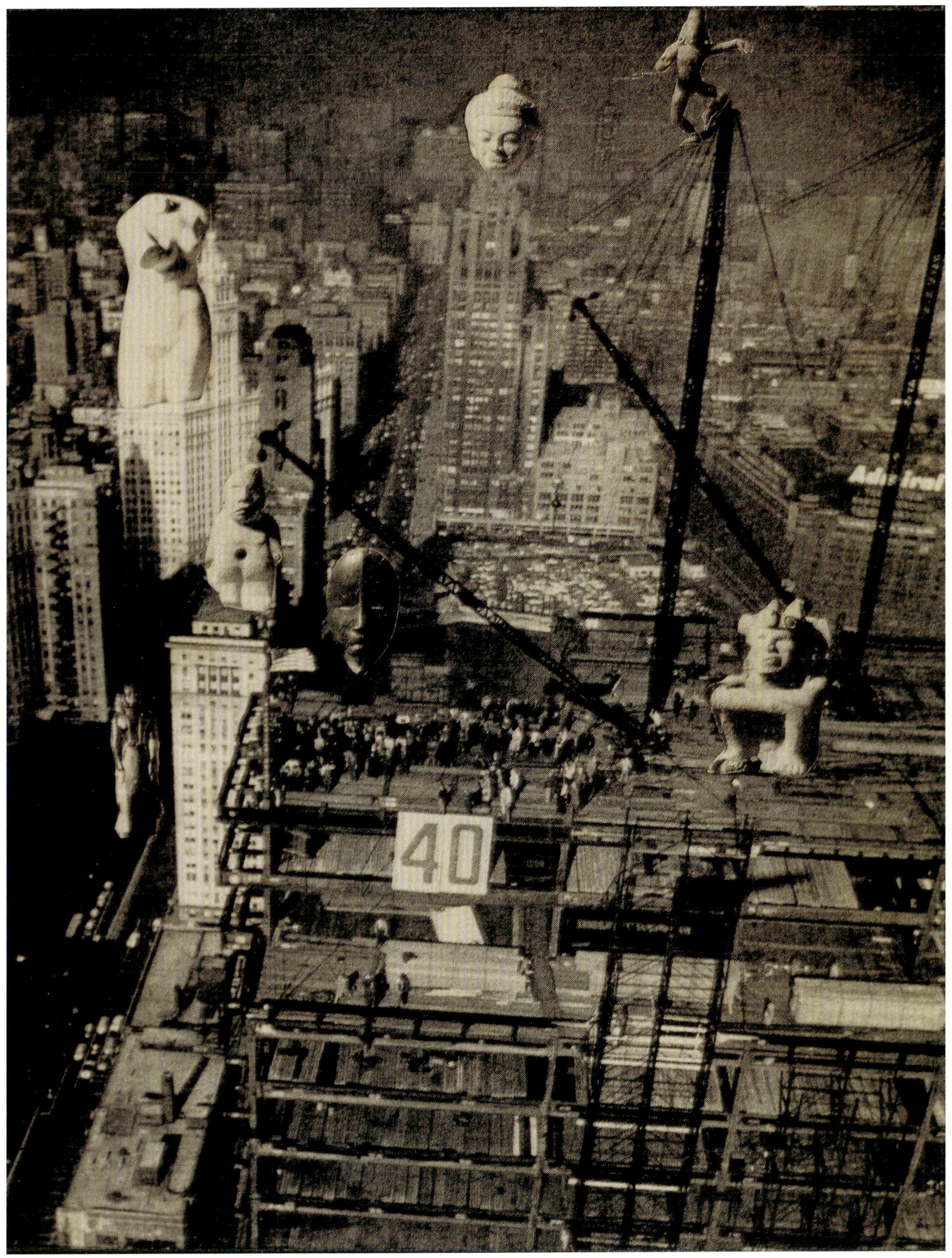

40

Robert Duncan

CAESAR'S GATE

POEMS 1949-1950

with collages by
Jess Collins

by ROBERT DUNCAN

Heavenly City, Earthly City, 1947
Medieval Scenes, 1949
Poems 1948-49, 1949
Song of the Borderguard, 1952
Fragments of a Disorderd Devotion, 1952
The Artist's View Nº 5, 1953
Faust Foutu, 1954

by JESS COLLINS

The Artist's View Nº 8

The Divers Press • 1955

inscribed March 1968
Robert Duncan

CIRCULATING LIGHTS

Well, how very well! An eye opens
with water flowing over rim of
cup, fountains of what is seen.
And the depths of the eye lie
in the darkest pulpy machineries
of brain. Convolutions of well
being from which tears rise.

In the distance we see all our
vacations, near to us. In the
foreground, an untranslatable
key. This is the healing out
of sleep, the Book that Writes
trees, lakes, mountains, vistas
of sun and moon, natural
letters to the illiterate deep.
Writes well.

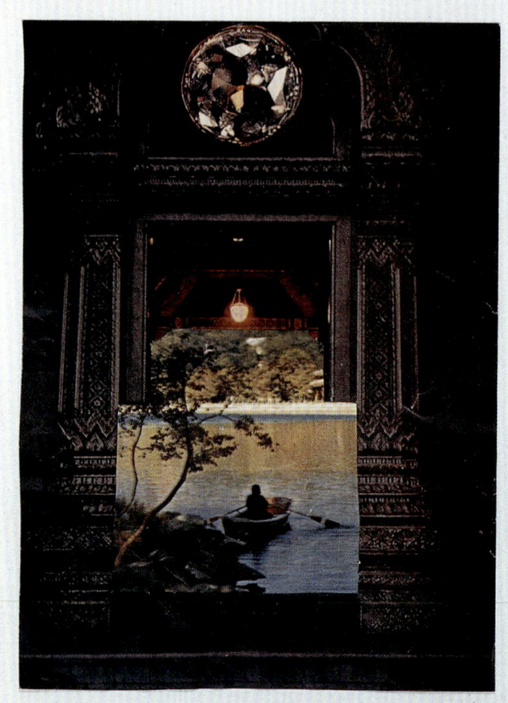

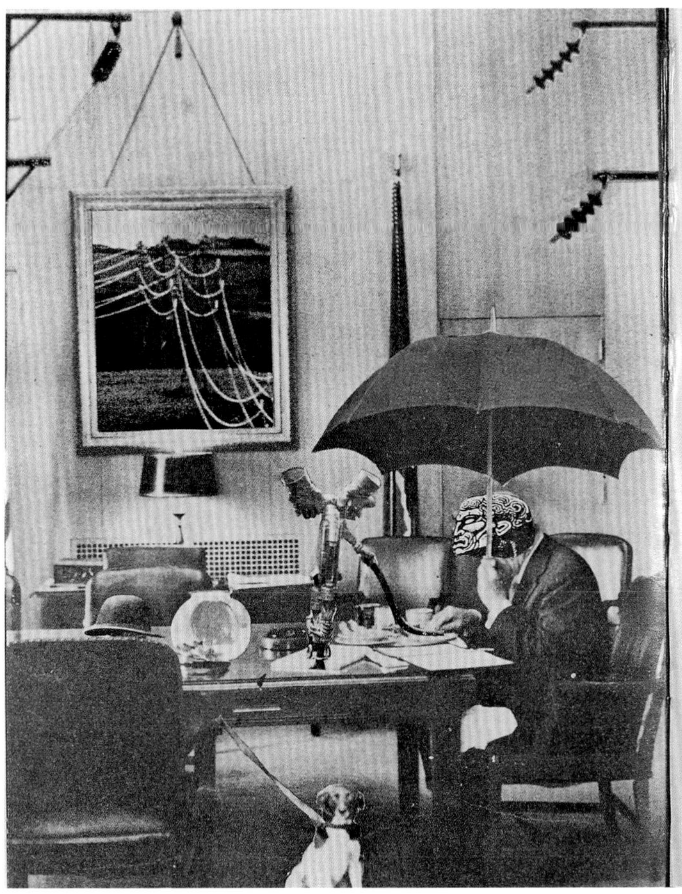

(opposite page)
Fig. 50 Robert Duncan and Jess, *Caesar's Gate* (spread details), 1955. Special edition book with original collages by Jess, 57 pages, 8 ⁵/₈ x 6 ⁵/₈ in. (21.8 x 16.8 cm). The Poetry Collection, State University of New York at Buffalo

(this page)
Fig. 51 Robert Duncan, *Caesar's Gate* (spread detail), 1972–73. Cloth-bound book with wraparound jacket and collage reproductions by Jess, 80 pages. 8 ³/₄ x 6 ⁵/₈ in. (22.2 x 16.8 cm). Collection of Steve Dickison

58. Jess's *Romantic* painting *The Place of the Lion*, 1958, is titled after a novel by Williams set in London, where platonic archetypes appear to wreak havoc on the city.
59. *The Four Seasons & other paste-ups* (New York: Odyssia Gallery, 1980).

No matter how it was told, the archetypal story for Jess was one of an innocent's wanderings, or fall, into realms of the imagination, the metaphysical, outer space, or the unconscious. Hence his devotion to the fairytale writings of George MacDonald, the Puritan gothic of Nathanial Hawthorne, the science fiction of J. U. Lloyd (a pharmacist who set stories in a land called "Etidorhpa," or "Aphrodite" spelled backwards), the mystical chronicles of C. S. Lewis and J. R. Tolkien, and the supernatural thrillers of Charles Williams. A scholar of Arthurian legends and Dante, Williams structured one of his own books after a reading of the Tarot.[58] But these are just a few of the popular, classic, obscure, and esoteric texts that are the Gnosis (to recast Duncan's term) of Jess's art.

A most revelatory reading can be found in a collection of quotes that Jess compiled for his 1980 exhibition catalogue *The Four Seasons & other paste-ups*.[59] Hooking and tumbling off of one another, the quotes cascade with meaning about Jess's art. Water is a recurrent motif. From the writer Dorothy Richardson, who is credited with having published the first so-called stream-of-consciousness novel, for instance: "Stream of consciousness is a muddle-headed phrase. It's not a stream, it's a pool, a sea, an ocean. It has depth and greater depth and when you think you have reached its bottom there is nothing there, and when you give yourself up to one current you are suddenly possessed of another." And so Jess plunges the depths of his own compositions by way of quotation.

A POEM IN STRETCHING

prophesying. Reading water or words, signs are cards in their multiple juxtapositions. Where we read into. Its not really there. Its nothing. A plate of disturbd sand. A landscape of sounds honks sigh a sigh. A plain stretch of time in which trees are not green but hesitate. A sign. The easy trees, houses, far away castles, a moat, a highway with car streams of, a high net of wires. It is nothing. Wires or eyes crosst giving rise to vision in the distortion of vision. Its not there. Its in the air. The rumor. It comes to our ears? A poem stretching out once crampt in the hand. Heard having been seen. Now it is seen that it has been heard. A card. Then another card. It is the queen of hearts not hurts and a seven, black. Spades. Other cards we are not seeing determine the scene. We are not looking at them. We were not looking for them. They tell us, remind us. Unseen words we have just seen not yet heard tell us. I know now. I know I mean I see it all. She is afraid. A game of chance. Shuffle the deck. In the shuffle of words losing the sense we sense.

Put your cards on the table. O.K. Signs of the times.

A cigarette first. Yes. Hands in their motion holding. A cigarette. Lighting. A match. Light cigarette. A hesitation. Pausing before striking. The hot smoke toxic we draw in. A gasp. Stop. A bitter gasp. The hand grasps the pencil,

·64·

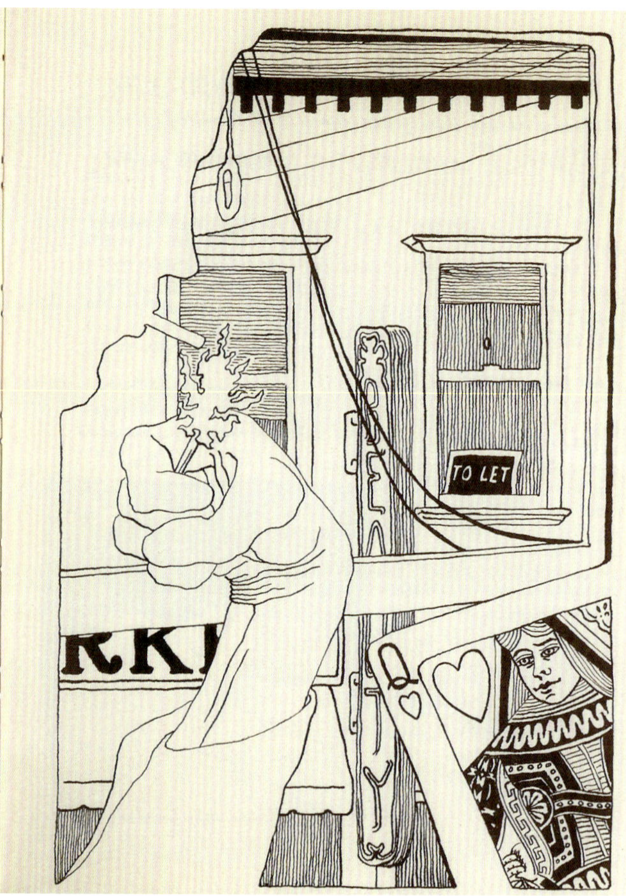

Fig. 52 Robert Duncan, *A Book of Resemblances: Poems: 1950–1953* (spread detail), 1966. Hardbound book with embossed cover and illustrations by Jess, 91 pages, 17 1/2 x 13 in. (44.5 x 33 cm). Collection of Michael Palmer and Cathy Simon

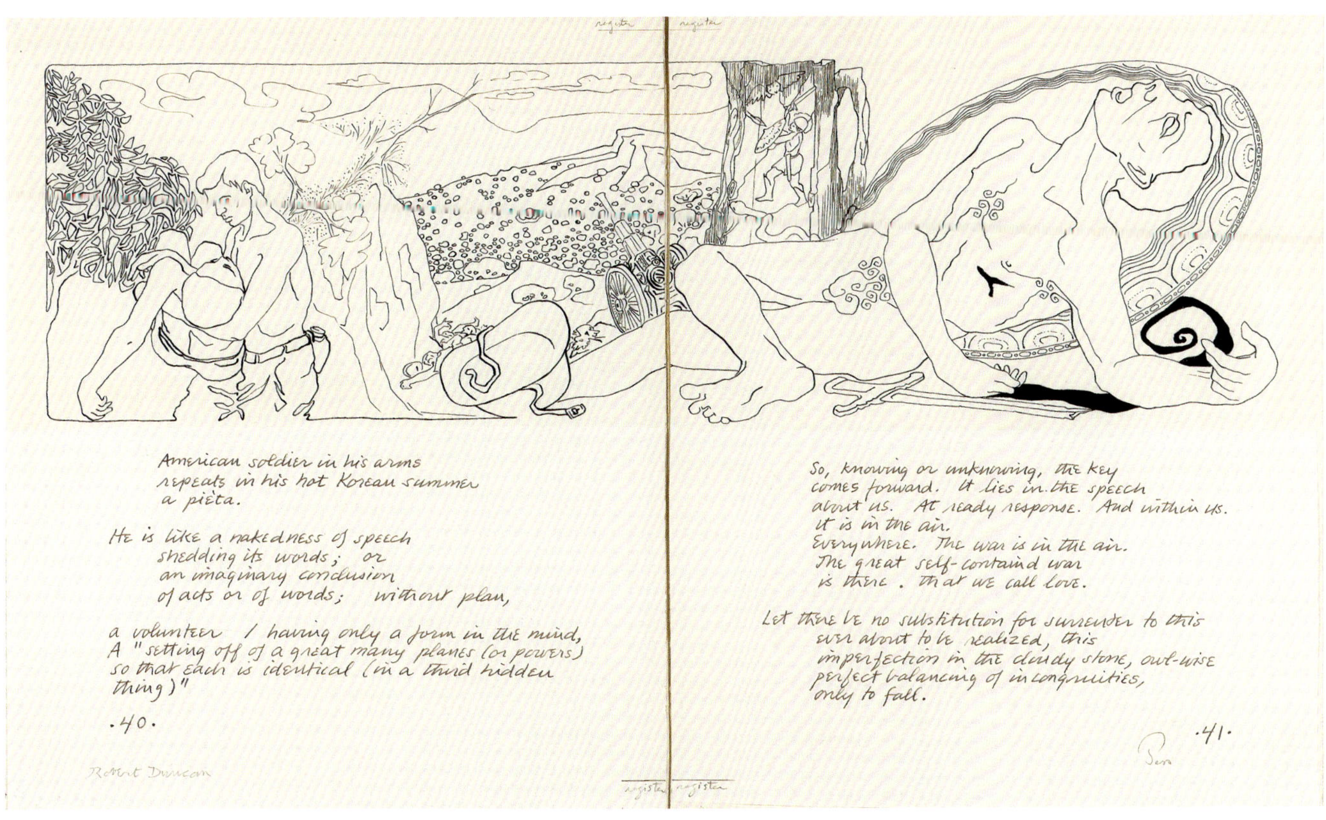

Fig. 53 Jess, *Untitled ("An Essay at War") from A Book of Resemblances*, 1966. Ink on paper, two sheets, each 21 1/2 x 13 in. (54.6 x 33 cm). Private collection

Fig. 54 Jess, *Decoration from A Book of Resemblances by Robert Duncan*, 1966. Ink on paper, 8 3/4 x 6 3/4 in. (22.2 x 17.1 cm). Private collection

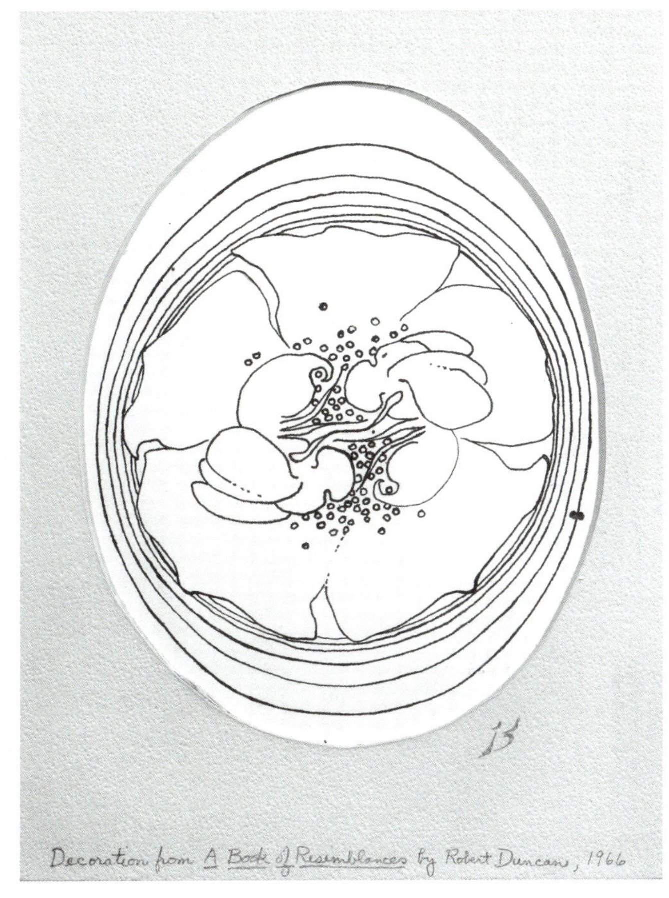

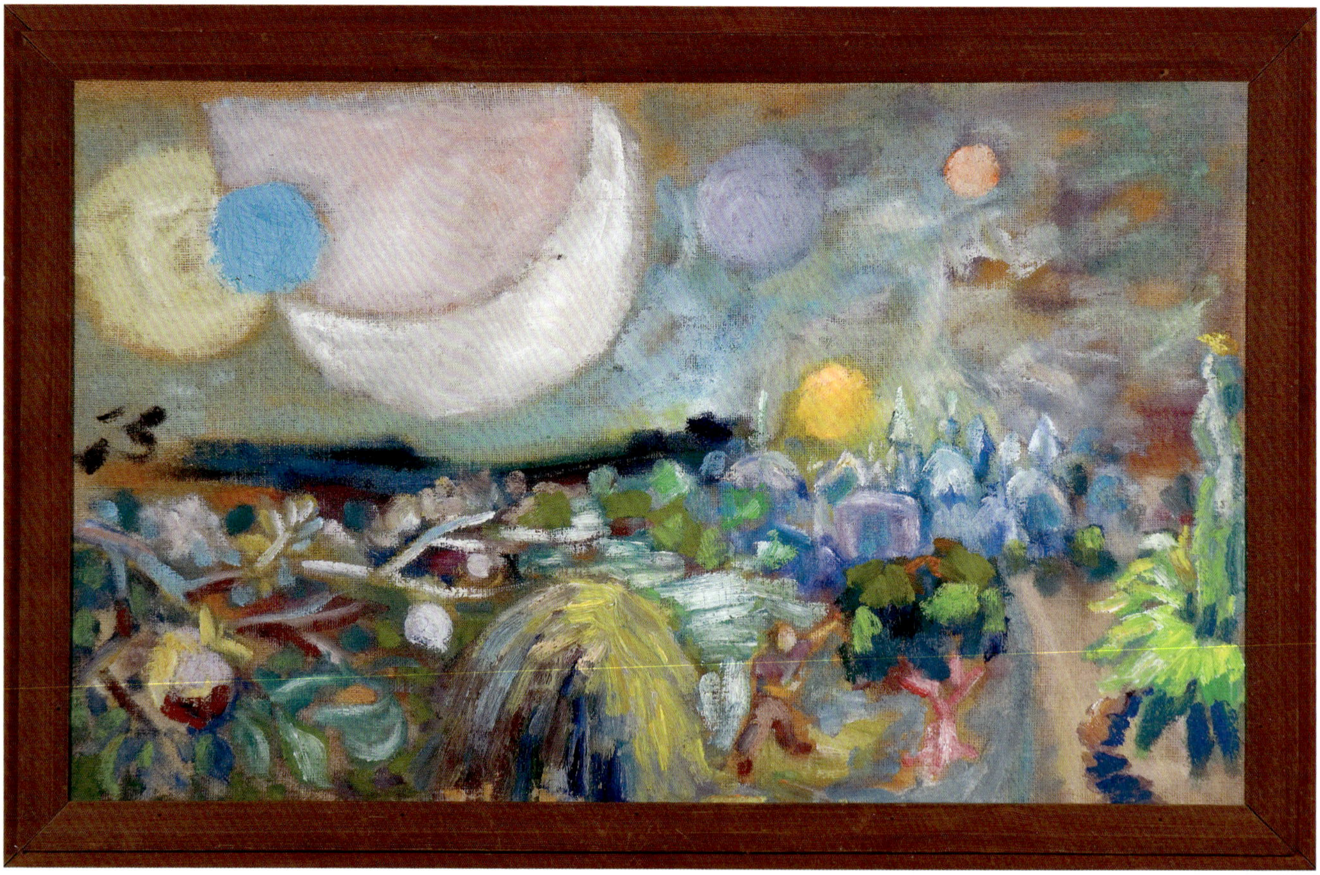

Fig. 55 Jess, *Land of the Mangaboos*, 1955.
Oil on burlap, mounted on plywood, 24 x
38 1/2 in. (61 x 97.8 cm). Private collection

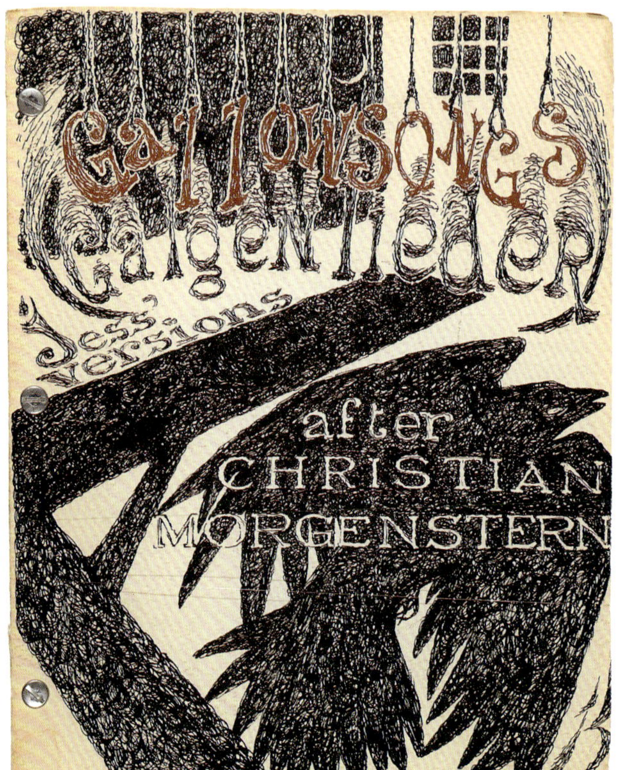

Fig. 56 Jess, *Gallowsongs: Galgenlieder by
Christian Morgenstern, Versions by Jess*, 1970.
Book bolted in paper wrappers, inscribed
by Jess, n.p., 11 1/4 x 8 3/4 in. (28.6 x 22.2 cm).
Collection of Dodie Bellamy and Kevin Killian,
San Francisco

Another quotation in Jess's montage comes from Charles Baudelaire, whose literary notion of "correspondences"—fugitive connections between words and images, sense and spirit, matter and music—is indispensable to any consideration of collage.[60] It's the mechanics behind Jess's montage of quotations that link him, by correspondence, to a whole history of visionary and literary artists whose work slips alongside conventional art history to communicate across its margins. From Jess back to Hieronymous Bosch, this tradition encompasses Henry Fuseli, William Blake, Max Klinger, Samuel Palmer, Albert Pinkham Ryder, Thomas Cole, and Odilon Redon. What unites their work is the sense that "imagination is an almost divine faculty which, without recourse to any philosophical method, immediately perceives everything: the secret and intimate connection between things, correspondences and analogies"—to quote Baudelaire.[61]

Another take on "correspondence" is the notion of corresponding with another's creativity, as Jess did particularly in his art of translation. Jess embarked on this activity quite literally with a 1970 book of drawings and verse that turned Christian Morgenstern's German nonsense poems inexactly into English (fig. 56). The last piece of the title gives away the jest: *Gallowsongs: Galgenlieder by Christian Morgenstern, Versions by Jess.* Using translation like a form of alchemy, Jess's renditions of the Romantic poet's works end up being unique works by Jess. He opens with something like a confession or apology to Erika Feist, whose 1951 recital of *Die Galgenlider* apparently got him going. "Here's hoping: she may not deplore the shadow-cast by sparks leaping the language gap. Like: a painter playing at poet-translator, I had to be divinitive not definitive." And so Jung and Freud appear together in a way that would be anachronistic to Morgenstern's 1905 publication, but is completely in keeping with Jess's modern translation of the "The Nasobēm": "It doesn't stand in Jung. / Nor even in Freud. / It came from my song / The first time to light."

Appropriation is a stock technique of modernist art and writing. It's interesting though to see Jess's acts of appropriation cast into the bookish light of translation. The practice emanates from Duncan's notion of the "derivative" as an essentially generative practice, but also from James Joyce's recasting of the Homeric tale of Ulysses into a tome-long account of a day of nothing special. Back in California, we can look to Jack Spicer's *After Lorca*, his book of "dictated poems" that were so way after Lorca they were written after he was dead. Spicer, channeling Lorca, complains in the book's introduction, "In even the most literal of [the poems] Mr. Spicer seems to derive pleasure in inserting or substituting one or two words which completely change the mood and often the meaning of the poem as I had written it. More often he takes one of my poems and adjoins to half of it another half of his own, giving rather the effect of an unwilling Centaur."[62] The cover of Spicer's *Lorca* features a drawing by Jess, who was evidently working within a very infectious context of literary translation and collage.

60. Ibid. Albeit the quotation from Baudelaire that Jess selected has only indirectly to do with correspondences: "There are those people who would steal a fragment from a picture by Rembrandt, and without modifying it, without digesting it, without even finding the glue to stick it on with, will incorporate it into a work composed from an entirely different point of view."

61. This is Baudelaire writing on Edgar Allen Poe, whose contemporaneous work Baudelaire translated into French, treating it almost as an extension of his own, so closely did he feel his imagination twinned by Poe's.

62. Jack Spicer, *After Lorca* (San Francisco: White Rabbit Press, 1957), n.p.

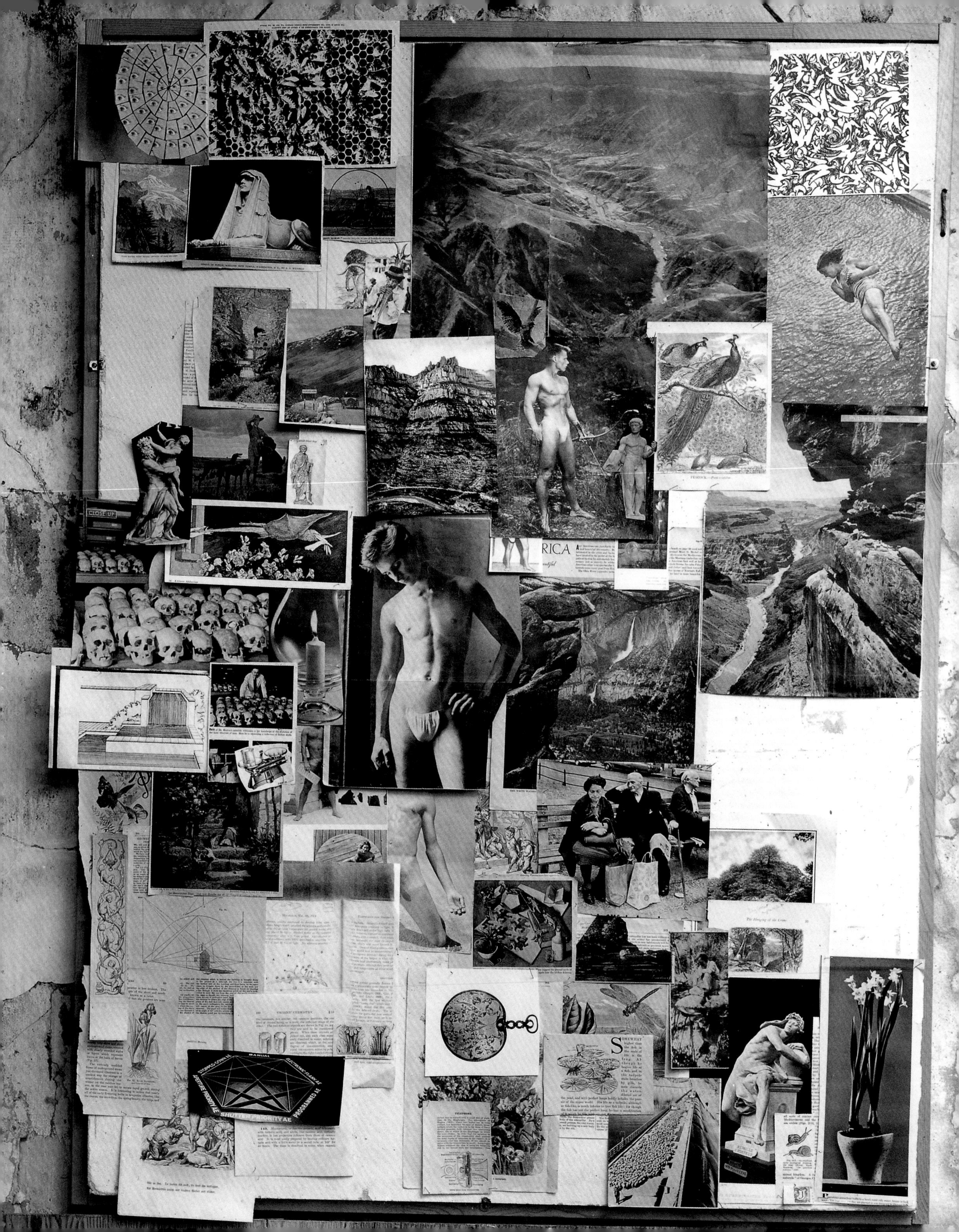

Narkissos Taking Form

Jess's most profound act of translation was his *Narkissos* project. Named for the myth of Narcissus (Jess spelled it the Greek way), it was part of a larger project he conceived to "learn how to paint." It also represents nothing less than his attempt to redeem a homoerotics of art. As early as 1952, Jess writes that he had been trying to create "homoerotic romances," citing his paintings *Café Sodom*, 1954, and *Boy Party*, 1954. He began *Narkissos* in 1959 when he was suddenly struck by the "inadequacy of expressionism to achieve censuousity without pornographic emphasis." (Jess's use of creative spelling was not limited to his paste-up poetry.) As part of the same overall conceptual project that year, Jess also laid out the images for his *Translations*. However time-consuming, the *Translations* were a snap compared to *Narkissos*. The goal was to make a single painting using "the translation technique, but composed of an interweaving of found black and white images, as if a complicated 'paste-up' had been TRANSLATED. Seeking finally to maintain intense homoeros unprofaned, sensuous, joyful and frearful."[63]

In 1959 he delineated the composition in a small pencil sketch.[64] A naked youth gazes into the water, from which a pair of arms reaches out to him. In the distance another youth hovers in front of a cliff that is crested by a crouching sphinx—an incarnation of the "muse amused" from Duncan's notebook. But it's not until 1976 that Jess began drawing for *Narkissos* in earnest (fig. 58). A photograph of the work in the studio shows the mind-boggling project underway. On one easel the elements of a paste-up collage, all hand-drawn by Jess, are in the process of being composed on paper. On the other easel a drawing of the handmade paste-up—its mirror image—is partly rendered directly onto primed canvas. Each work measures over five feet square. In between the two easels, pinned to the wall, is what appears to be the drawing that Jess is cutting up into collage elements. Another photograph shows a bulletin board with the actual source material pinned relatively into place (fig. 57). Nestled in the center is a photograph of a nearly naked youth, who bears a strong but coincidental resemblance to young Jess. Amid myriad surrounding images one might spot the "Abduction" scene from Max Klinger's print cycle *The Rape of the Glove* near Bernini's sculpture of the *Rape of Persephone*. In the upper left-hand corner, a photograph by Berenice Abbott of a parabolic mirror casts multiple watchful eyes over all.

Progress moved at snail's pace—Jess's signature speed, as one might gather by the snail in the lower right-hand corner of the composition.[65] And life intervened. In 1984 Duncan suffered kidney failure and Jess stopped all work to care for him until Duncan's death in 1988. To help steady his grief and "regain concentration," Jess resumed work in 1989, when he reported that he was again "embarked on a large composite Translation . . . undertaken partly as the medieval guild artist was required to make his masterwork, except that here the journeyman's own work has set the specifications."[66] The project was again brought to a halt in 1989, after the October earthquake left Jess with the Herculean task of

63. Jess's notes on the work's genesis come from his statement "*Narkissos* taking form," which is part of the *Narkissos Notebook*. Guided by the *Narkissos Notebook*, Michael Palmer offers a reading that details how intricately and on many levels the imagery has been pieced together to create a world of mythic imagination. Michael Palmer, "On Jess's Narkissos," in *Jess: A Grand Collage*, pp. 93–103.
64. An exquisite line drawing, *Study for Narkissos*, 1964, gives further compositional detail.
65. In his notes, Jess writes of the physical challenges of making the work: "1975 Doubts as to physical ability to undertake the *Narkissos*, the size . . . requiring too far a reach while bending the back."
66. Jess, "Biography," 1989.

Fig. 58 Jess, *Narkissos: The Last Translation*, 1978/1991. Graphite on primed linen, 70 x 60 in. (177.8 x 152.4 cm). The Museum of Modern Art, New York. Gift of Odyssia Skouras

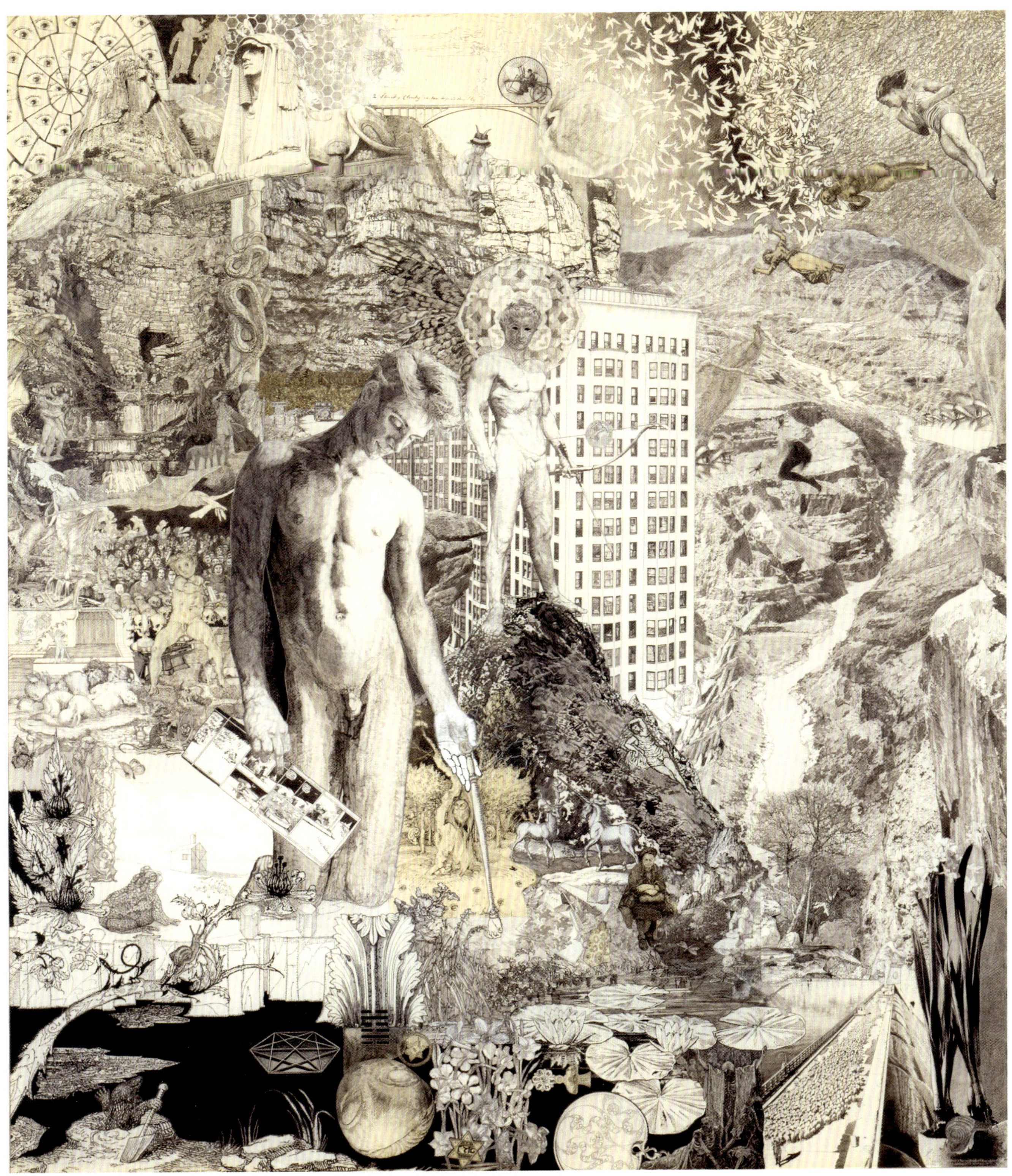

Fig. 59 Jess, *Narkissos*, 1976-1991. Collage and graphite on paper, 70 in. x 60 in. (177.8 cm x 152.4 cm). San Francisco Museum of Modern Art. Purchased through the gifts of Phyllis Wattis, Elaine McKeon, Judy and John Webb, Bobbie and Michael Wilsey, Jean and Jim Douglas, Susan and Robert Green, Pat and Bill Wilson, and the Accessions Committee Fund: gift of Frances and John Bowes, Shawn and Brook Byers, Emily L. Carroll and Thomas W. Weisel, Doris and Donald G. Fisher, Diane and Scott Heldfond, Maria Monet Markowitz and Jerome Markowitz, and the Modern Art Council

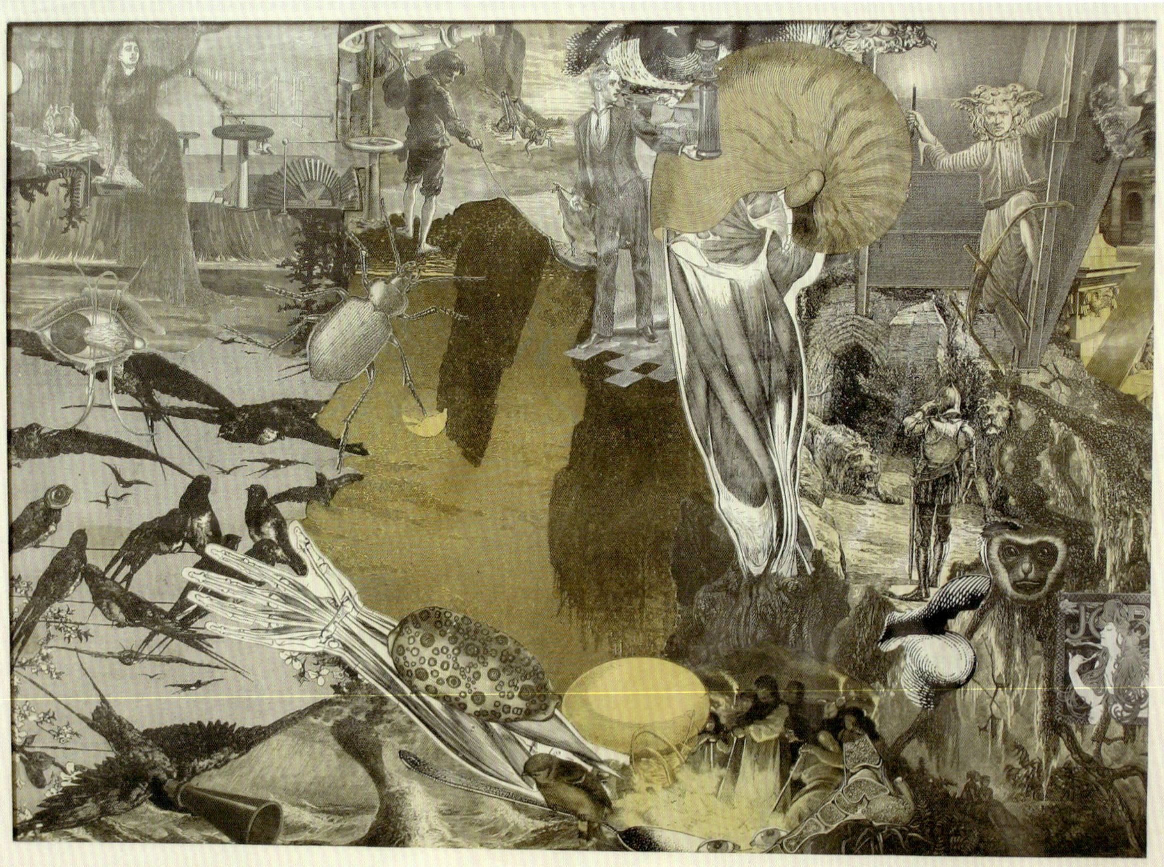

refiling his studio archive. In 1990 he determined to "broadcast decision to give up painting *Narkissos*." And so he finishes the collage (fig. 59) and pencil drawing, but never realizes his ultimate ambition of translating them into a monumental painting.[67]

Jess's *Narkissos Notebook*, 1959–90, a plain three-ring binder divided into sections, with a reference sheet on locating books in the San Francisco Public Library tucked into the front, represents Jess's far-reaching research. In it, he traced the Narcissus myth and its iconography from ancient times to contemporary readings, through texts by Melville, Blake, and Freud right up to Herbert Marcuse's *Eros and Civilization*. In page after page of notes and quotes, he cites writings on the art of Leonardo, Poussin, Brancusi, Dalí. One section of the *Notebook* is an "Image Reservoir" with George Herriman's cartoon *Krazy Kat* "testing the Narcissus legend" among the many citations. Various subsections ("Narkissos' reflection," "Watchers," "Meddlers," "Flowers and Insects") itemize the total pictorial contents. In the back of the *Notebook*, a scrapbook of images shows just how far Jess was willing to pursue his myth. After botanical prints and pages cut from a very tame adult magazine called *After Dark* is a page from a Victorian catalogue advertising a bathtub model called "The Narcissus."

Embodying the archival nature of his practice, based as it was on reading and research, cutting and compiling, Jess's *Narkissos Notebook* is an extraordinary

Fig. 60 Jess, *Echo's Wake, Part IV*, 1961/1966. Collage, 10 1/4 x 14 1/2 in. (26 x 36.8 cm). Collection of Paule Anglim, San Francisco

67. The collage *Narkissos* is in the collection of the San Francisco Museum of Modern Art; the drawing *Narkissos* is in the collection of the Museum of Modern Art, New York.

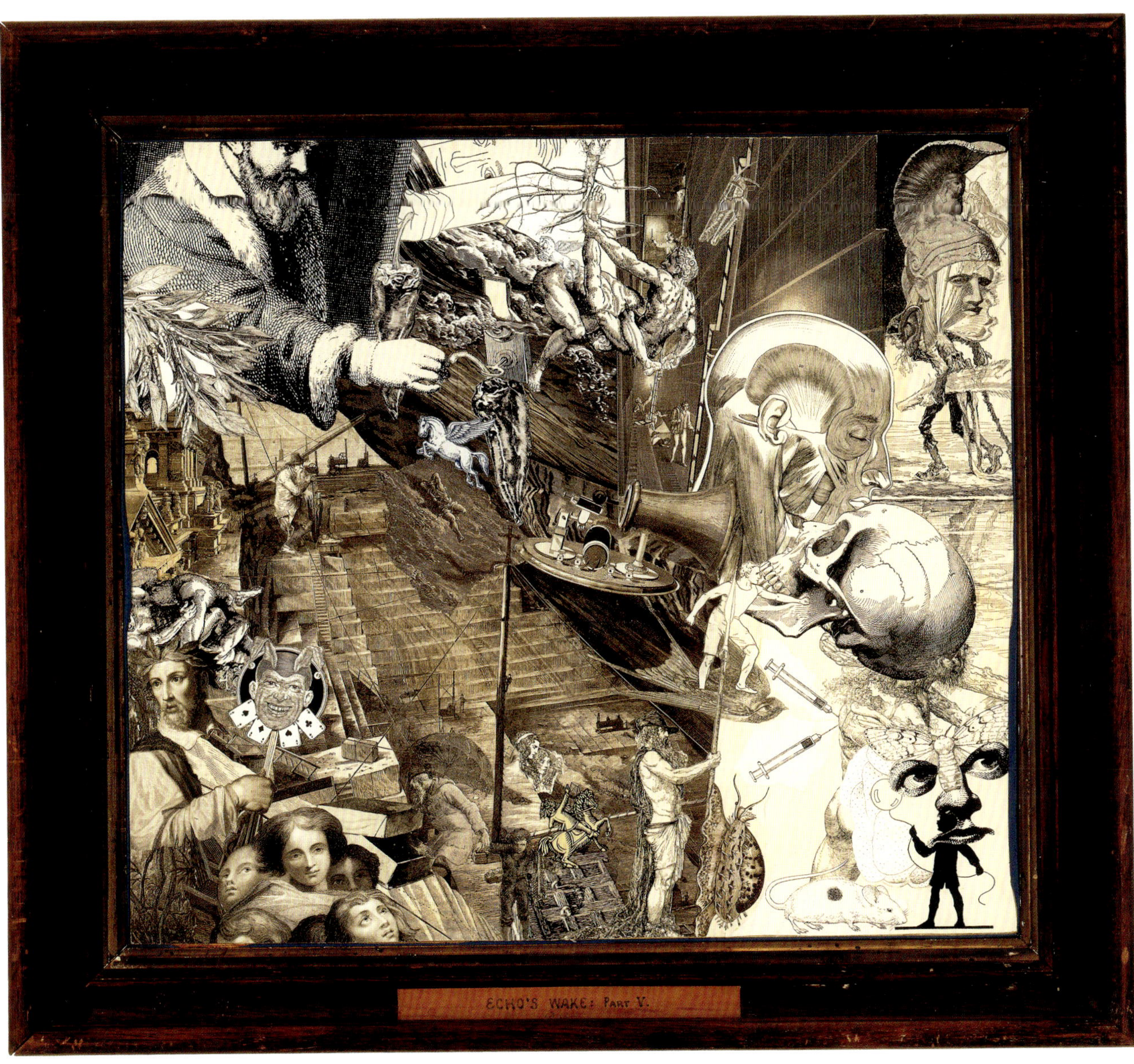

Fig. 61 Jess, *Echo's Wake: Part V*, 1966. Collage, 17 ½ x 19 in. (44.5 x 48.3 cm). The JPMorgan Chase Art Collection

work of process art. And though the *Narkissos* project stopped short of its final translation into paint, the two existing iterations powerfully express Jess's "homoeros" of art. His was an exquisitely time-consuming act of reproduction that delectated in indirect processes, hermetic meanings, and layered images that both reveal and conceal their sources and identities. Jess's art of duplication was not determined by making a new original—by being procreative—but aimed to reflect in a different light what already exists. Like the homoerotic act, Jess's homoeros is in essence a mirroring: the beautiful twin brothers the Dios Kuroi mirrored in one another, and, of course, Narkissos mirrored back at himself. The complexity of the *Narkissos* composition is disorienting in a way that is itself charged with possibility. Offering no traditional ground to stand on

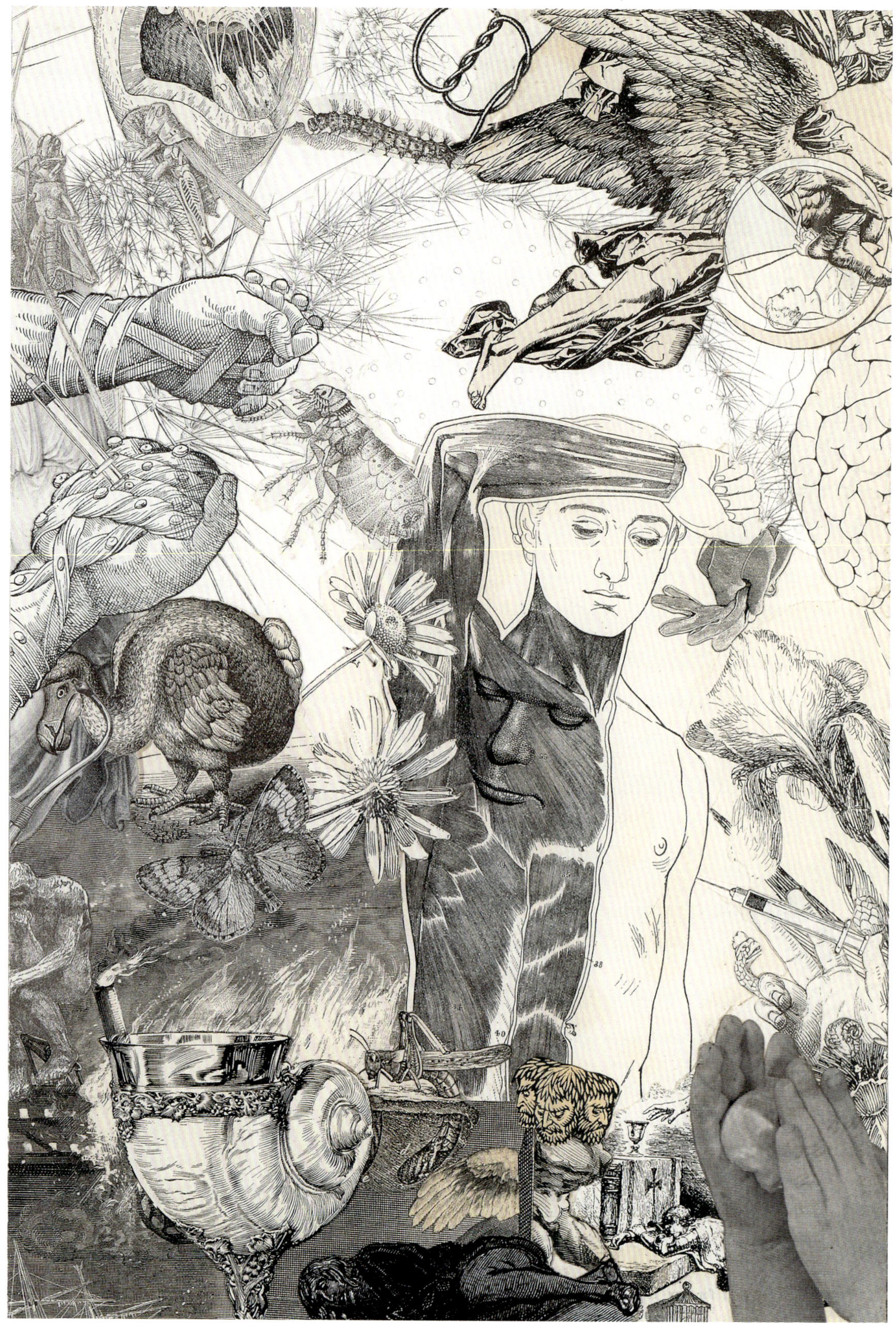

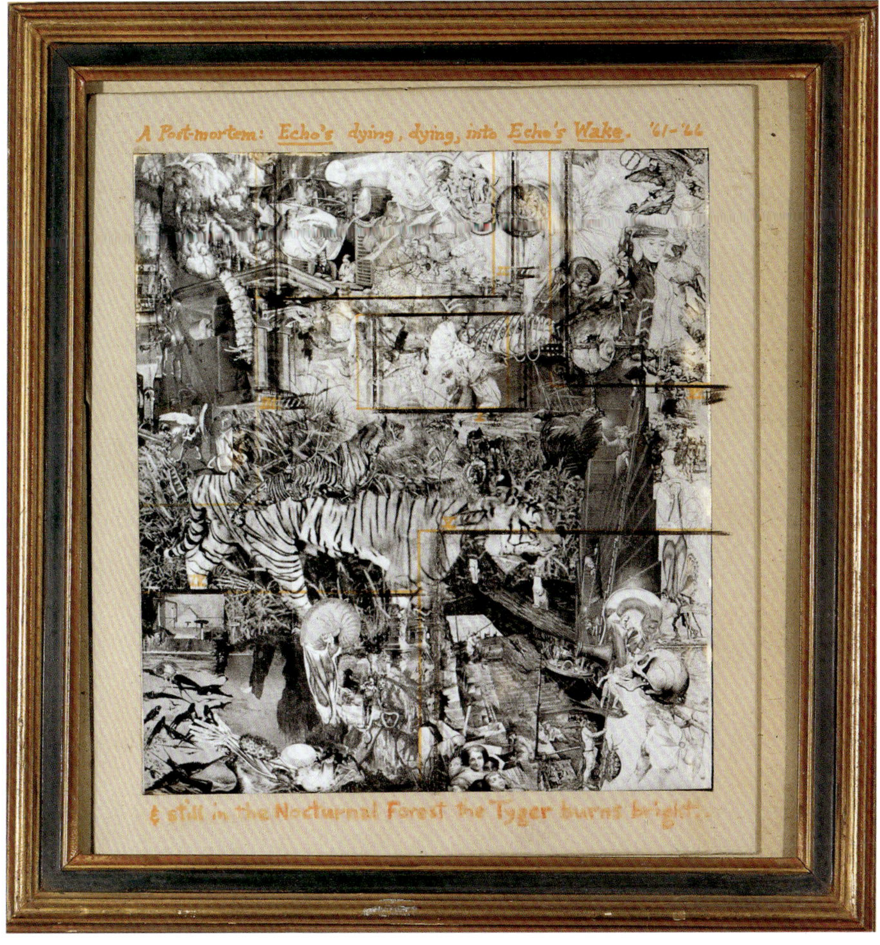

(opposite page)
Fig. 62 Jess, *Echo's Wake, Part VI*, 1961/1966.
Collage, 18 ½ x 14 ½ in. (47 x 36.8 cm)
Courtesy Odyssia Gallery, New York

(this page)
Fig. 63 Jess, *A Post-mortem: Echo's Dying,
Dying, into Echo's Wake: '61–'66*, 1966. Ink on
photograph and cardboard in frame with
crayon on glass, 12 ¼ x 11 ½ in. (31.1 x 29.2 cm).
Courtesy Odyssia Gallery, New York

or conventional narrative paths to follow, these works enforce an open mode of
exploration across deliberately slippery terrain. The poet Robert Glück tapped
into the eruptive erotic force of Jess's art in writing on his first paste-up, *The
Mouse's Tale*, 1951, a work titled after a bit of concrete poetry by Lewis Carroll
that Glück describes as being "embedded in a swarm of Lilliputian exhibition-
ists, tireless multipliers of sexual urge."[68]

Narkissos relates to another body of work that *was* completed—by the very
process of being cut apart. According to the myth, Narcissus was so infatuated
with his beauty that he perished gazing at his own reflection in a pool of water.
His narcissism had already proved fatal to Echo, the nymph who loved him.
Succumbing to the callousness of his rejection, she faded to pieces, leaving only
her disembodied voice to echo among the rocks and stream. Echoing the title of
his beloved James Joyce, Jess created *Echo's Wake*, six collages cut from a single
paste-up of 1961 (figs. 60, 61, 62). *A Post-Mortem: Echo's Dying, Dying into Echo's
Wake: '61–'66*, 1966 (fig. 63), commemorates the gesture with a photograph
of the original paste-up under glass, marked with crayon showing which parts
made the cut. Who knows what happened to the unused fragments, which,
like Echo's body itself, all seem to have disappeared.

68. Robert Glück, "Jess: The Mouse's Tale, 1951,"
Artforum (March 2000), p. 119.

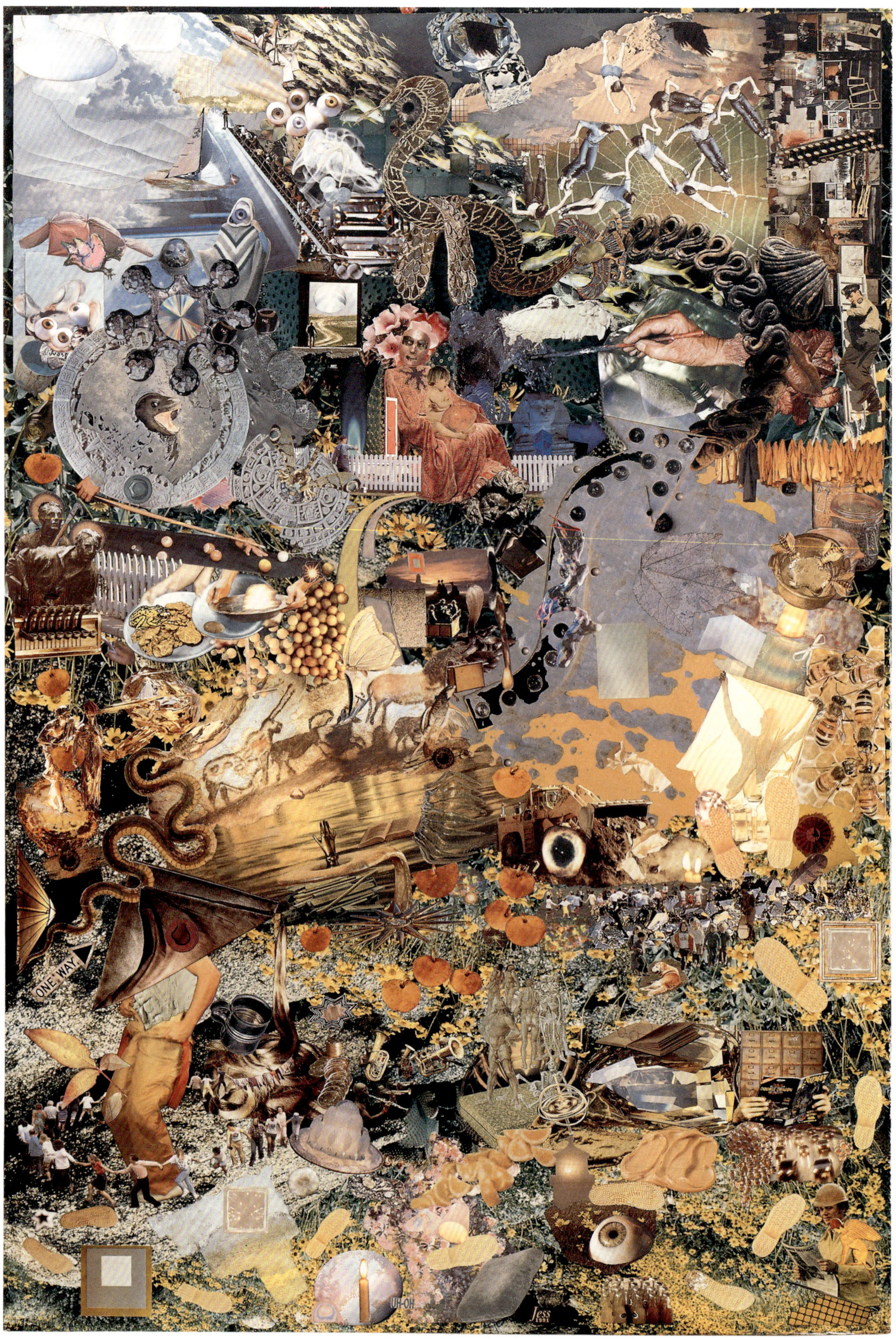

Dyslecstasy

Rife with literary references, Jess's work also offers pure reading pleasure. For anyone who loves a good story, it's like "reading a fantasy novel," as the artist Bruce Conner once said of looking at Jess's art.[69] Duncan linked the reading of Jess's art "to the great primary tradition that extends from the illustrated walls of Cro-magnon man's galleries."[70] *Dyslecstasy*, 1991 (fig. 64), one of Jess's late, great collages, epitomizes the pleasure. Requiring no outside sources or guide to apprehend and enjoy, *Dyslecstasy* features a cave painting at its center, directly above a hand that is reaching out of water. Nearby shines a naked youth (another reflection of *Narkissos*). The rest of the composition swirls with emblems of Eros and apocalypse: a burning candle, a mushrooming cloud, winding snakes, eyes and "o" shapes. There are no words, save the title. A "centaur" expression—half didactic (dyslexia) and half ecstatic—it embodies the dual ways of being read that Jess constructed in his work, and instructs us in the pleasures of corrupted syntax that is the grammar of collage.

As *Dyslecstasy* implies, what is collage if not a queer way of reading? Collage syntax flows its own way, flouting assumptions about how things should go together, whether the parts of an image or a sentence, words and pictures, visual and literary frames of reference, or a couple. Jess once said, "Robert and I would often discuss a particular image from reading or television and follow its line back in time using our library here. We would always be fascinated by how the imagination travels through time, the image being a constant vehicle."[71] His syntax was an associative one; each image of a collage was connected—through time and like pieces of a puzzle. An avid jigsaw puzzle doer, Jess knew that each puzzle company used the same cutout template on many different pictures. His *Deranged Stereopticon*, 1974 (fig. 66), one of his mind-boggling picture-puzzle collages, replicates this duplication: it is two different collages, each with same-shaped pieces, assembled side by side into a perfect fit of scrambled images.

Perhaps this associative scramble is why Jess's art looks so queerly correct right now. We live in world not just of books, but of flux, in which pictures constantly cascade and swell amid ever expanding boundaries of global and media cultures. I am writing this text on my computer, having turned frequently (and conveniently) for information in my research of Jess's art to the collage space that is the Web. And don't we navigate the Web steered by the vernacular of collage: searching, finding, copying, cutting, pasting, grabbing, stealing, filing, archiving, linking, and sharing? These days, one can even translate texts on-line—albeit the results are often most queer. Translated into today's critical language, the Web-like structure of Jess's *Dyslecstasy* might be called "rhizomatic." It certainly appears to embody the notion of the horizontally dispersed media that is digital culture, though Jess would have preferred "polysemous," after a favorite term of Duncan's for imagery that flows in all directions while accruing a multiplicity of meanings. Alongside his art's relationship to history and narrative, which gives it such accessibility and relevance, Jess's work seems tuned to a future that is now present.

69. Conner quoted in Jesse Hamlin, "A Look into the Secluded Life of Jess," *San Francisco Chronicle*, February 24, 1994, p. E1; another interesting take on reading Jess is in Barrett Watten, "Derivations," *Artweek*, April 21, 1994.
70. Robert Duncan, "Iconographical Extensions," in Jess, *Translations* (Los Angeles: Black Sparrow Press, 1971), p. i.
71. Jess quoted in Auping, *A Grand Collage*, p. 26.

In his 1936 essay "The Storyteller" Walter Benjamin predicted the modern-day doom of oral tradition. But perhaps this tradition just changed forms. Steeped in literary culture, Jess's art emerges as a visual form of dyslecstatic storytelling for postmodern times. His compositions are dense yet porous, with diverse narrative possibilities that we readers may surf or analyze, stream or search, and piece together as we will. Redeemed from a life submerged in printed matter, they are narratives forged to represent the limitlessness of a universe connected through correspondences. Onto this universe—full of the sublime sense of pleasure and terror that unbounded spaces seem to hold—Jess's art opens like a book that enjoins each of us viewers to be our own storyteller.

Fig. 65 Jess, *Brimo of Colchis*, 1954. Collage, 23 x 12 ³/₄ in. (58.4 x 32.4 cm). Courtesy Odyssia Gallery, New York

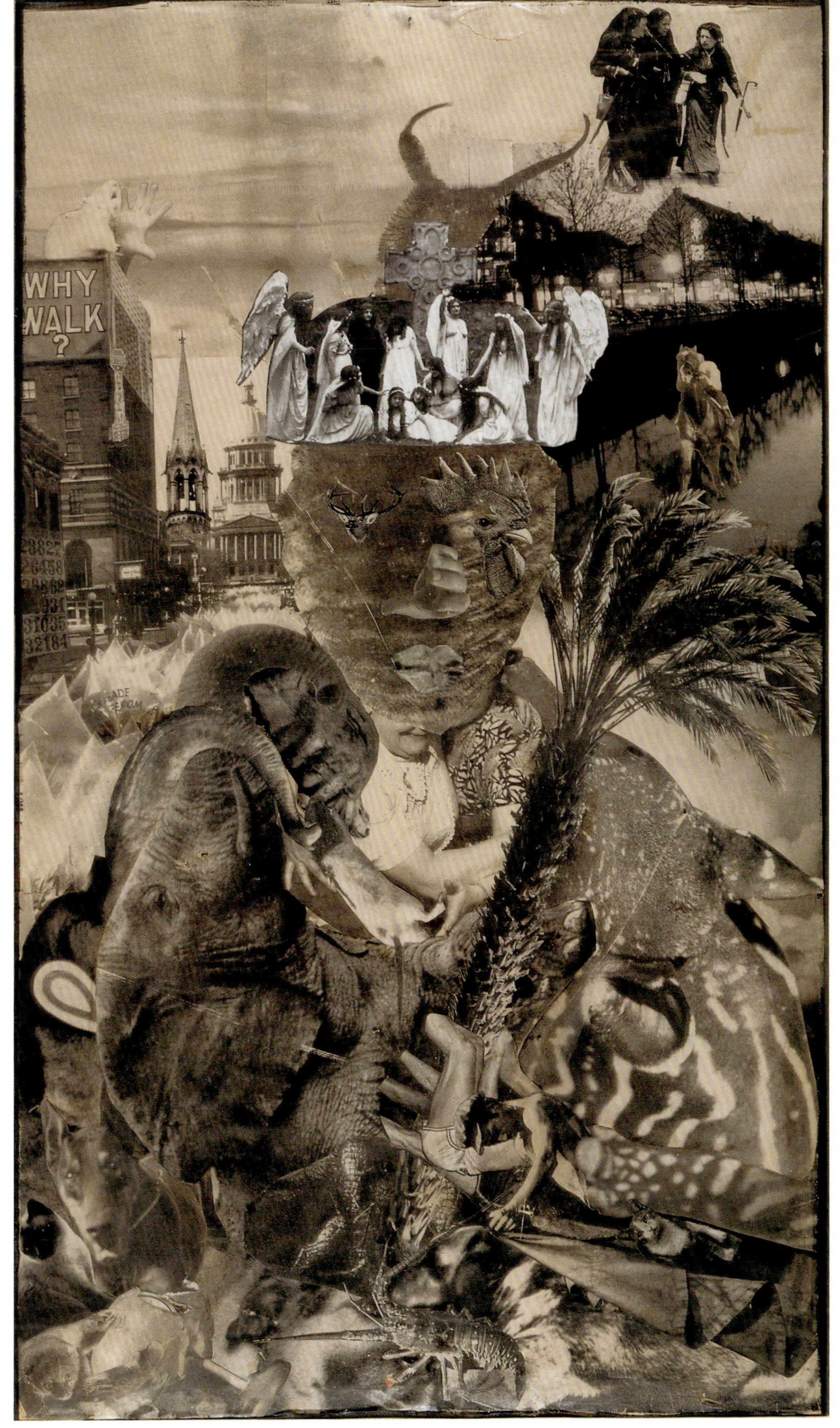

WHY
WALK
?

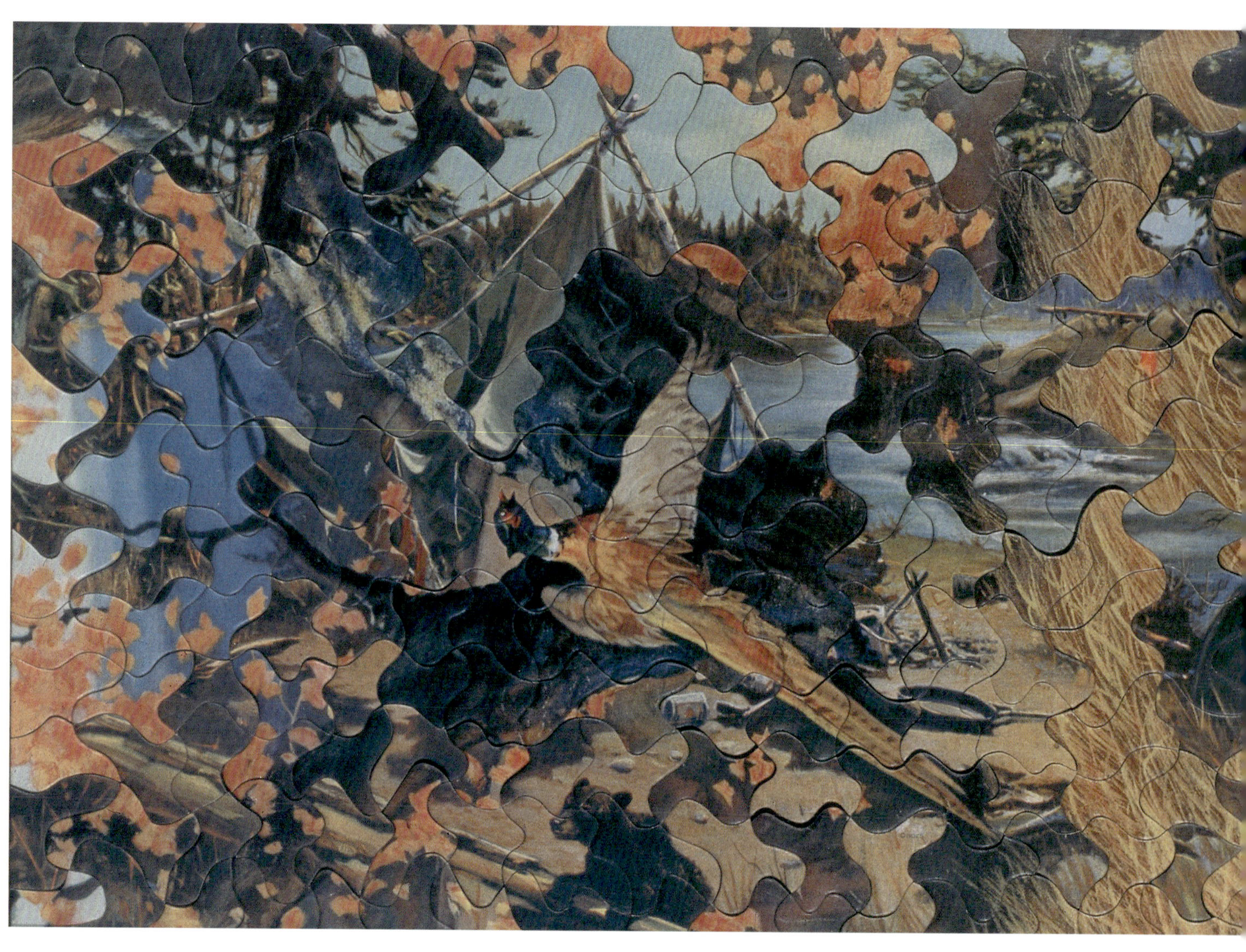

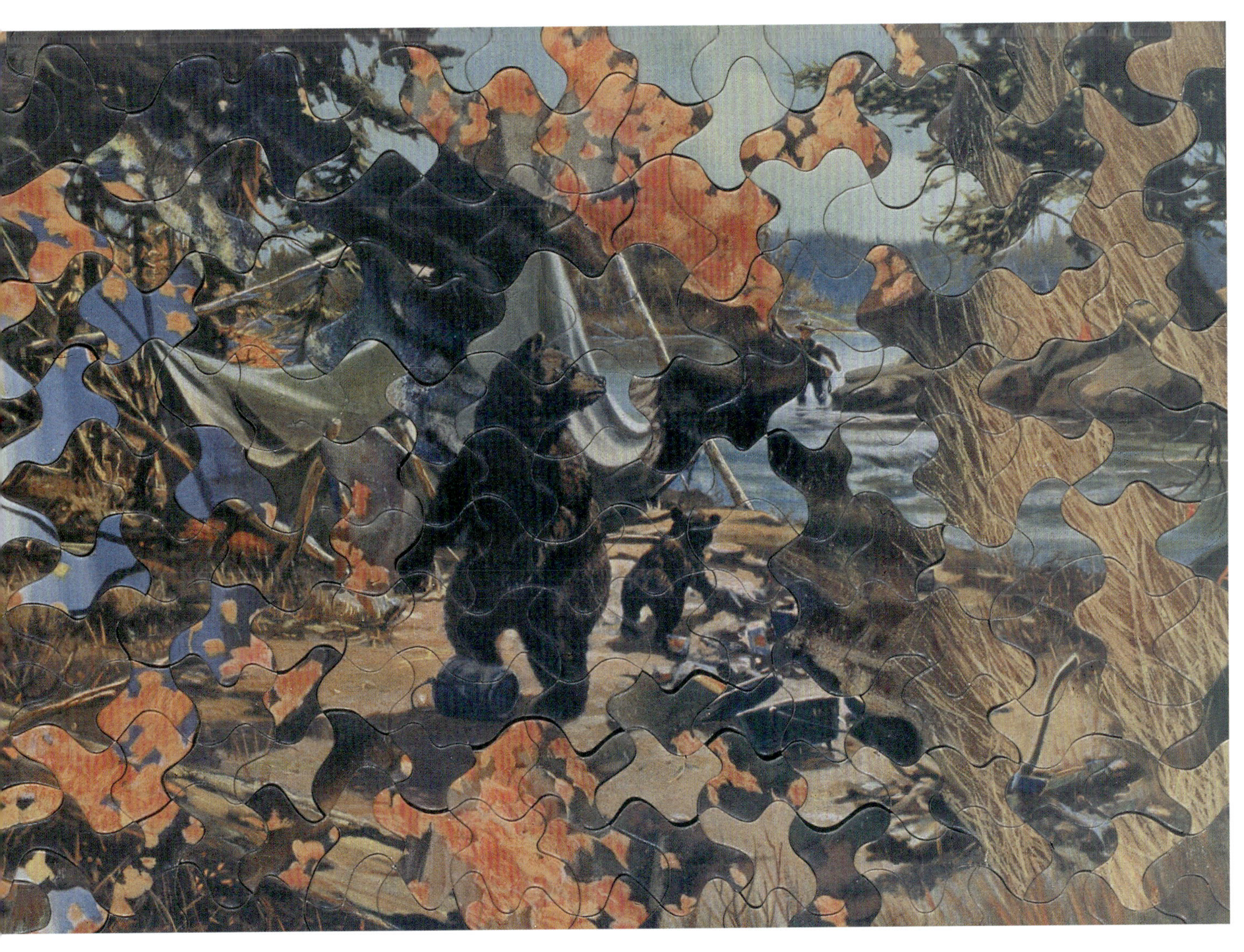

Fig. 66 Jess, *Deranged Stereopticon*, 1974.
Collage, 15 1/2 x 34 1/2 in. (39.4 x 87.6 cm).
Courtesy Odyssia Gallery, New York

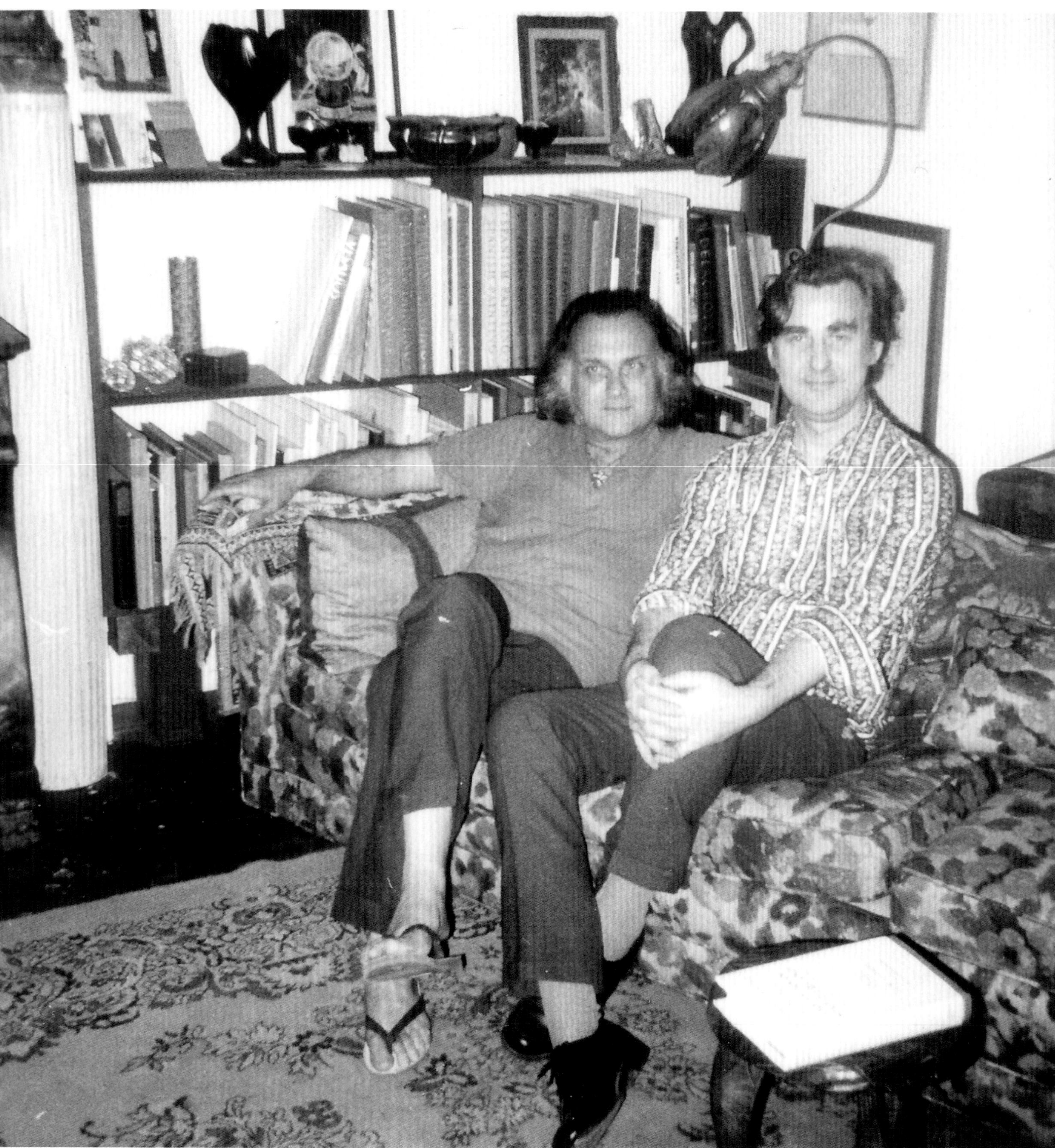

JESS AND HIS LITERARY MILIEU

BY LISA JARNOT

The household that Jess shared with Robert Duncan was from its beginning a magnet for a host of creative presences.[1] When the two men took marriage vows in January 1951, both brought with them the social relationships they had cultivated during the previous decade. Jess formed his community of painters, including Brock Brockway, Lynne Brown (later Lyn Brockway), and Harry Jacobus while studying at the California School of Fine Arts in San Francisco.[2] Duncan, during his abbreviated undergraduate career at the University of California, Berkeley (1937–39), and his subsequent residence in and around New York City (1939–46), met a number of writers and editors who ushered him into his professional life as a writer. At Berkeley, his peers included painter Virginia Admiral, who went on to become one of Hans Hofmann's New York protégés, and Pauline Kael, the nascent film critic.[3] When Duncan arrived on the East Coast in 1939, he joined the Woodstock artists' and anarchists' commune of *Phoenix* magazine editors James and Blanche Cooney, and made himself at home in New York City circles that included diarist Anaïs Nin, novelist Henry Miller, poet Kenneth Patchen, playwrights James Baldwin and Tennessee Williams, and essayist Paul Goodman. The city, with its wartime influx of European refugees, including Salvador Dalí and André Breton, also offered Duncan entrance into a world of Surrealist enchantment.

In 1946, returning to Berkeley with a vague plan to complete his education, Duncan instead found himself a key player in a confluence of events and gatherings partly inspired by elder poets Kenneth Rexroth and Madeline Gleason, and fueled by a younger generation of Bay Area writers including Jack Spicer and Robin Blaser.[4] Duncan, Spicer, and Blaser formed the core of what came to be known as the Berkeley Renaissance, a congregation of writers who developed an aesthetic that might be characterized as a West Coast mid-century experimental poetics. San Francisco would soon have the distinction of being a "poet's town," and the three young poets were instrumental in paving the way for verse that challenged traditional ideas of form and meter while at the same time telling traditional stories from new perspectives. Medieval history, gnostic religion, linguistics, homosexual reveries, snippets of Shakespeare, and bits and pieces of pop culture all flowed into the poems of the Berkeley companions, who imagined themselves as fellows of an Arthurian roundtable.

Duncan and Jess first crossed paths in 1949 at a reading on the campus of the University of California, Berkeley. There, Duncan performed a long piece called "The Venice Poem," which encapsulates the themes and formal innovations of Berkeley Renaissance writing. Jess, captivated by the poem and the poet, later recalled that he had "fallen in love" with Duncan on the spot.[5]

1. The term "household" is used throughout this essay to describe the physical space and artistic works that Duncan and Jess shared and created during the course of their marriage. For both men, the word evoked an understanding of the sacred place of Eros and imaginative intent.

2. For more on Jess's relationships with painters in the Bay Area, see Michael Auping's main essay in *Jess: A Grand Collage 1951–1993*, exh. cat. (Buffalo, N.Y.: Albright-Knox Art Gallery, 1993), pp. 31–65.

3. Regarding Duncan's Berkeley circle in general, see Robert Duncan, *Drawings and Decorated Books*, ed. Christopher Wagstaff (San Francisco: Rose Books, 1992).

4. During the early 1940s, young writers and activists congregated at the Libertarian Circle meetings held at Rexroth's San Francisco apartment. Gleason's Bay Area Poetry Festivals of the late 1940s served as a model for The Poetry Center of San Francisco State College, established in 1954.

5. Jess, in conversation with the author, August 1988; see also, Lewis Ellingham and Kevin Killian, *Jack Spicer: Poet Be Like God* (Middletown, Conn.: Wesleyan University Press, 1998), p. 40.

Duncan, by nature gregarious, obsessively vocal, and socially hyperactive, was surrounded by a rambunctious, erudite group of writers and thinkers. Jess, fiercely reclusive and easily distressed by noisy crowds, depended on extended periods of solitude to complete his work. During the early part of the couple's relationship, they negotiated rituals of household work practices and boundaries of social engagement. Jess was quick to ban unruly individuals from the household, and Duncan was careful to extend invitations only to sanctioned guests.[6] Jess's dalliances in Duncan's circle of friends in fact came most comfortably in the form of his behind-the-scenes contributions to books, magazines, and collaborative projects over nearly forty years. While his contributions to and participation in Duncan's social world were selective, he drew from and was drawn to a handful of writers and visual artists who shared his delighted devotion to do-it-yourself endeavors of the imagination.

In a household that grew as an art project by its very design, Jess found his key collaborator and confidant in Duncan. In addition to the domestic projects they completed together (including stained-glass window designs, backyard gardens, and extravagant meals), the two shared a deep love of storytelling. Accumulating books as sacred objects, they placed a few select texts at the heart of the household; L. Frank Baum's *Oz* series (which both men had cherished during childhood) and George MacDonald's Scottish fantasy tales took a special place in the master bedroom. Inspiration for Jess's paintings, collages, books, chapbooks, magazines, assemblages, plays, and films resonated from the bookshelves that lined nearly every wall of the house. As each man's career flourished—Duncan becoming a major contemporary American poet, and Jess an internationally recognized painter—their affinities deepened and their collections of treasured objects grew.

During the first year of their marriage, the couple moved from Jess's studio at 1350 Franklin Street in San Francisco (a looming artists' flop known as the Ghost House) to James Broughton's apartment at 1724 Baker Street. Broughton, a poet, playwright, and experimental filmmaker then on an extended trip to Europe, left Duncan and Jess with the business responsibilities related to his Centaur Press, and with a large living space ripe for entertaining guests. Among those the couple welcomed into the household were the young filmmakers Stan Brakhage and Lawrence Jordan (arriving from Denver in 1953 and 1954, respectively) and Kenneth Anger, whose first film, *Fireworks* (1947), later became a milestone in avant-garde American cinema. Jess, who took a liking to the fairly inexperienced artists, collaborated with all three on a number of film projects.[7] During the same period, Duncan and Jess ventured into another ambitious project, with painter Harry Jacobus, opening King Ubu Gallery, an independent artists' space that provided a valuable and rare public forum for seeing works by Jess, Jacobus, and others from their circle at the California School of Fine Arts.

During the spring of 1955, Duncan and Jess traveled across the United States, en route to the Spanish island of Mallorca for a yearlong stay. Both

6. Many of Duncan and Jess's friends and students tell stories of Jess's selectivity in accepting newcomers into the household. This recollection comes via the author's conversations with Jess as well as Mary Margaret Sloan, Norma Cole, and Christopher Edwards.

7. Anger and Brakhage completed an untitled film (circa 1953) in which they used Jess's collage *The Mouse's Tale* as the main visual image. This film was never shown and is now missing, though Brakhage said he thought it was somewhere in his vast archive. (Brakhage, in conversation with the author, 2000). Jess and Brakhage made a film called *In Between* (1954/55). Jess's collaborations with Jordan stretched into the following decades and included the films *The 40 and 1 Nights, or Jess's Didactic Nickelodeon* (1955–62) and *Finds of the Fortenight* (1980).

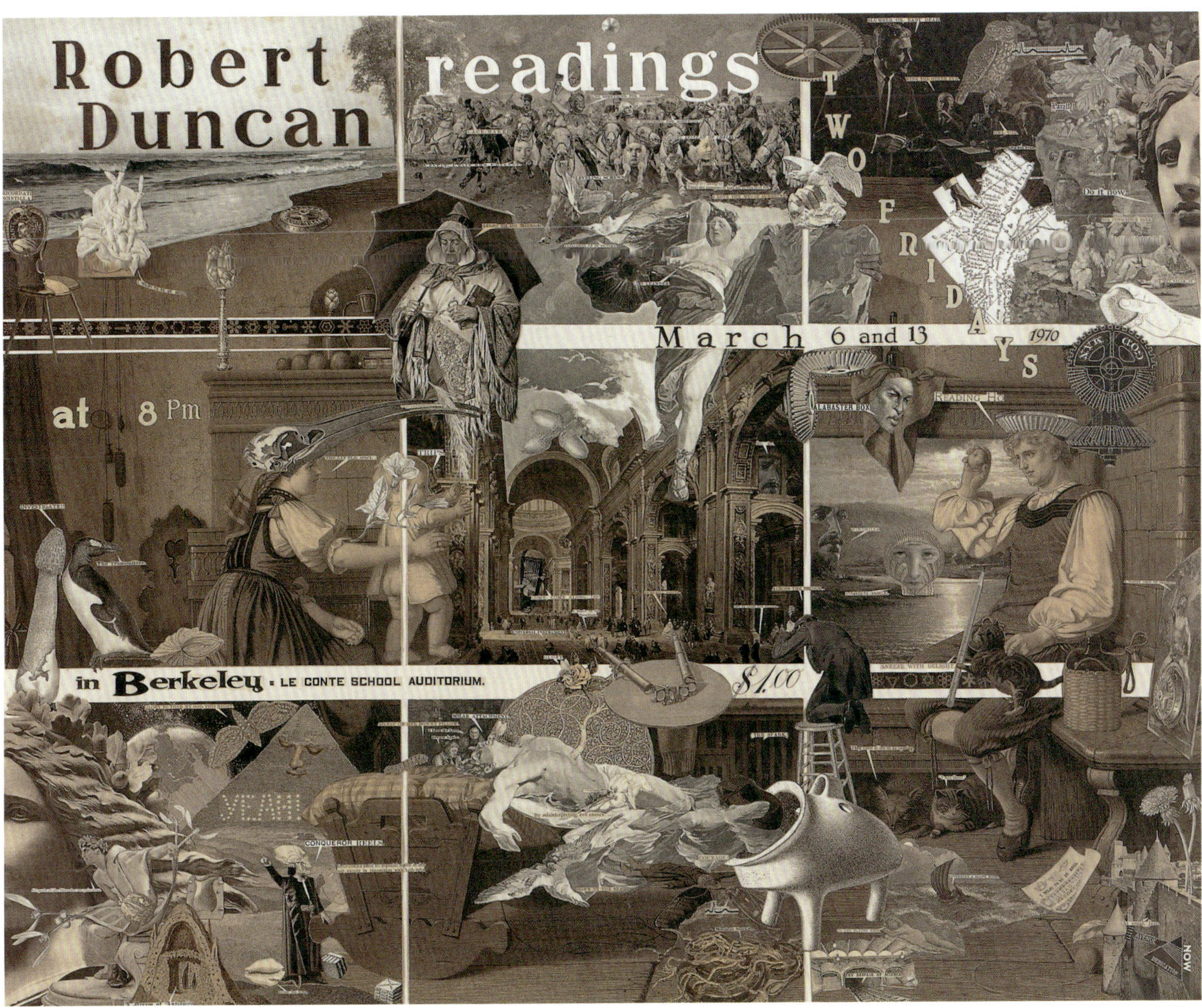

Fig. 68 Jess, *Robert Duncan Reading at Le Conte Auditorium*, 1970. Collage, 30 ¼ x 38 ¼ in. (76.8 x 97.2 cm). University of California, Berkeley Art Museum; gift of the artist

non-drivers, they enlisted Jacobus to escort them and made several sightseeing stops, including a short detour to Black Mountain College outside of Asheville, North Carolina. There, they visited the poet Charles Olson, who had first crossed paths with Duncan in 1947 in Berkeley, and had been named rector at Black Mountain in 1951. A father figure for a generation of writers interested in history, myth, and the craft of the open form poem, Olson inspired a clear shift in Duncan's preoccupations as a writer. The two men, well matched in physical and intellectual energies, were instrumental in developing a projective "field poetics." For Jess too the pilgrimage to Black Mountain was significant. In addition to meeting with Olson, he had the thrill of visiting the campus where Josef Albers had taught color theory and the Abstract Expressionists explored non-linear visual narratives.

Duncan and Jess's next stop was New York City, where they introduced themselves to another poet soon to be associated with Black Mountain College, Denise Levertov. Born in England and raised in a bookish family, Levertov

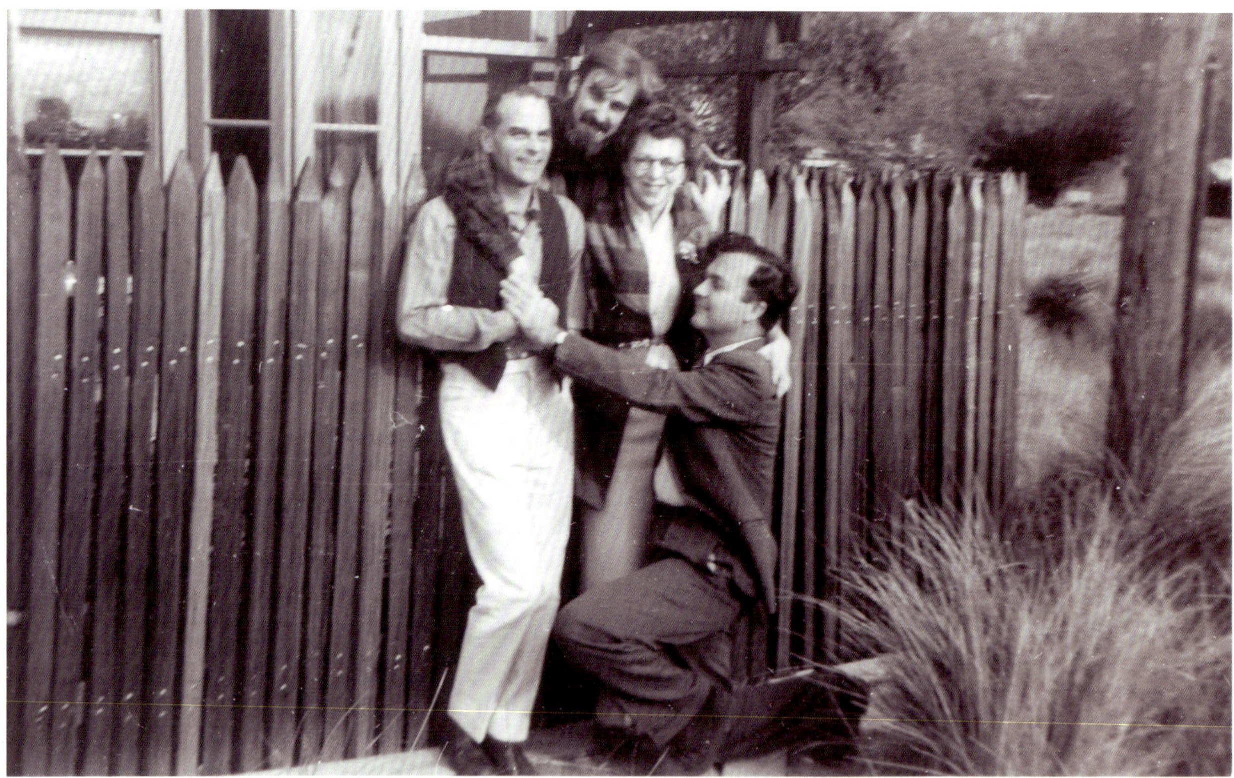

Fig. 69 James Broughton, a bearded Jess, Ida Hodes, and Robert Duncan at the Elfmere Cottage in Stinson Beach, California, 1960

Fig. 70 Robert Creeley, editor, *Black Mountain Review* (page detail), no. 4, Winter 1954. Magazine with collage reproduction by Jess, 64 pages, 8 ½ x 6 ½ in. (21.6 x 16.5 cm). Collection of Steve Dickison

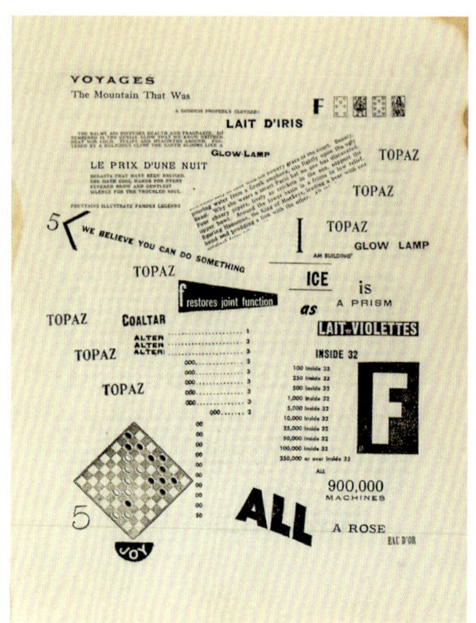

began a friendship with Duncan and Jess that revolved around devotion to creative activity and a fierce determination toward integrating intellectual and political preoccupations. In Levertov, Duncan and Jess found a peer whose commitment to her art as a primary expression of her existence paralleled their own daily practices of reading, writing, and painting.

On landing in Mallorca, Duncan and Jess made the acquaintance of yet a third poet associated with Black Mountain, Robert Creeley. Creeley, then the editor of the *Black Mountain Review* (fig. 70) and the Divers Press, was eager to have the companionship of both men. A few years younger than Duncan and Jess, he leaned on them for relationship advice, composed poems in call and response to Duncan's work, and subsequently began a vibrant correspondence with the two that lasted for thirty years. The stay in Mallorca opened the way for an early collaborative book project between Duncan and Jess, *Caesar's Gate* (Divers Press, 1955). During the production of the book, a comfortable division of labor fell into place: Jess composed original collages to be bound between the pages of Duncan's poems (see fig. 49), while Duncan solicited subscriptions to the publication via illustrated letters mailed to friends in the United States and Europe. The project laid the foundation for Jess and Duncan's later collaborations, from Christmas cards to chapbooks to announcements of poetry readings (see fig. 68).

When the couple's travel funds ran dry, Duncan accepted a brief teaching job at Black Mountain College during the spring of 1956, after which the couple returned to San Francisco. There, Duncan assumed the role of assistant director of The Poetry Center at San Francisco State College, working alongside English professor Ruth Witt-Diamant and poetry enthusiast Ida Hodes, whom Duncan had been introduced to via a mutual friend, novelist Henry Miller. Duncan and Jess's return to the Bay Area coincided with the beginning of the San Francisco Renaissance, heralded by Allen Ginsberg's historic reading of *Howl* at the Six Gallery the previous fall. In a scene infused with the energy of another visitor, Jack Kerouac, younger writers shed the conventions of formal narrative poetry and prose and focused their energies on critiquing American suburban cold war culture. The North Beach poetry community, centered around Lawrence Ferlinghetti's City Lights bookstore and a growing number of bohemian-friendly bars and galleries, drew flocks of younger writers interested not only in the Beats, but in Duncan and Spicer. Spicer, a formidable poet and professional linguist, remained one of Duncan's great companions in the realm

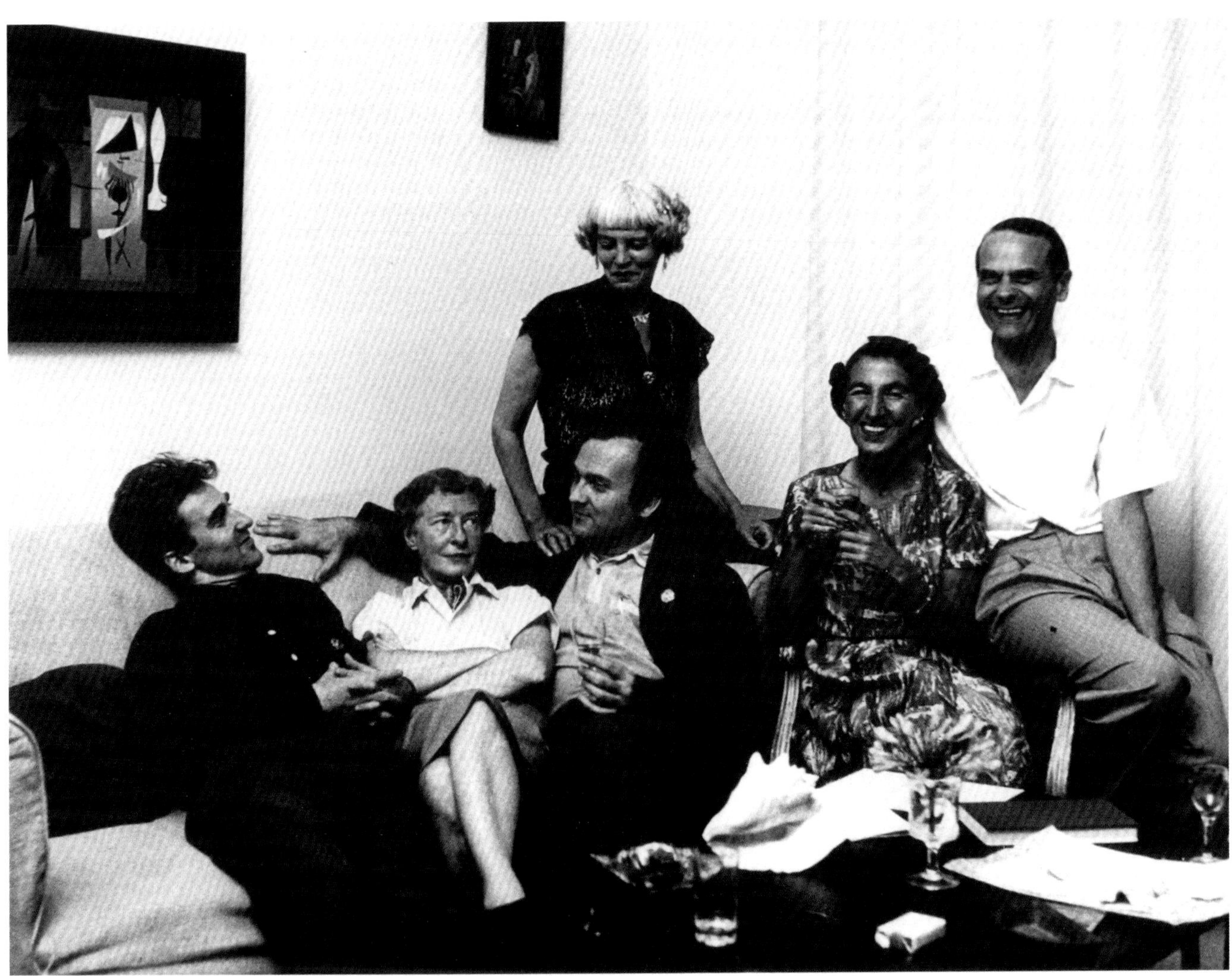

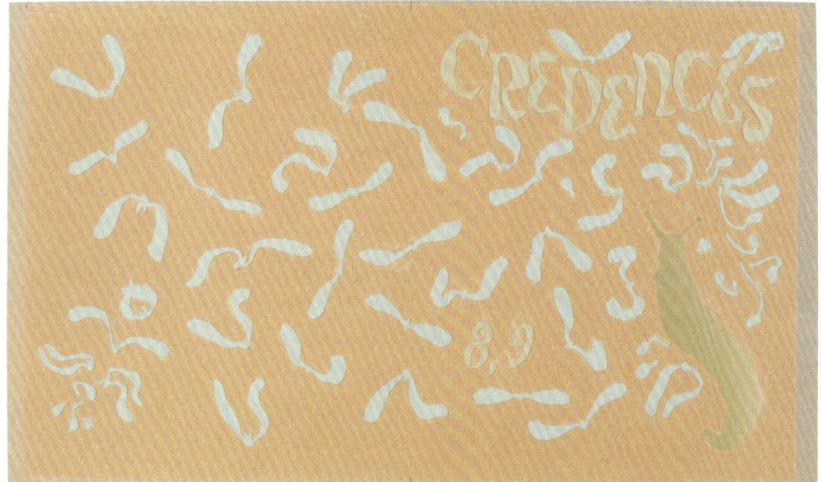

Fig. 72 Jess, *Cover for Credences 8/9*, 1980. Collage, 10 ½ x 14 in. (26.7 x 35.6 cm). Collection of Anne and Robert Bertholf, Buffalo, New York

of poetry, despite their increasing personal estrangement.[8] The two became rival mentors at late-1950s informal Sunday poetry gatherings, which drew a number of fledgling writers, including Joanne Kyger (one of the central younger women writers of the Beat scene).[9] Out of those workshops and subsequent group outings to North Beach bars, the White Rabbit Press, first run by Boston poet Joe Dunn, emerged. Renamed Enkidu Surrogate (a "surrogate" of Dunn's project) under Duncan's editorship in 1958, the press operated from a cottage in Stinson Beach to which Duncan and Jess had moved the same year (fig. 69). With Jess contributing illustrations and Duncan promoting the press and selling books, Enkidu Surrogate became yet another extension of cooperative household activities.

A further collaboration within the San Francisco community came in the form of a group called The Maidens (fig. 71), whose gatherings resembled a Victorian tea klatch with a penchant for camp. The Maidens included James Broughton, Helen Adam, Eve Triem, Madeline Gleason, Duncan, and Jess, who met on occasion to share meals and recite poems they had composed for each other.[10] Jess preferred such intimate groups of Bay Area writers. Resistant to the "sex and drugs" aesthetics of the San Francisco Beat movement, he gravitated toward the company of women, and toward those who shared his affection for the genteel pleasures of domestic life. In these respects, Helen Adam and her sister, Pat, became two of Jess's closest friends. Having arrived in the United States from Scotland in 1939, the sisters soon moved to San Francisco with their elderly mother in tow. Helen, proclaimed a child prodigy with the publication of a collection of poems called *The Elfin Pedlar and Tales Told by the Pixie Pool* in 1923, wrote in the tradition of Scottish border ballads throughout her life's work. Also a playwright and collage artist, she had a macabre sensibility and a love for the Victorian, which entered into deep conversation with Jess's work.[11] Both Adam and Jess furnished their collages with images culled from mainstream magazines, reconstructing visual sequences that mocked the preoccupations of the dominant culture.

8. Spicer struggled with alcoholism throughout his adult life and died in 1965 at the age of forty.
9. Ellingham and Killian's *Jack Spicer* is among the most detailed sources on the San Francisco poetry scene of the 1950s and 1960s.
10. For more on The Maidens and Duncan's relationship with James Broughton, see Broughton's memoir *Coming Unbuttoned* (San Francisco: City Lights Books, 1993), p. 64.
11. See Kristen Prevallet's "Helen Adam's Sweet Company," www.heelstone.com/meridian/adam4.html.

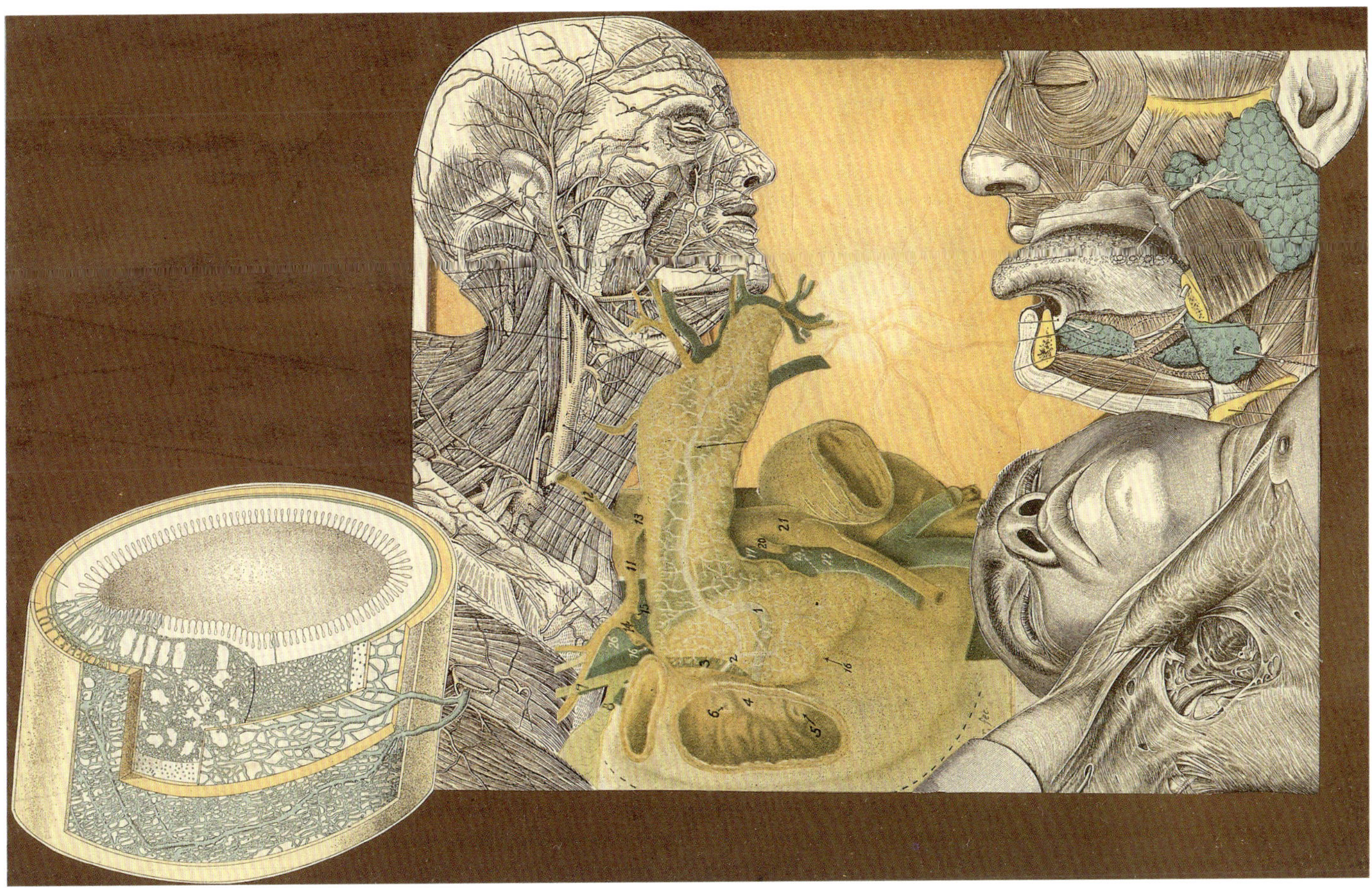

Fig. 73 Jess, *Once Upon a Time . . . For Robert*, 1966. Collage, 10 ½ x 6 ¾ in. (26.7 x 17.1 cm). Collection of Mr. and Mrs. Federico Quadrani, New York

12. Denise Levertov's anti-war activism during the late 1960s and early 1970s had, by Duncan's charge, placed her devotion to the craft of the poem in jeopardy. See *The Letters of Robert Duncan and Denise Levertov*, eds. Robert J. Bertholf and Albert Gelpi (Stanford, Ca.: Stanford University Press, 2003), p. 629.

With the Adam sisters' move to New York City in 1964, Olson's death in 1970, and a growing rift between Duncan and Levertov during the late 1960s, a new set of acquaintances filled Duncan and Jess's household.[12] By the early 1970s, Duncan had a busy professional life, giving readings and lectures throughout the United States and gathering around himself a number of young scholars who were interested in his work and in Jess's work as well. Editors at a range of new independent experimental poetry magazines (many inspired by Donald Allen's 1960 *New American Poetry* anthology) were eager to claim Duncan (and sometimes Jess) as contributors. Clayton Eshleman's *Caterpillar*, founded in 1967, featured works by both Jess and Duncan, as did Kent State English professor Robert Bertholf's *Credences* magazine (see fig. 72). Poet Michael Davidson (later a professor at the University of California, San Diego), and San Francisco poet Michael Palmer (fondly referred to as "the Michaels") became household intimates beginning in the early 1970s. When composer Pauline Oliveros introduced Jess and Duncan to writer Lynn Lonidier, she too became a frequent guest.

In 1980, Duncan became a founding member of the New College of California's Poetics Program, bringing another wave of writers into Jess's life. Duncan's afternoon lunches with his students, held in the sunny kitchen nook of the couple's house at 3267 Twentieth Street in San Francisco's Mission District, were on occasion punctuated by Jess's emergence from his studio to have a peek at the company. A handful of Duncan's New College students formed friendships with Jess, as did Canadian poet and translator Norma Cole, who appeared on the periphery of the New College scene in the early 1980s.

Throughout his career as a teacher, Duncan insisted that his students tend to the linguistic and metrical intricacies of language and recognize the continuity between successive generations of writers. Jess shared such attention to detail and tradition in his own work as a collage artist, and responded positively to the likeminded young writers who made their appearances in the household as Duncan's guests. Jess's meticulous cover designs for books by Michael Davidson, Norma Cole, and Lynn Lonidier all exuded his delight in his creative correspondence with a younger generation of poets. After Duncan's death in 1988, many of those writers formed the backbone of Jess's household community.

One of Jess's late projects, a series of emblems originally slated to adorn the covers of Duncan's multi-volume *Collected Writings*, offers a final view into the depth of the couple's intimacy (fig. 74). Conjuring images from the household library and from their rich shared history, *Emblems for Robert Duncan I*, 1989, sketches out the tenderness of the couple's thirty-eight-year emotional and creative collaboration. Placing images of his partner amid masters such as Shakespeare and Dante, Jess released Duncan into the pantheon of writers he most admired.

(opposite page and overleaf)
Fig. 74 Jess, *Emblems for Robert Duncan I*, 1989. 6 of 7 collages, 6 1/4 x 5 5/8 in. (15.9 x 14.3 cm) each. Courtesy Odyssia Gallery, New York

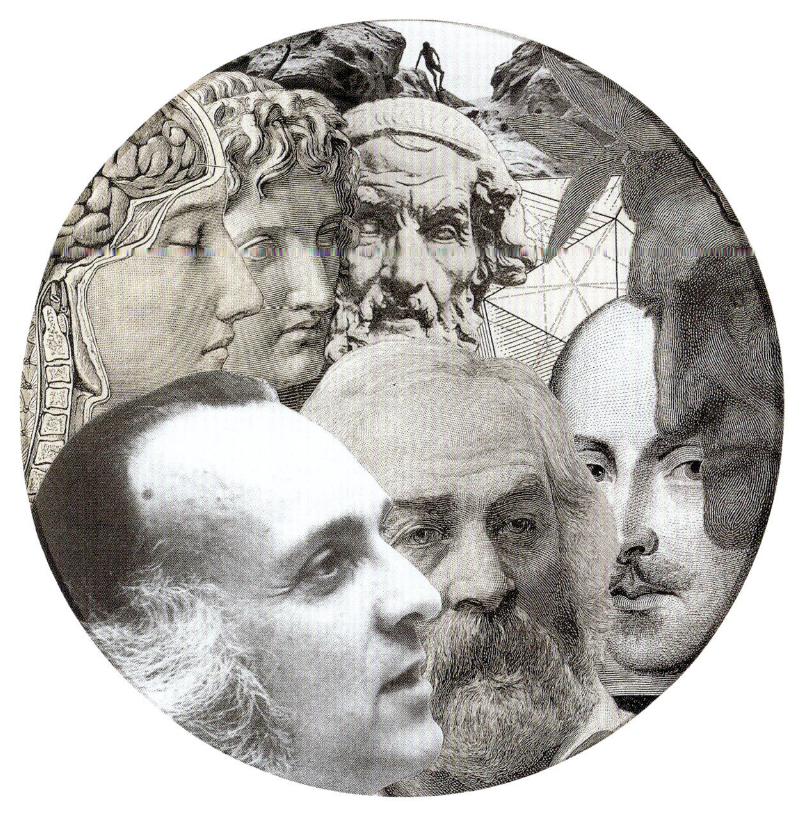

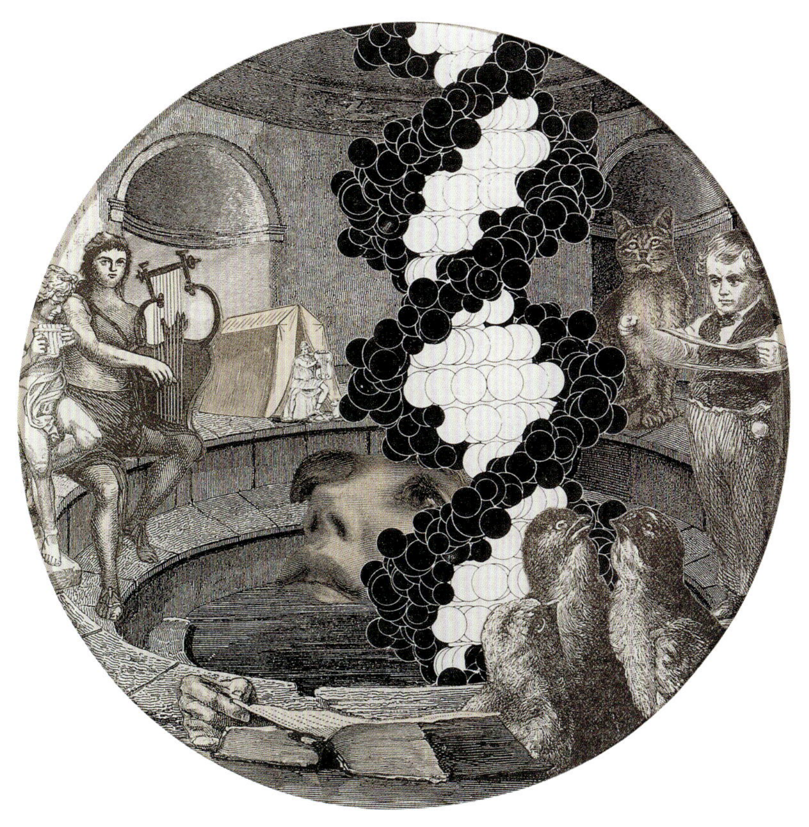

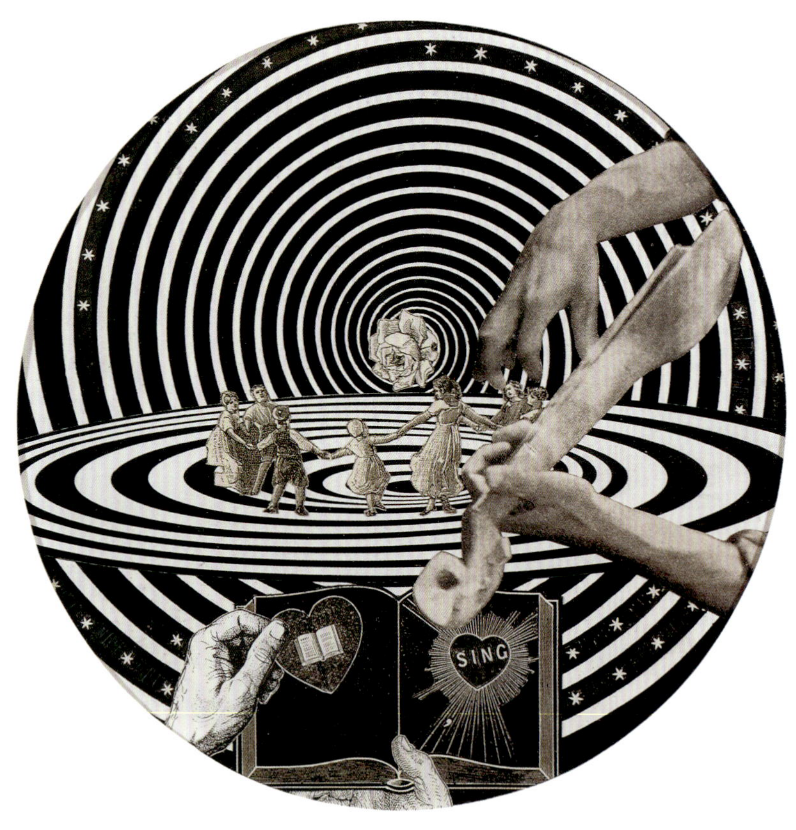

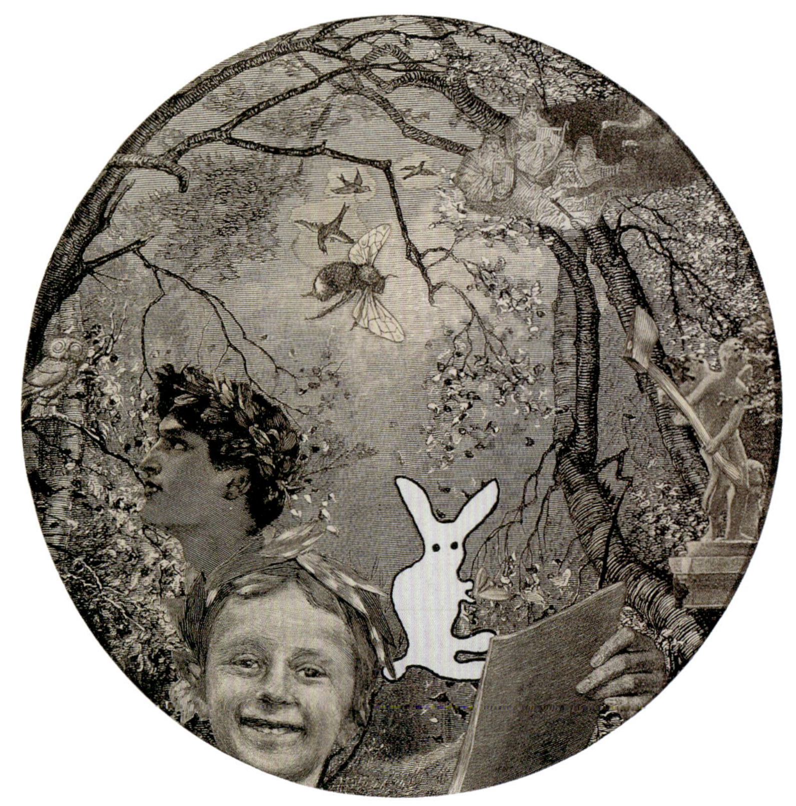

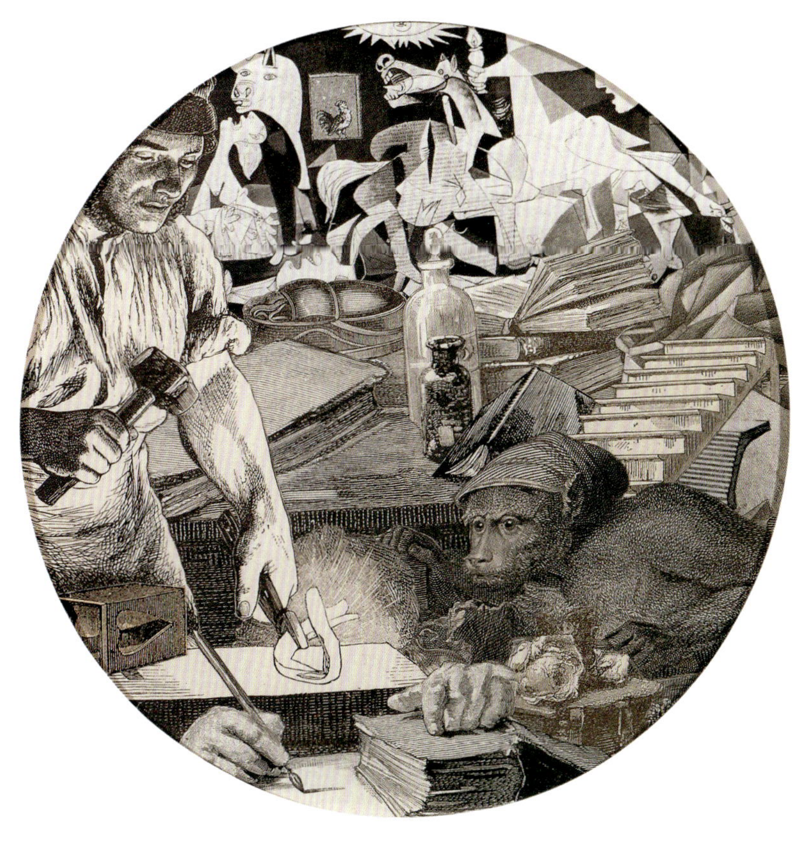

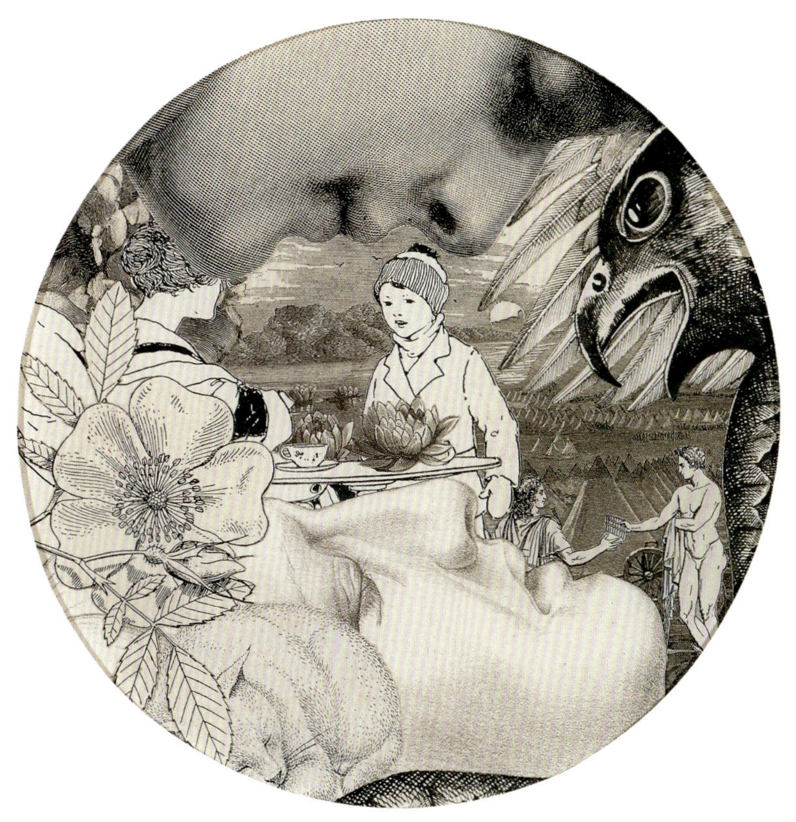

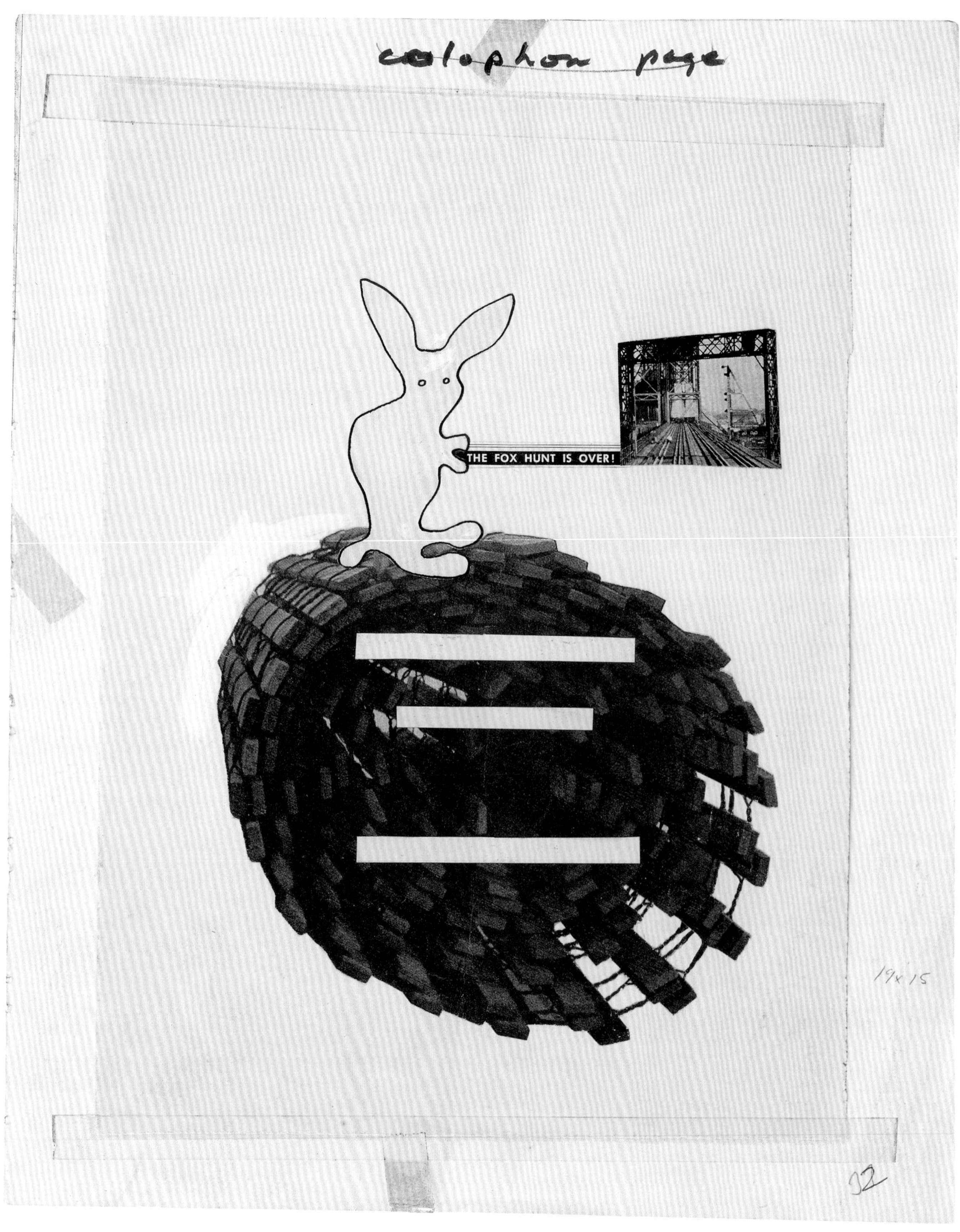

Fig. 75 Jess, *The Fox Hunt Is Over*, 1959. Collage and ink on board, 11 ¾ x 8 ½ in. (29.8 x 21.6 cm). Courtesy Odyssia Gallery, New York

COMPILED BY THOMAS EVANS AND BRANDON STOSUY

This glossary offers a loose matrix of sites, persons, and terminologies associated with Jess's life and work.

Helen Adam

Scottish-born Helen Adam (1909–1993) began writing poems at the age of four; by the time she arrived in the U.S. in 1939 she had already published three collections. In autumn 1954 Adam attended Robert Duncan's poetry workshop at The Poetry Center at San Francisco State College and impressed him with her ballad-derived poems and occult affiliations. Becoming close friends with Jess and Duncan, Adam also collaborated with the couple on several projects. She performed in Duncan's play *Faust Foutu* at the Six Gallery in January 1955; Jess illustrated the text of her play *San Francisco's Burning* and drew covers and illustrations for her White Rabbit chapbook *The Queen o' Crow Castle* (fig. 76); and in 1958 he composed an *Imaginary Portrait* of Adam (fig. 22). Adam also made important contributions to Jess and Duncan's reading: she introduced them to the Scottish border ballad tradition, and to the fantasy novels of George MacDonald (both important resources for Jess's own poems, as was Adam's poetry). (See Jarnot, p. 82)

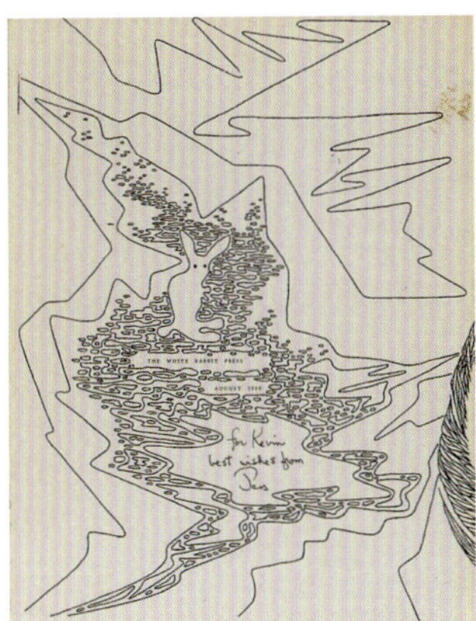
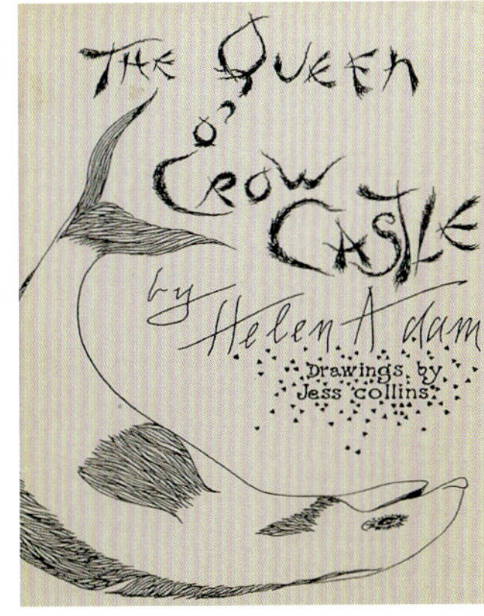

Fig. 76 Helen Adam, *The Queen o' Crow Castle: A Ballad for Jess Collins* (front and back cover), 1958. Book with cover and illustrations by Jess, sewn in paper wrappers, 16 pages, 8 ¹/₂ x 6 ¹/₂ in. (21.6 x 16.5 cm). Collection of Dodie Bellamy and Kevin Killian, San Francisco

The Artist's View

A different artist or writer was given full control of editing and designing each issue of this Tiburon, California–based journal, edited by Claire Mahl and published by Painters Poets Sculptors from 1952 to 1954. Jess contributed a paste-up poem to the inaugural issue, which is now almost impossible to find. Robert Duncan's issue no. 5 included a Jess collage, and Jess constructed a sprawling, four-page broadside for the final issue, no. 8. *The Artist's View* no. 8 (see fig. 2) includes reproductions of some of Jess's own works (*A Feignting Spell*, *Mary Butts Landscape*, *Seventy XXth Success Story*), a cell from "Dick Racy," illustrations for Duncan's poetry, paste-up elements (natives at the feet of someone in bed—with a frog), a number of sententious sayings, fairy tale quotes, jumbled maxims ("Honesty is the best fallacy"; "Love cankers all"), and philosophical puns and straight talk ("Imagination is the magic, is my nation").

"Assembly"

Like the work of other artists associated with California Assemblage—Wallace Berman, George Herms, Bruce Conner—Jess's junk sculptures (which he called "assemblies") reflect a distinctly West Coast affection for dilapidated and encrusted surfaces. Where Berman's sculptures are characterized by inscribed surfaces and Conner's by erotic and fetishized materials, what binds Jess's assemblies is simply a love for putting things together. Jess first exhibited a group of assemblies, along with early paste-ups, at King Ubu Gallery in 1953, titling the display "Necro-Facts," i.e., dead artifacts.

Largely built between the mid-1950s and 1960s, the playful, three-dimensional sculptural objects include a variety of found materials (see fig. 37). Rather than seek any sort of sculptural permanence, Jess kept the assemblies fairly fluid. In his *Log* he notes: "In general, the parts are not permanently joind, rather they are balanced, intertwined, jammd, lockd, screwd, hung, loopd, linkd, tied; rarely cemented, taped." In fact, many are a daredevil balancing act of multiple, moveable parts. Some assemblies are especially elaborate: *A Letterbox for Hellgate*, 1961, is comprised of a Dictaphone casing, a bookend, a carved-wood tray, an oyster shell, pliers, hinges, clock springs, screws, clips, jewelry, a saltshaker depicting a bear sitting on top of a honey comb, hanging crystals, a hypodermic needle loaded with a dead locust, a pot-metal elephant head wearing dark glasses, and more. Others involved fewer parts: *Hiawatha*, 1962, for example, is a found bust of an Indian chief, to which Jess added a horse head as a hat and a marble in the horse's mouth.

Jess also built ten or so functioning assembly lamps. (Determining the exact number of any of Jess's assemblies is difficult; as Jess noted in his *Log*, many of the fragile, precarious artworks are currently "Smasho!") *Assembly Lamp #7*, 1963, combines a cast pot-metal police-dog lamp base, lamp fittings, a small white lotus globe, anchovy key, brass thimble, clam-shell, and a toy roulette marker, among other pieces. Pull the chain decorated with four cat heads, and it turns right on.

The assemblies were photographed—by Ben Blackwell, for the 1984 catalogue *Jess: Paste-Ups (and Assemblies)*—in situ at Jess's home, among photographs and Victorian paraphernalia; they make particular sense as an extension of the household's proliferation of arranged knickknacks and mementos.

Black Mountain Review

Robert Creeley edited the seven issues of *Black Mountain Review* between spring 1954 and fall 1957. As a crucial expression of the literary and artistic ferment roused by Charles Olson's rector-ship (1951–1956) of the now famous North Carolina college, the magazine helped to define a community of loosely affil-iated poets including Creeley, Ed Dorn, Denise Levertov, Jonathan Williams, and Robert Duncan—most (but not all) of whom had attended Black Mountain College as students or teachers. Duncan published several poems and essays in *Black Mountain Review*. Jess published one paste-up poem in no. 4 (Winter 1954; fig. 70) and four paste-ups in no. 6 (Spring 1956).

Black Sparrow Press

John Martin founded the Santa Rosa, California–based Black Sparrow Press in 1966, on the proceeds from the sale of his D. H. Lawrence first-edition collection to University of California, Santa Barbara. Expanding beyond his primary aim of publishing the writings of the then unknown Charles Bukowski, Martin published several books (*Christmas Present, Christmas Presence!*, *Epilogos*, *Names of People* [illustrated by Jess], *65 Drawings*, and *Tribunals*) and broadsides by Robert Duncan, books by several of Duncan's associates (William Everson, James Broughton, Charles Olson, Robert Creeley, Robert Kelly, Michael Palmer), Ekbert Faas's biography *Young Robert Duncan*, and Robert Bertholf's *Robert Duncan: A Descriptive Bibliography*. In September 1970 Black Sparrow published Jess's translations from Christian Morgenstern, *Gallowsongs* (fig. 56), and in 1971 produced Jess's catalogue *Translations* for the Odyssia Gallery.

Boob

Collaborative verbo-visual paste-ups Jess and Robert Duncan initiated in 1952, the *Boob* series (figs. 9, 10, 11) began with the punk-primitive *Boob #1*, which was distributed as a pair of free broadsides with *Boob #2*, a twenty-nine-line poem by Duncan accompanied by Jess's image of a bird. In 1954 Jess produced the more complex *Boob #3*, which echoes James Joyce's *Finnegans Wake*. (See Schaffner, p. 20)

James Broughton

James Broughton (1913–1999) was a Californian poet, film-maker, and publisher. His books of poetry include *True and False Unicorn* (1957), *A Long Undressing* (1971), and *Packing Up for Paradise* (1997). His best known films are *Mother's Day* (1948), *The Pleasure Garden* (1953), and *The Bed* (1968). With his partner, Kermit Sheets, Broughton founded Centaur Press, publishing volumes by Anaïs Nin, Madeline Gleason, Muriel Rukeyser, and Robert Duncan's *Medieval Scenes* (1950).

Throughout the 1950s Broughton was particularly close to Jess and Duncan: he participated in The Maidens group and exchanged poems and paste-ups with them; he gave Jess a set of early *Scientific American* magazines, which Jess put to extensive use in paste-ups and *Translations*; Duncan dedicated poems to him; and Jess made the paste-up book *A Birthday Pillow Book for James* (1956). While Broughton and Sheets were in Paris and London (from 1952 to 1954), Jess and Duncan sublet their San Francisco apartment at 1724 Baker Street, and ran Centaur Press in their absence. (See Jarnot, p. 78)

Caterpillar

Published and edited by poet, critic, and translator Clayton Eshleman in New York City and later in Sherman Oaks, California, *Caterpillar* began in 1966 as Caterpillar Books, an imprint Eshleman continued until 1968 that included titles by authors such as David Antin, Jackson Mac Low, and Louis Zukofsky. In October 1967, Eshleman began publishing *Caterpillar* magazine (fig. 77), a quarterly, perfect-bound journal focused on trans-lation and on a convergence of artists, prose writers, and poets. Contributors included Vito Acconci, Stan Brakhage, Charles Bukowski, Robert Creeley, Robert Duncan, Allen Ginsberg, Leon Golub, Robert Kelly, Denise Levertov, Gerard Malanga, Gary Snyder, Jerome Rothenberg, Gilbert Sorrentino, Jack Spicer, and Diane Wakowski. There were twenty issues, including the double issue no. 8/9 (October 1969), to which Jess contributed the front and back paste-up covers. No. 18 (April 1972) featured Jess's wraparound paste-up *Notice. No Eggs Required. By Order* (fig. 45). The same issue included a photo of Antonin Artaud and his long poem, "Artaud le the Momo" in both French and

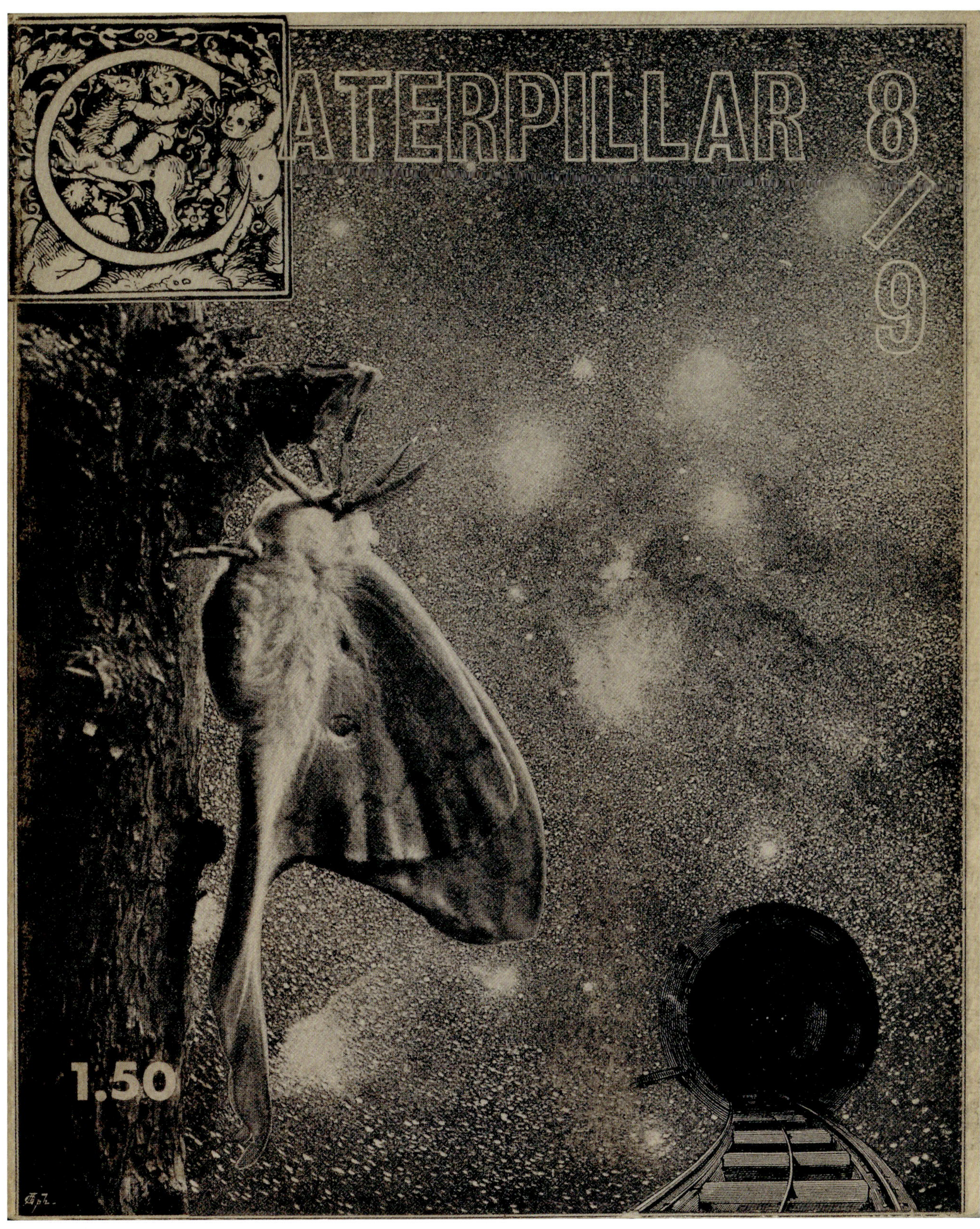

Fig. 77 Clayton Eshleman, editor, *Caterpillar*, no. 8/9, October 1969. Magazine with cover by Jess, 256 pages, 7 x 5 1/2 in. (17.8 x 14 cm). Collection of Steve Dickison

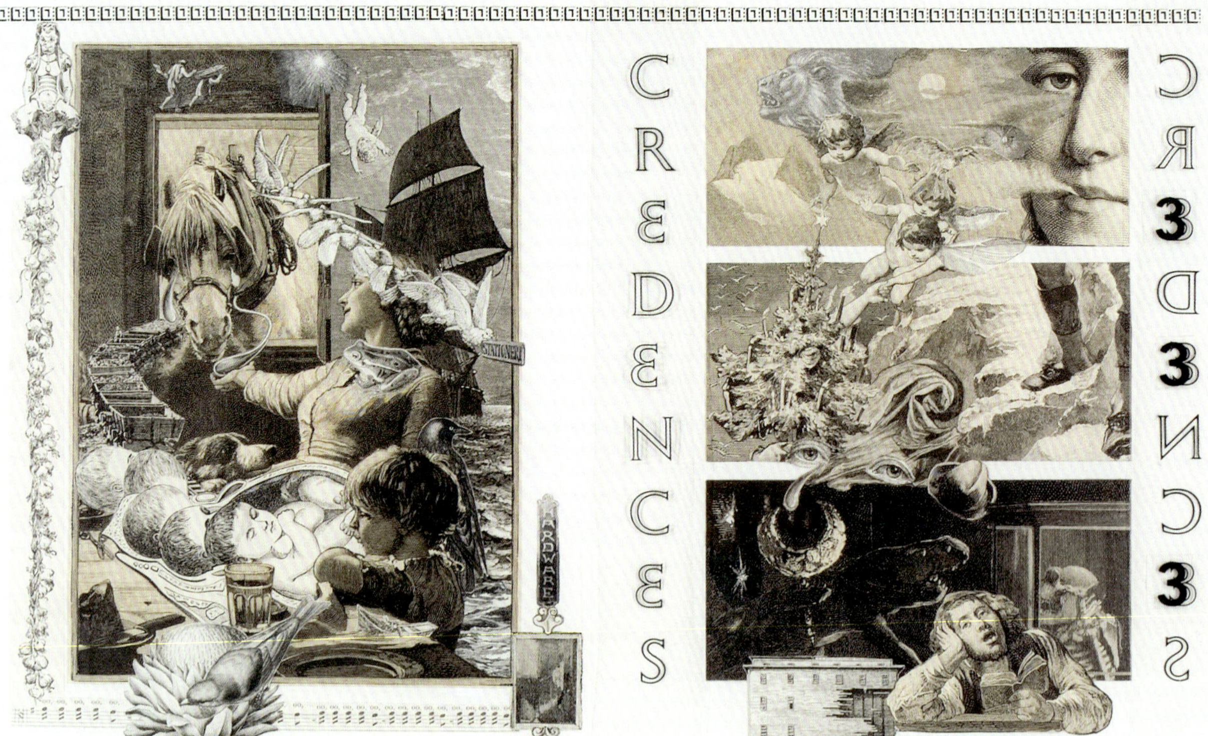

Fig. 78 Jess, *Cover for Credences 3*, 1976. Collage, 8 ½ x 14 in. (21.6 x 35.6 cm). Collection of Anne and Robert Bertholf, Buffalo, New York

English, followed by Eshleman's critical analysis of and notes on the work, as well as "details" from an Artaud "painting-collage" series by Nancy Spero. In 1971, Doubleday published *A Caterpillar Anthology*, which included nos. 1 through 12. The journal ceased publication in 1973. Eshleman went on to edit forty-six issues of the California-based journal *Sulfur* from 1981 to 2000.

Norma Cole

Poet, artist, and translator from the French, Norma Cole (b. 1945) was an intimate of Jess and Duncan's in San Francisco throughout the 1980s and '90s. She is the author of *Metamorphosia*, *Mars*, *Contrafact*, *Spinoza in Her Youth*, and several other books of poetry and translation. In 1993 Jess composed the paste-up cover for Cole's poetry collection *Mars* (Listening Chamber, 1994; figs. 35, 36), and in 1994 they collaborated on *Catasters*, a paste-up by Jess with poems by Cole on inset panels, published as Morning Star Folio 6/4 by Alec Finlay's Edinburgh-based Morning Star Publications in 1995. This was to be Jess's last paste-up. (See Schaffner, pp. 41–42)

Credences

The literary journal *Credences* was edited by Robert Bertholf from Kent, Ohio, and Buffalo, New York, in twenty-three issues published from 1975 to 1985. Jess made collage covers for nos. 3 (May 1976) and 8/9 (March 1980) (fig. 78; fig. 72). *Credences* also published poems, essays, and an interview by and with Duncan, as well as writings by several members of his immediate circle in the 1970s, such as Aaron Shurin, Steve Abbott, and David Levi-Strauss.

Robert Creeley

A major American poet, Robert Creeley is well known for his spare, unadorned poetic voice and for his sixty-plus books of poetry, prose, and essays, a novel, and a collection of short stories. Creeley (1926–2005) was born in Arlington, Massachusetts, and enrolled at Harvard University before graduating from Black Mountain College and the University of New Mexico. He and his first wife, Ann MacKinnon, founded the Divers Press in 1953 in Mallorca, Spain, maintaining the imprint for three years and publishing more than a dozen titles, including Robert Duncan's fifth collection of poetry, *Caesar's Gate Poems 1949–1950* (1955), which included seventeen paste-ups by Jess (later editions varied) (figs. 49, 50, 51). Creeley edited the *Black Mountain Review* from 1954–1957, publishing Jess in issues no. 4 and 6. While living with Duncan in Mallorca from 1955 to 1956, Jess used earth-toned magazine-print clippings to construct the paste-up *A Paranoiac Portrait of Robert Creeley*, 1955 (fig. 19). (See Jarnot, p. 80)

Didactic Nickelodeon
Jess produced forty-one paste-ups comprising *The 40 and 1 Nights, or Jess's Didactic Nickelodeon,* 1955 (fig. 28), for his collaboration with the filmmaker Lawrence Jordan. *Jess's Didactic Nickelodeon, Series Two: "The Guardian Angels' Guide-book"* (fig. 29) is a series of thirty-seven variously sized paste-ups made that same year. (See Schaffner, p. 34)

Dilexi Gallery
Artist and poet Robert Alexander and musician and entrepreneur James Newman founded the Dilexi Gallery in 1958 in San Francisco's North Beach neighborhood, on Broadway. Alexander found the gallery's Latin name in a dictionary (as he had for the famous Ferus Gallery in Los Angeles a year earlier): "*dilexi,* to select, to value highly." Jess, Jay DeFeo, Robert Morris, Hassel Smith, and Irving Petlin all had solo shows there. After a few months Alexander resigned and Newman moved the gallery to Union Street, running it there on his own until 1970. Jess's exhibition *Paste-Ups and Assemblies* was held at the Union Street space from December 12, 1960, to January 7, 1961 (see fig. 79).

Robert Duncan
Robert Duncan (1919–1988) was a poet, playwright, teacher, and scholar associated with the Berkeley Renaissance, the San Francisco Renaissance, and the Black Mountain school of poetry. He lived with Jess from 1950 until his death in 1988, collaborating with him on numerous books and artworks. Among his best-known collections are *Opening of the Field* (1960), *Bending the Bow* (1968), and the two *Groundwork* volumes, *Before the War* (1984) and *In the Dark* (1988). (See especially Jarnot, pp. 76–87)

Joe Dunn
Poet, publisher, and painter Joe Dunn (1932–1997) was born in Boston, where as a teenager he was closely affiliated with the poets Steve Jonas, Gerrit Lansing, and John Wieners. Having been introduced to the work of the Black Mountain poets by Jonas, Dunn attended Black Mountain College in 1956, its final year, and took Robert Duncan's writing class. He moved to San Francisco after the college closed, embracing the communities around Duncan, artist Wallace Berman, and poet Jack Spicer. Dunn founded White Rabbit Press after one of Spicer's Magic Workshops in June 1957, on Spicer's suggestion. He operated the press until 1958, when the cost of his methedrine dependence brought publication to a halt; his writing and publication thereafter was intermittent. In later years he returned to Boston and worked occasionally with local theater companies. His only publication was *The Better Dream House*, a collaboration with Jess that a revived White Rabbit published in April 1968 (fig. 32).

Hawk's Well Press
Poet, translator, editor, essayist, and anthologist Jerome Rothenberg ran Hawk's Well Press in New York City from 1958 to 1964. He also edited five issues of the magazine *Poems from the Floating World* under the imprint. Hawk's Well published books including Rothenberg's *Black Sun, White Sun* (1960), Robert Kelly's *Armed Descent* (1961), Diane Wakowski's *Coins & Coffins* (1962), and Jess's *O!* (1960), a book-length offset publication of paste-ups, poems, "o" words, and overwrought poetic lines (fig. 31). *O!* sold for 50 cents at the time of its publication. It is reprinted in *A Book of the Book*, co-edited by Rothenberg and Steven Clay for Granary Books in 2000.

Ida Hodes
Ida Hodes (b. 1914) met Robert Duncan in Chicago through their mutual friend Henry Miller in 1945. She later lived in Los Angeles and Big Sur, before moving to San Francisco in the early 1950s. While Jess and Duncan were in Mallorca they kept up an almost daily correspondence with Hodes, who looked after their cat, Princess, and solicited subscriptions for *Caesar's Gate.* In 1957 Duncan asked Hodes to join him as secretary at The Poetry Center, where she arranged reading tours for visiting poets. Hodes played Marguerite in Duncan's *Faust Foutu* and also acted in his *Adam's Way* (1962). In 1966 Jess painted *Fig. 3—Ida, Duncan, and I: Translation #18* from a 1957 photograph taken by Helen Adam of the trio beneath the Golden Gate Bridge (fig. 24).

Imaginary Portraits
The *Imaginary Portraits* are a series of some twenty paintings made between 1952 and 1960 in which Jess depicted friends, associates, Robert Duncan, the children of friends, his cousin, a cat, and himself. Many of his subjects are well-known poets and artists of the period—Lyn Brockway, Robin Blaser, Denise Levertov (fig. 21), Gina James, James Broughton, and Helen Adam (fig. 22), among others. Jess relied on memory to create

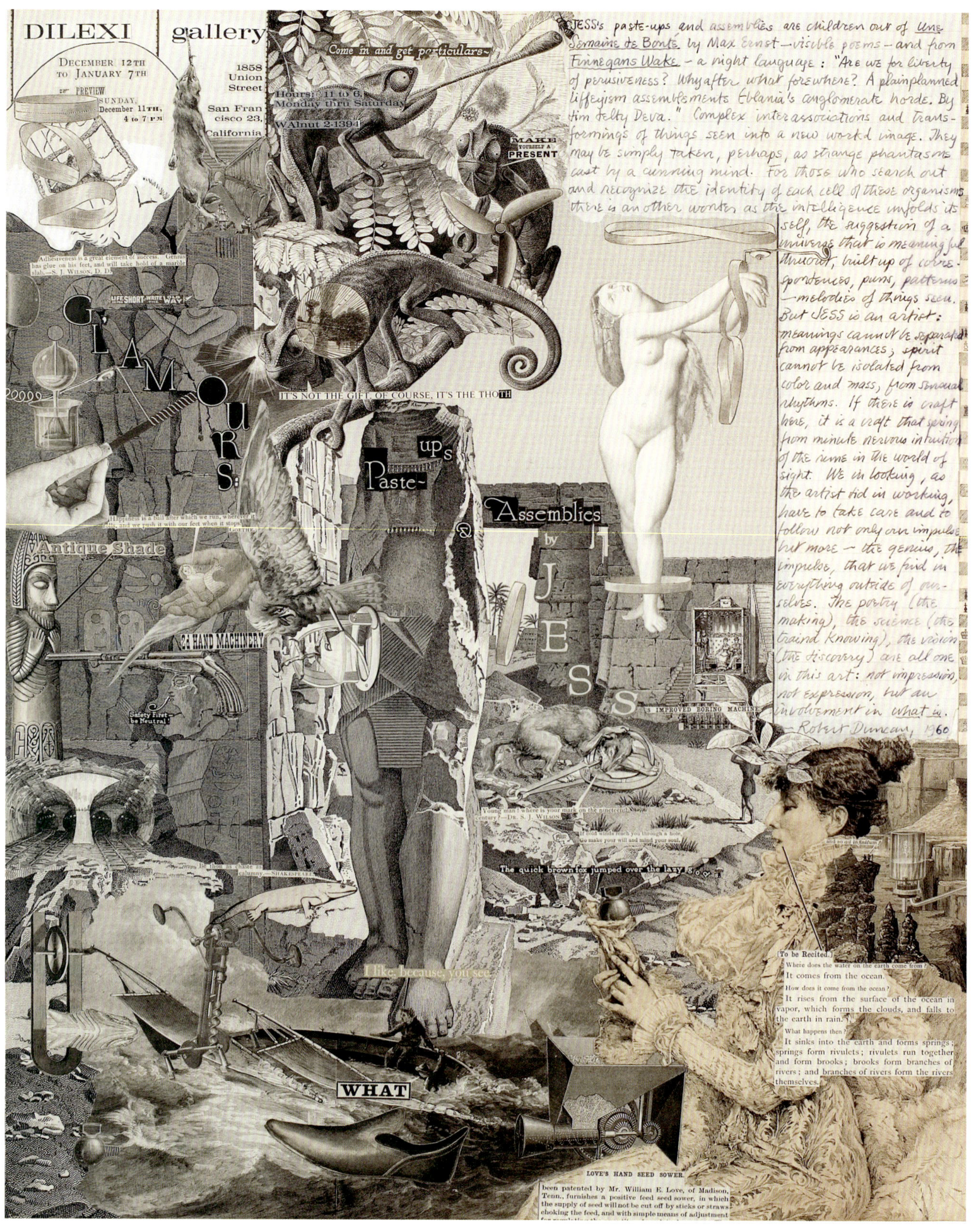

Fig. 79 Jess, *Collage for Paste-Ups and Assemblies at Dilexi Gallery*, 1959. Collage, 20 ⅛ x 15 ⅞ in. (51.5 x 40.5 cm). Collection of Jim Newman and Jane Ivory

impressionistic, romantic, unusual "portraits." The titles, too, give the pieces an otherworldly, mythic feel: for example, *The Nasturtium that Dissolved the World: Imaginary Portrait #13: Denise Levertov*, 1955; and *Angel Captain Hornblower: Imaginary Portrait #17: James Broughton*, 1957, in which a winged hero, in full cherubic splendor, abuts an oversized peacock.

J

Poet Jack Spicer launched *J* magazine in September 1959 with the announcement: "*J* will be a 16-page mimeographed flyer very much like *Beatitude*. It will sell for the same price or lower." The success of *Beatitude* (edited by Bob Kaufman) on the North Beach scene had spurred Spicer into counter-action, but it took the practical assistance of collage artist Fran Herndon to get production underway. Spicer selected submissions from contribution boxes installed at bars including The Place, and also solicited manuscripts from poets such as Robert Duncan, George Stanley, Richard Brautigan, Joe Dunn, and Robin Blaser. Herndon designed the covers. Spicer set geographic limits on distribution (*J* was available almost exclusively in the Bay Area): "New York contributions are not forbidden. But quotaed."

Jess's essay "I Ups to Myself And" (a mischievous meditation on his practice) appeared in *J* no. 2, and his comic strip "The Poet Scorner" in *J* no. 5 (fig. 42), the last issue to be edited by Spicer. All five had been published within the last few months of 1959; three further issues were published by Spicer's colleagues George Stanley and Harold Dull in 1960 and 1961.

Lawrence Jordan

Born in Denver, Colorado, where fellow filmmaker Stan Brakhage was a high-school friend, Lawrence Jordan (b. 1934) met Jess and Duncan after moving to San Francisco in 1954. While Jordan was close to other artists in the Bay Area, such as Jay DeFeo, Wallace Berman, and Bruce Conner (with whom he founded the Camera Obscura cinema), he and Jess were especially akin in sensibility, sharing delight in fairytales, Victoriana, and the collages of Max Ernst. Jess's paste-ups moved Jordan to animate collage in films such as *Minerva*, *Duo Concertantes*, and *Rime of the Ancient Mariner* (in which Orson Welles reads the poem over animated collages derived from Gustav Doré's illustrations). He made two collaborations with Jess: *The 40 and 1 Nights, or Jess's Didactic Nickelodeon* (1962; fig. 28) and *Finds of the Fortenight* (1980), which features paste-up texts by Jess (made in 1960) that function as subtitles: "Here I come, Daddy!" "Aren't you ashamed?" "Impossible!" In the 1950s and '60s Jordan spent time in New York, where he assisted Joseph Cornell with his films (including *Legends for Fountains*) and his boxes. He currently teaches at San Francisco Art Institute. (See Schaffner, p. 34)

King Ubu Gallery

Jess, Robert Duncan, and the artist Harry Jacobus founded this gallery, named for the French author Alfred Jarry's nineteenth-century absurdist play, *Ubu Roi*, in December 1952 at 3119 Fillmore Street, San Francisco. (See Schaffner, p. 51; see fig. 46)

Denise Levertov

Poet Denise Levertov (1923–1997) was born in England and migrated to the U.S. in 1948. Among her best-known poetry collections are *O Taste and See*, *To Stay Alive*, and *Freeing of the Dust*. Her memoir *Tesserae* was published in 1995.

Robert Duncan initiated a correspondence with Levertov after reading her poem "The Shifting" in *Origin* in 1953. He and Jess first met her and her husband, Mitch Goodman, in New York in 1955, on their way to Mallorca. A regular correspondence and close friendship arose between Levertov and Duncan, and subsequently between Levertov and Jess. While in Mallorca Jess painted *The Nasturtium that Dissolved the World*, which included a figure that Duncan thought resembled Levertov— and so the painting was subtitled *Imaginary Portrait #13: Denise Levertov* (fig. 21).

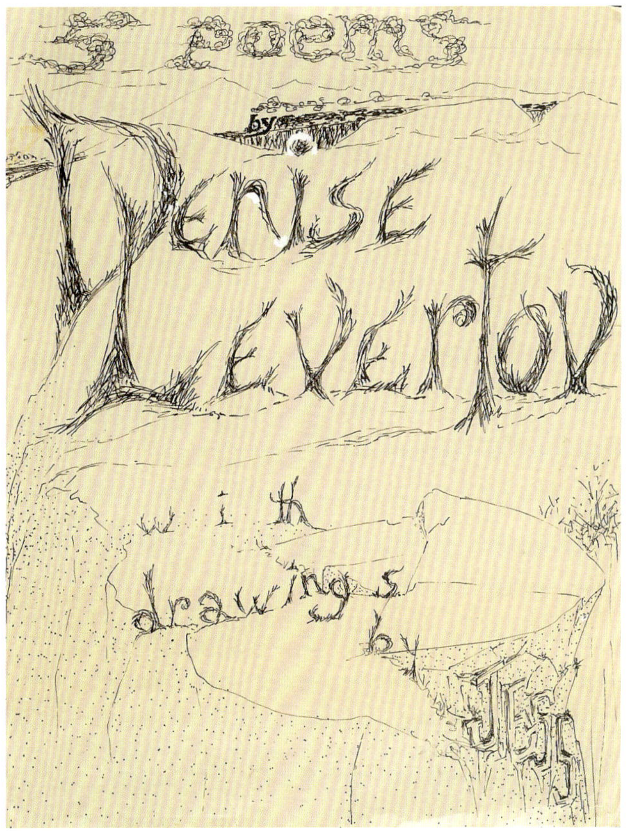

Fig. 80 Jess, *Untitled* (cover for *5 Poems* by Denise Levertov), 1958. Ink on paper, 17 x 13 in. (43.2 x 33 cm). Courtesy Odyssia Gallery, New York

For Levertov's 1958 San Francisco Poetry Center reading, Joe Dunn proposed a White Rabbit publication, and Jess made drawings for the book, *5 Poems* (fig. 80). The trip cemented her friendship with Jess in particular, and after her departure he sent her a painting titled *Majorcan Pastorale*. In 1959 Levertov attempted to persuade New Directions to publish Jess's "versions" of Morgenstern's *Gallowsongs*, though to no avail (Black Sparrow eventually published them in 1970). Levertov and her family often received gifts from Jess, including drawings, paintings, collages, and *Oz* books. (See Jarnot, pp. 79–80)

Log

Divided into sections—"Paintings and Crayon Works," "Paste-Ups," "Sculpture & Constructions," and "Assemblies"—Jess's *Log* was a detailed, handwritten listing of his works that also included a brief bio, a "Chronicle" of his exhibitions from 1950 to 1997, and the addresses of his early collectors ("Patrons' Addresses"). The cover page is an "Invocation" that includes dialogue from L. Frank Baum, verse from the seventeenth-century Japanese poet Ransetsu, and Jess's own "This Book Belong Stoo Jess." Each entry includes title, measurements, media, an inventory number, and where the work resided at that time. If the reverse side of the canvas included a longish quote or literary excerpt, this was also included. For the *Translations*, the source image is reprinted. The *Log* does not include every work Jess ever made—he excluded what he viewed as minor works. As he notes at the start of the "Paste-Ups" section: "Paste-ups are not numbered other than in this book; many slighter ones are not listed, & many not remembered."

"The Maidens"

The name Helen Adam, James Broughton, Eve Triem, Madeline Gleason, Jess, and Duncan took for their group, which met monthly to share lunch and recite poems. (See Jarnot, p. 82; fig. 76)

Narkissos

Jess's teeming, intensely personal re-imagining of the Narcissus myth was his most ambitious project, spanning more than three decades of his career. (See Schaffner, pp. 62–69; figs. 57, 58, 59.)

Odyssia Gallery

Founded in Rome as Galleria Odyssia in 1957 by Federico Quadrani and Odyssia Skouras Quadrani, Odyssia Gallery relocated to New York in 1964 and began representing Jess in 1968, organizing his first New York solo exhibition in 1971.

"Paste-up"

Jess made his first paste-up, *The Mouse's Tale*, in 1951, and went on to make hundreds more in various formats. He derived his paste-up materials from Victorian engravings (correspondents would mail him pages from *Punch* and *The Strand*), comics, contemporary magazines such as *Life*, and, in the 1970s and '80s, jigsaw puzzles. Jess was fastidious in cutting out his images, which—after a long period of selection and arrangement— were held in place with pins, then, after further consideration, pasted down. (He disguised the pin punctures with a moistened Q-tip.) One of Jess's most renowned paste-ups is the *Tricky Cad* book sequence (see fig. 16), made at the kitchen table at Baker Street in 1954. Recomposing *Dick Tracy* cartoons, Jess foiled the swagger of the original, rerouting its noir vocabulary into such reconstructions as: "I just shot to the sun deck!" and "Had to hide their secret exit and I'm glad you've enquired!" *Tricky Cad* was included in John Coplans's 1963 exhibition *Pop Art USA* and is widely acknowledged a Pop precursor.

The scale and density of the paste-ups increased in the 1970s, and in series such as *Four Seasons*, 1971–1980, imagery began to spill out onto the frames. In this decade Jess also favored black-and-white Victorian engravings, and making book covers for friends such as Michael Davidson (*The Mutabilities & the Foul Papers*; fig. 34) and Lynn Lonidier (*A Lesbian Estate*; fig. 81). The epic work *Narkissos*, completed in 1991, is the most ambitious paste-up (fig. 58).

Romantic

In a letter published in Stan Persky's magazine *Open Space* in 1964, Jess declared himself "insistently a Romantic artist." Though this comment may better describe an attitude than a style, his *Romantic* paintings, which span the 1950s and early '60s, can be characterized by looser brushwork than, say, the *Translations* or the *Salvages*, and by their more pronounced preoccupation with landscape. As he later reflected (in an interview with Michael Auping), the series grew out of his earlier, non-objective works: "The more I painted 'non-objectively,' the more I began to see my image complex, telling or suggesting a story." Romance for Jess suggested narrative motifs such as castles and children, and mythic beasts like owls and snakes. His affinity for the hallucinatory Symbolist scenarios of Odilon Redon and Gustav Moreau, and for the interiors of Edouard Vuillard, affirmed this narrative tendency. Jess's "romantic" stance in interviews and writings was almost defiant (perhaps fortified by Duncan's insistence that poetic Modernism was a continuation of poetic Romanticism), and while the term applies to a specific body of work, he frequently characterized all of his works under this rubric.

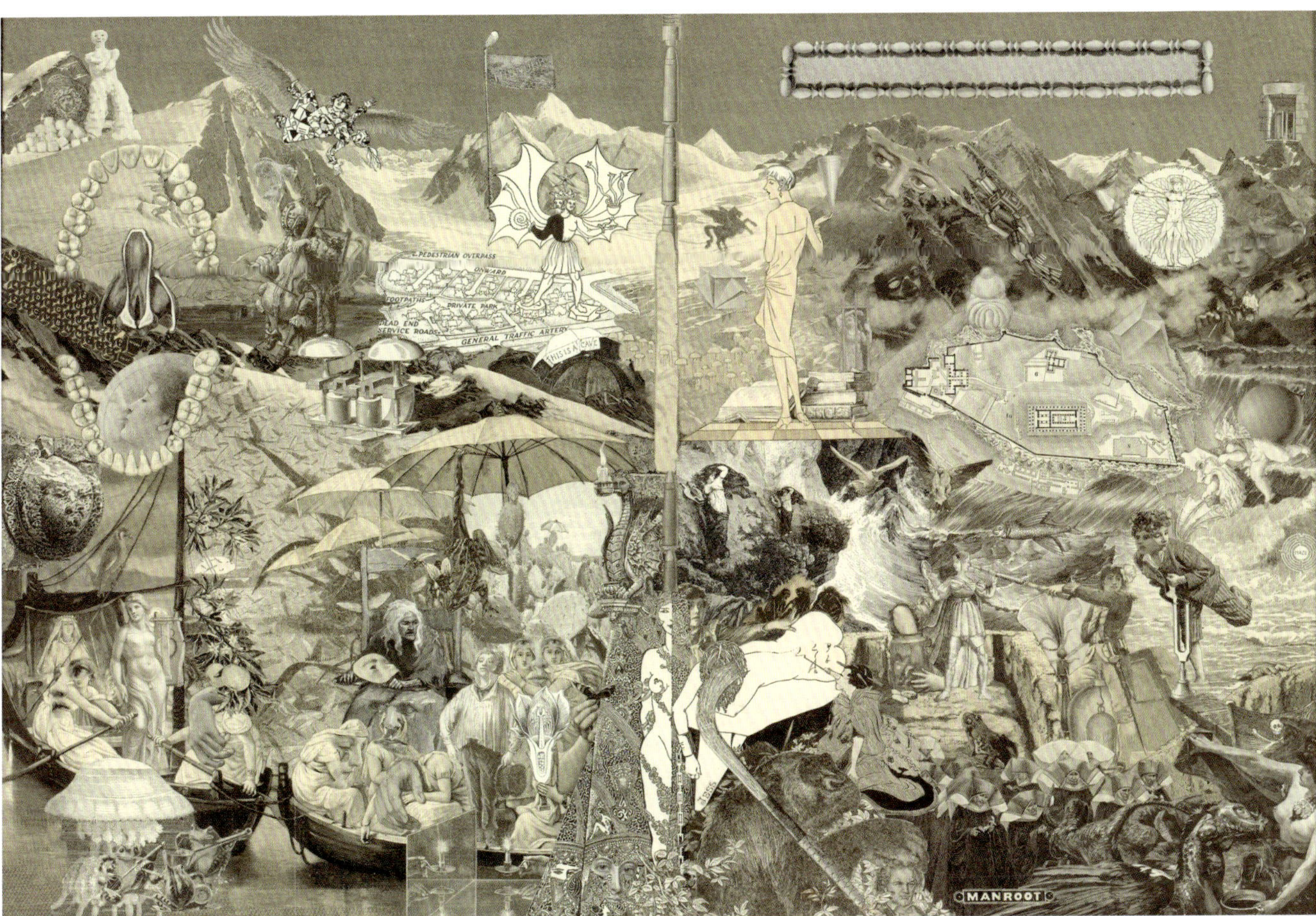

Salvages

In an interview with Michael Auping (for the exhibition catalogue *A Grand Collage*) Jess noted, "All of my work comes from
salvaging." This intention is most explicit in the *Salvages* (see
fig. 5), a series of just eight paintings begun in the early 1970s,
overlapping with the last of the *Translations*. For these works,
Jess took incomplete canvases acquired from local thrift stores
in the 1950s and '60s (as well as some of his own discarded
canvases), and "salvaged" them through the addition of
images that pursued the suggestions (in terms of color or line)
of the partially completed originals. With their inclusion of
narrative elements, the *Salvages* echo the earlier *Romantic*
paintings. They differ, however, in their open mingling of
unfinished areas with crisp depiction. (See Shaffner, p. 16)

Jack Spicer (entry by Kevin Killian)

Jack Spicer (1925–1965) was born in Hollywood, California,
and arrived at the University of California, Berkeley in 1945. At
twenty-one he met Robert Duncan, who was auditing some of
the same courses Spicer was taking. The two poets grew
close, and with another undergraduate, Robin Blaser, devised
a poetic school they only half-facetiously called the "Berkeley
Renaissance." The three poets pioneered a conceptual and
practical poetic "dictation," a theory that poetry reaches us
from a mysterious, ill-defined "outside," and Spicer promul-
gated this theory among younger poets, as well as among the
artists he worked with at the California School of Fine Arts
(now the San Francisco Art Institute).

Despite an initial leeriness, Spicer and Jess became intimately involved in each other's practices in the 1950s. Spicer
encouraged Jess to write, and published some of his poetry
in *J*. Jess tried to teach Spicer how to paint, and executed
drawings for the first edition of Spicer's *Billy the Kid* (1959;
fig. 82). During his lifetime, Spicer published only a handful
of books, among them *After Lorca* (1957), *The Heads of the
Town Up to the Aether* (1960–1961), *The Holy Grail* (1962), and
Language (1963–1965). His "serial poems" were published
posthumously. (See Jarnot, pp. 77, 81)

Fig. 81 Jess, *Cover for A Lesbian Estate*, 1977. Collage, 13 ¾ x 19 ¾ in.
(34.9 x 50.2 cm). The Museum of Modern Art, New York. The Judith
Rothschild Foundation Contemporary Drawings Collection Gift

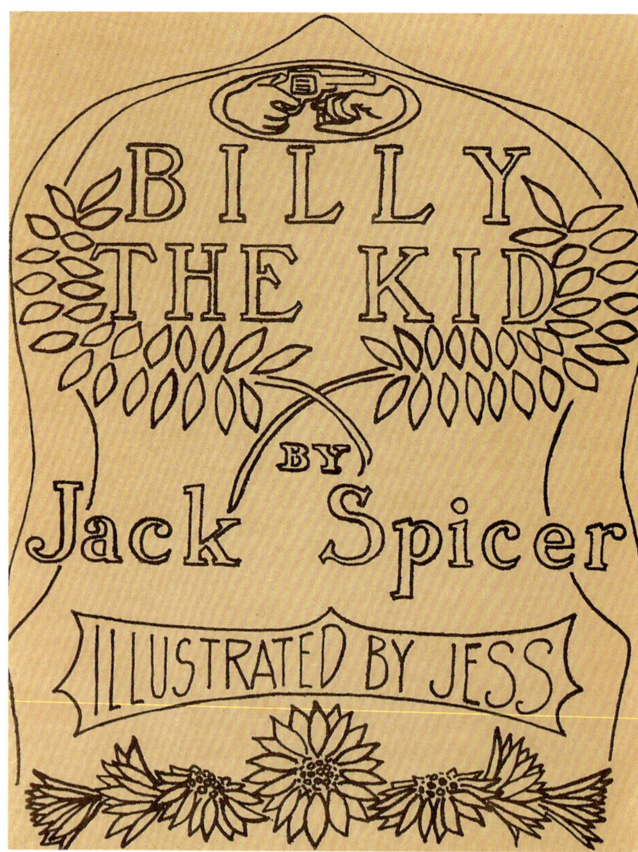

Fig. 82 Jack Spicer, *Billy the Kid*, 1959. Book with cover and illustrations by Jess, bound in paper wrappers, stapled, 16 pages, 8 ½ x 6 ½ in. (21.6 x 16.5 cm). Collection of Dodie Bellamy and Kevin Killian, San Francisco

Translations

For his *Translations* series, 1959–1976, which number thirty-two paintings in all (not including *Narkissos*, which is sometimes considered a *Translation*), Jess "translated" images from printed matter (book illustrations, postcards, or photographs) into painterly terms, enlarging and rendering them onto canvas in thick whorls of oil, often in a pastel palette, with care and exactitude. Themes include physics, occultism, and childhood, and images from various Victorian publications reinvigorate such neglected masterpieces as John Uri Lloyd's science-fiction novel *Etidorhpa* and Gelett Burgess's *Burgess Nonsense Book*. The literary connotation of "translation" is therefore appropriate, all the more so as texts often accompanied reproductions of the paintings in catalogues and exhibitions, expanding the occasion of each painting and almost parodying explication. (See Schaffner, p. 30; see figs. 24, 33, 84, 85.)

White Rabbit Press

Under Joe Dunn's direction, White Rabbit produced ten titles, beginning with *Love, the Poem, the Sea, and other Pieces Examined*, by Dunn's Boston colleague Steve Jonas. Lithographed from author typescripts or manuscripts and uniform in size (6 ½ x 8 ½ inches), the series included chapbooks by Helen Adam, Robert Duncan, Charles Olson, George Stanley, and Richard Brautigan. In 1962 the printer Graham MacIntosh revived the press, publishing further titles by Spicer and Duncan, as well as Dunn's aforementioned collaboration with Jess, *The Better Dream House* (fig. 32). Seven other White Rabbit titles feature covers or illustrations by Jess: Steve Jonas's *Love, the Poem, the Sea, and other Pieces Examined*, Jack Spicer's *After Lorca*, Denise Levertov's *5 Poems* (see fig. 80), Charles Olson's *O'Ryan* (in two parts), Robert Duncan's *The Cat and the Blackbird* (fig. 83), and Helen Adam's *The Queen o' Crow Castle* (fig. 76). After a hiatus of more than thirty-five years, MacIntosh revived White Rabbit Press again in 2005 with a broadside excerpt from Jack Spicer's book-length poem *Language*. (See Jarnot, p. 82)

3267 Twentieth Street

Jess and Duncan purchased a house at 3267 Twentieth Street, San Francisco, in January 1967, with the assistance of a wealthy friend, Barbara Joseph. The then predominantly Latin neighborhood was isolated from bohemia, which provided Jess with the solitude he sought for work. It was also rife with thrift stores for collecting collage and assemblage materials.

The house, a three-storey white Victorian built in the 1890s, with a garden and a gazebo at the rear, grew into a densely inhabited assemblage of resources and pleasures. It offered visitors an adventure (and an education) to move through, from the entrance hall onward. Jess's assemblies, photographs of Ezra Pound and Wallace Berman, and the art library were some of the living room's salient features; between the living room and the kitchen was a smaller room devoted to a large record collection. Guests were received in the kitchen, with its stained-glass windows made by Duncan and Jess.

Jess's studio was on the second floor, overlooking the street. Taking Leonardo's famous advice, he left its peeling walls to inspire painterly fantasies. The studio came to resemble the prospector's cabin Jess visited as a child, with its incremental layers of postcards, photos of friends, reference books, and paste-ups. Drawers were full of cut-out images categorized by subject, and on one wall hung a hand-lettered sign that read:

The Seven Deadly Virtues of Contemporary Art:
Originality
Spontaneity
Simplicity
Intensity
Immediacy
Impenetrability
Shock

Jess and Duncan's bedroom next door to the studio contained the children's books from which they would read to each other in the evenings. On the third floor, a hallway—which featured Duncan's crayon drawings and occult books—led to a guest bedroom, Duncan's study, and further sections of the library: the "Modernist room," which housed James Joyce and Gertrude Stein, and the "French room." The art collection, dispersed throughout the house, comprised a significant gathering of postwar Bay Area art, with works by Harry Jacobus, Edward Corbett, George Herms, Wallace Berman, and Dean Stockwell, as well as prints by R. B. Kitaj and a Goya etching. In its totality the household embodied Jess and Duncan's shared appetite for arrangement, amusement, and discovery.

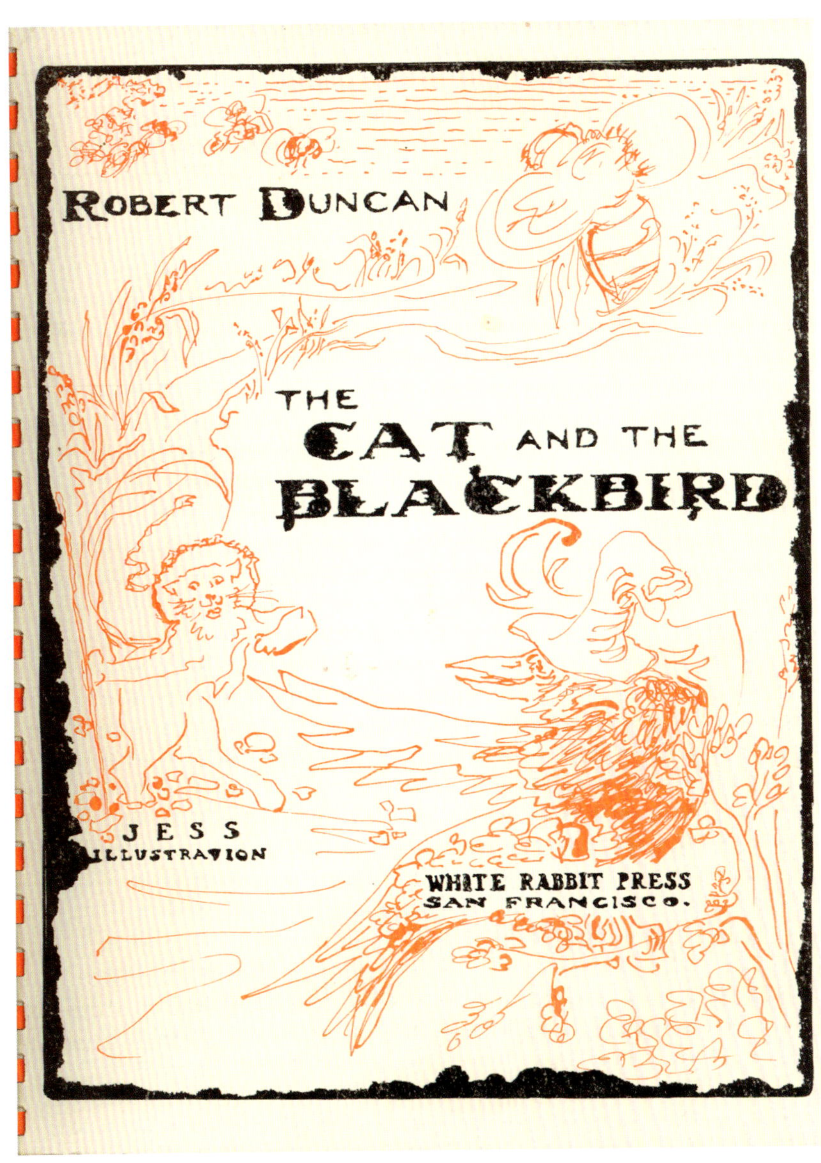

Fig. 83 Robert Duncan and Jess, *The Cat and the Blackbird*, 1967. Book with cover and illustrations by Jess, bound in glossy paper with plastic foldout spine, n.p., 12 ¼ x 9 ¼ (31.1 x 23.5 cm). Private collection

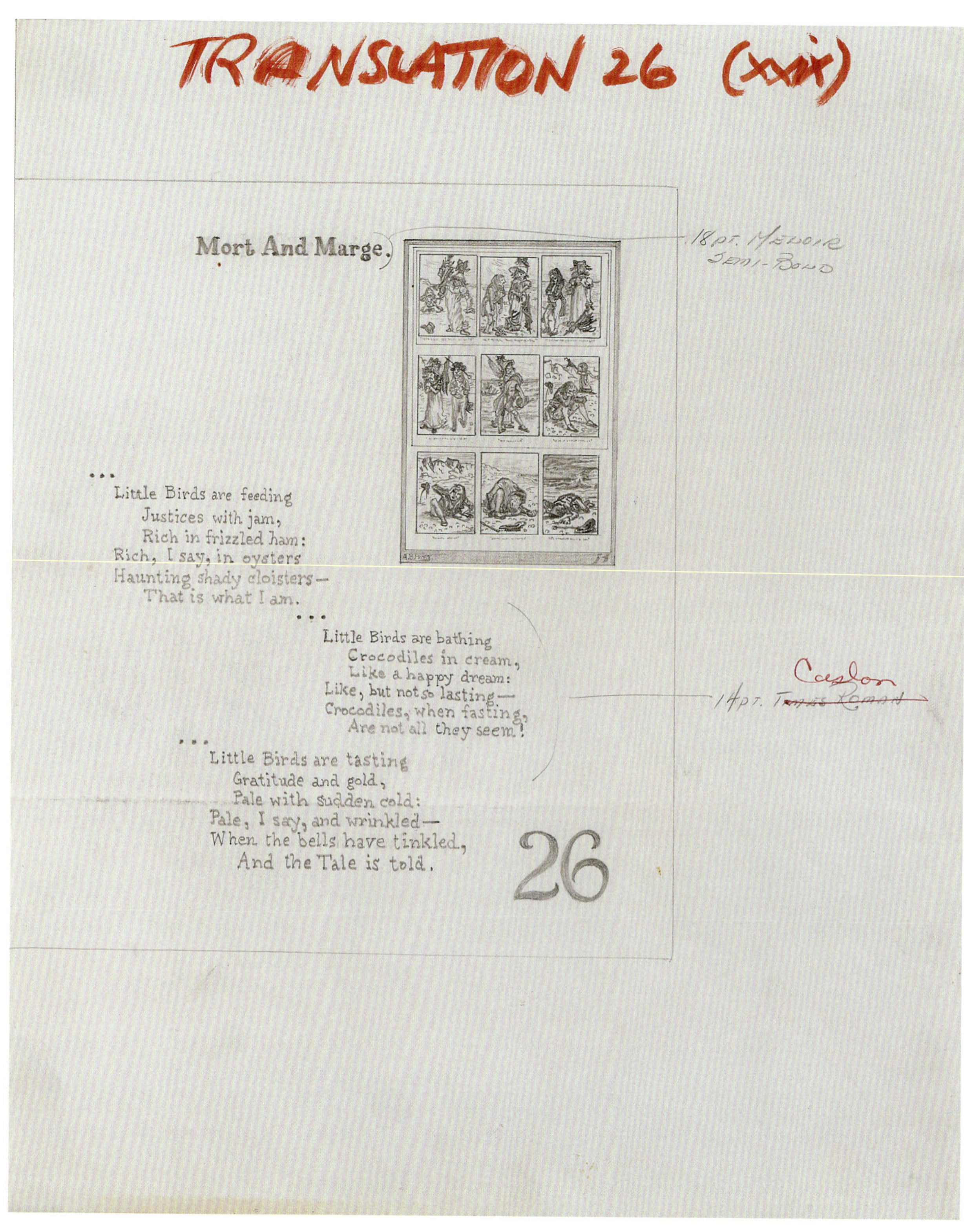

Fig. 84 *Imaginary Dummy of the Catalogue for "Translations by Jess"* (detail), 1969–71. Catalogue proof with handwritten notations and inset letter, 45 pages, 14 x 11 ½ x ½ in. (35.6 x 29.2 x 1.3 cm). Courtesy Odyssia Gallery, New York

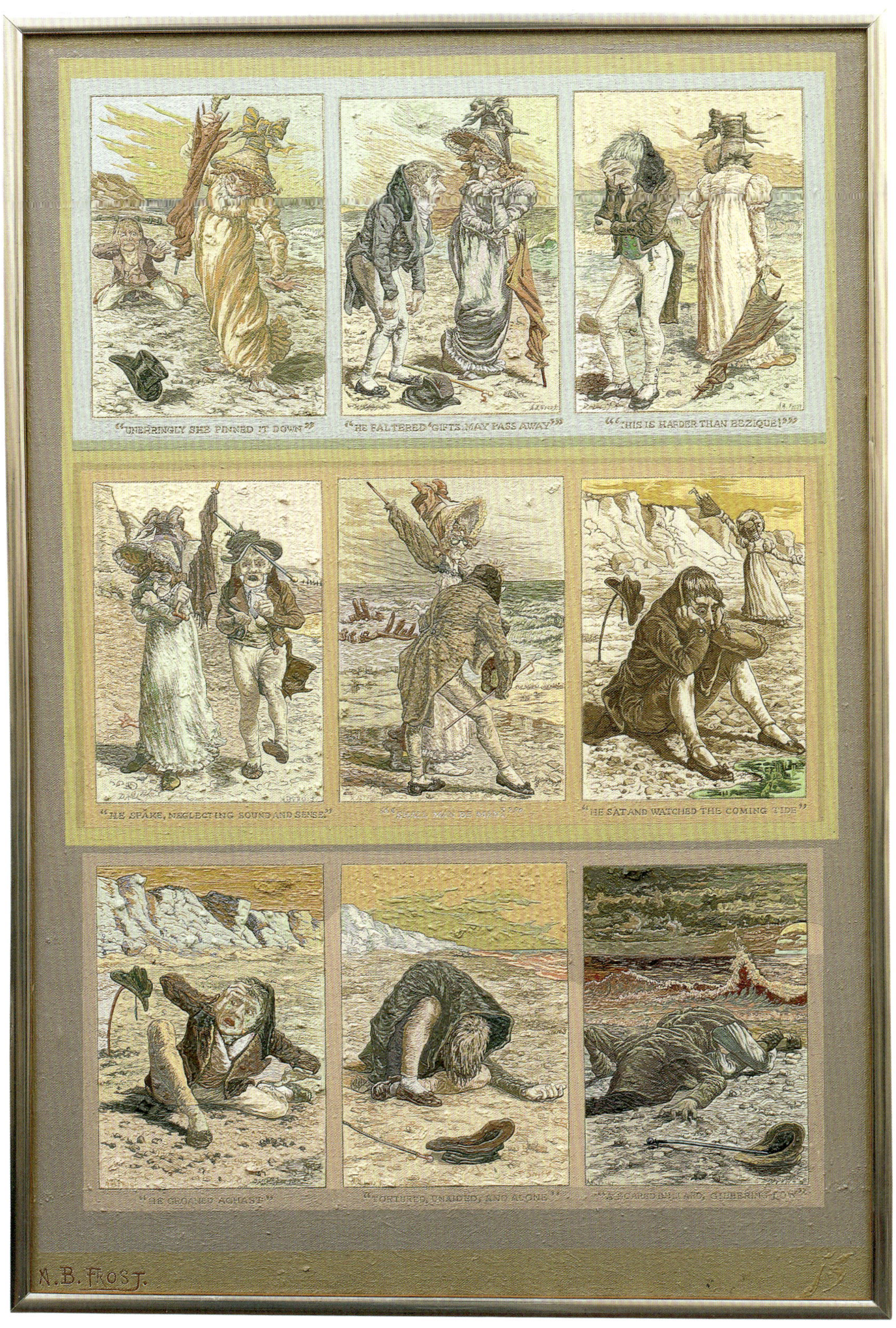

Fig. 85 Jess, *Mort and Marge: Translation #26*, 1971.
Oil on canvas, mounted on wood, 30 x 20 in.
(76.2 x 50.8 cm). Courtesy Odyssia Gallery, New York

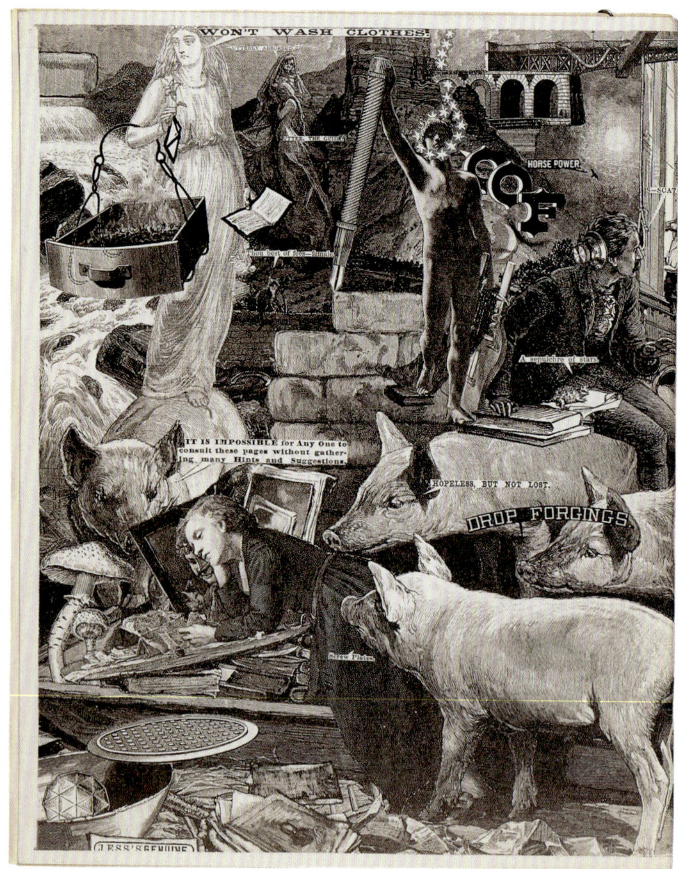

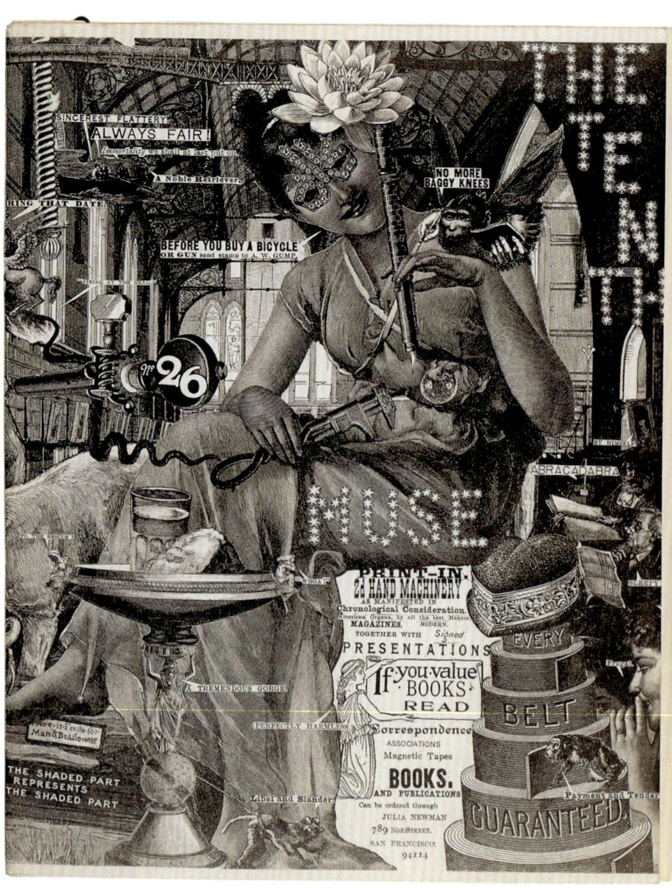

PUBLICATIONS WITH WORKS JESS MADE FOR REPRODUCTION

Jess created many works of art specifically for reproduction. A key reference in creating this list of publications in which they appear was an unpublished bibliography by Catherine Burnett on file at Odyssia Gallery, New York. An invaluable aid to Jess scholarship and research, Burnett's bibliography, which is annotated by Jess, cites both primary and secondary sources, provides descriptive commentary, and seems to be comprehensive up to around 1985. I have been unable to further identify the author, and would like to acknowledge my indebtedness to her work. Citations are chronological and alphabetical by title. Those in the exhibition are marked with a ***bold title***.
—Ingrid Schaffner

Fig. 86 Julia Newman, editor, *The Tenth Muse*, no. 26, 1969 (front and back covers). Catalogue with cover by Jess, loose-leaf paper and cardstock cover, 29 pages, 11 x 8 1/2 in. (27.9 x 21.6 cm). Collection of Christopher Wagstaff, Berkeley, California

The Artist's View 0. Tiburon, Ca.: Painters Poets Sculptors, 1952. Collage for publication edited by Claire Mahl.

Boob #1. San Francisco: Jess and Robert Duncan, 1952. Collage with Robert Duncan, privately issued as a broadside by the authors in an edition of 250.

Boob #2. San Francisco: Jess and Robert Duncan, 1952. Photographic image for poem by Robert Duncan, privately issued as a broadside by the authors in an edition of 250.

The Artist's View 5. Tiburon, Ca.: Painters Poets Sculptors, 1953. Cover drawing for issue dedicated to Robert Duncan.

The Artist's View 8. Tiburon, Ca.: Painters Poets Sculptors, 1954. Collage for never-distributed issue dedicated to Jess's art and writing.

Black Mountain Review 4. Black Mountain, N.C.: Black Mountain College, Winter 1954. Word collage for publication edited by Robert Creeley.

Caesar's Gate. Palma de Mallorca, Spain: The Divers Press, 1955. Collages for poems by Robert Duncan. Regular edition plus a limited edition of 13 copies (A–C, 1–10), each with an original collage and holograph poem, signed by the artist and the author.

Publication announcement for *Caesar's Gate*. Palma de Mallorca, Spain: The Divers Press, 1955. Collage that does not appear in the book.

Black Mountain Review 6. Black Mountain, N.C.: Black Mountain College, Spring 1956. Collages.

The Boobus and the Bunnyduck. Unpublished, 1957. Drawings for a children's book with Michael McClure.

After Lorca. San Francisco: White Rabbit Press, 1957. Cover drawing for poems by Jack Spicer.

Love, the Poem, the Sea, and Other Pieces Examined. San Francisco: White Rabbit Press, 1957. Cover drawing for poems by Steve Jonas.

5 Poems. San Francisco: White Rabbit Press, 1958. Cover and drawings for poems by Denise Levertov.

O'Ryan 2-4-6-8-10. San Francisco: White Rabbit Press, 1958. Cover drawing for poems by Charles Olson.

The Queen o' Crow Castle: A Ballad for Jess Collins. San Francisco: White Rabbit Press, 1958. Cover and drawings for ballad by Helen Adam.

Announcement for *Paste-Ups and Assemblies*. San Francisco: Dilexi Gallery, 1959. Collage.

Billy the Kid. Stinson Beach, Ca.: Enkidu Surrogate, 1959. Cover and drawings for poems by Jack Spicer.

Folio 3. Bloomington, Ind.: Indiana University, Summer, 1960. Collage for publication edited by Clayton Eshleman, published by the Department of English.

J **5**. San Francisco: Jack Spicer, 1959. Cover and comic strip, "The Poet Scorner by Jess," for mimeograph publication edited by Jack Spicer with Fran Herndon.

O!. New York: Hawk's Well Press, 1960. Collages and poems for chapbook by Jess.

The Opening of the Field. New York: Grove Press, 1960. Frontispiece drawing for poems by Robert Duncan.

Northwest Review 4. Eugene, Oreg.: Edward van Aelstyn, Fall 1963. Collage book, *The Dios Kuroi*, for magazine edited by Edward van Aelstyn. Initially a feature, the collage was also privately issued as an off-print edition.

A Poetry Folio. San Francisco: San Francisco Four Seasons Foundation, 1963. Drawing for Robert Duncan's poem "Unkingd by Affection," published as a broadside for the San Francisco Arts Festival's portfolio.

Rivoli Review 1. San Francisco: Richard Duerden, 1963. Cover drawing for publication edited by Richard Duerden.

San Francisco's Burning. Berkeley, Ca.: Oannes, 1963. Cover and drawings for poem opera by Helen Adam and Pat Adam. First edition limited to 500. Reprinted in 1983 by Hanging Loose Press.

Semina 8. Los Angeles: Wallace Berman, 1963. Collage for 149 copies of publication edited by Wallace Berman.

12 Poets & 1 Painter. San Francisco: Four Seasons Foundation, 1964. Six drawings for publication edited by D. M. Allen.

Ballads. New York: Arcadia Press, 1964. Cover and drawings for poems by Helen Adam. Additional limited edition of 50 includes two additional drawings and is hand-tinted by Jess.

Open Space. San Francisco: Stan Persky, 1964. Jess contributed to six issues of the publication edited by Stan Persky: 6 (June 1964), pencil drawing; 7 (July 1964), cover drawing; 8 (August 1964), comic-strip paste-up; 9 (September 1964), ink drawing; 10 (October 1964), cover ink drawing and paste-up poem; 12 (December 1964), ink drawing.

A Poetry Folio. San Francisco: East Wind Printers, 1964. Drawing for Ebbe Borregaard's poem "When did morning wind rip callow flower," published as a broadside for the San Francisco Arts Festival's portfolio.

The Floating Bear: A Newsletter 31. New York: The Poets Press, June 1965. Cover drawing, *Barely Afloat*, for mimeograph newsletter edited by Diane di Prima and LeRoi Jones. This issue guest edited by Alan Marlowe.

Insect Trust Gazette 2. Philadelphia: Jed Irwin and William Levy, 1965. Prose text, *Osap's Faebles*, for magazine edited by Jed Irwin and William Levy.

O'Ryan 1-10. San Francisco: White Rabbit Press, 1965. Cover drawing for poems by Charles Olson.

A Book of Resemblances: Poems: 1950–1953. New Haven, Conn.: Henry Wenning, 1966. Drawings, ornaments, and design for poems by Robert Duncan. Limited edition of 203.

some/thing 1. New York: Jerome Rothenberg and David Antin, Winter 1966. Collage, *Ragnarok*, for journal edited by David Antin and Jerome Rothenberg.

The Cat and the Blackbird. San Francisco: White Rabbit Press, 1967. Cover and drawings for children's book designed by Jess with story by Robert Duncan.

Announcement for *Paste-Ups by Jess*. Spokane, Wash.: Eastern Washington Historical Society, Cheney Cowles Museum, 1967. Collage.

The Tenth Muse. San Francisco: The Tenth Muse, 1967–68. Jess contributed cover art to four catalogues for Julia Newman's San Francisco bookstore: 14 (1967), mimeograph drawing; 15 (1967), ink drawing; 21 (1968), ink drawing; **26 (1969),** collage.

*The **Better Dream House***. San Francisco: White Rabbit Press, 1968. Cover and collages for text by Joe Dunn.

Names of People. Los Angeles: Black Sparrow Press, 1968. Drawings for poems, "Stein Imitations," by Robert Duncan. Limited edition of 250 numbered and 26 lettered copies, signed by the artist and author.

Brochure for *Paste-Ups by Jess*. San Francisco: San Francisco Museum of Art, 1968. Wraparound cover collage, *Alone in a Crowd*. The same brochure design was used for *Jess: Paste-Ups*. Chicago: Museum of Contemporary Art, 1972.

***Caterpillar** 8/9*. Sherman Oaks, Ca.: Clayton Eshleman, October 1969. Collage front and back covers for magazine edited by Clayton Eshleman.

Announcement for poetry readings by Robert Duncan at Le Conte School Auditorium. Berkeley, Ca.: Le Conte School, 1970. Readings March 6 and 15. Collage for broadside.

Gallowsongs: Galgenlieder by Christian Morgenstern, Versions by Jess. Los Angeles: Black Sparrow Press, 1970. Poems, drawings, and design. Limited editions of 600 paper and 175 cloth, plus 26 copies (A–Z) signed by the artist.

From a Suite of Metaphysical Poems to the Seventeenth Century Genius in Poetry. San Francisco: Robert Duncan, 1971. Drawing, *The Burning Babe*, for broadside publication privately issued by the author, Robert Duncan.

Paste-Ups by Jess. New York: Odyssia Gallery, 1971. Collage for exhibition broadside at Odyssia Gallery, New York.

Translations. Los Angeles: Black Sparrow Press, 1971. Design for book accompanying his exhibition at Odyssia Gallery, New York. Additional cloth edition of 100 copies signed by the artist and Robert Duncan.

***Caterpillar** 18*. Sherman Oaks: Clayton Eshleman, April 1972. Wraparound cover collage, *Notice. No Eggs Required. By Order*.

Caesar's Gate. Berkeley, Ca.: Sand Dollar, 1972–73. New collages for revised edition of poems by Robert Duncan. Announcement for reprint features the same collage as announcement for the original 1955 edition.

***Credences** 3*. Kent, Ohio: Credences Press, May 1976. Collage for front and back covers of magazine edited by Robert Bertholf.

The Mutabilities & the Foul Papers. Berkeley, Ca.: Sand Dollar, 1976. Wraparound cover collage for poems by Michael Davidson.

A Lesbian Estate: Poems 1970–1973. South San Francisco: Manroot, 1977. Wraparound cover collage for poems by Lynn Lonidier.

Announcement for *Jess: Translations, Salvages and Paste-Ups*. Berkeley, Ca.: University Art Museum, 1977. Collage.

***Credences** 8/9*. Kent, Ohio: Credences Press, March 1980. Wraparound cover drawing.

Ironwood 22 (*Robert Duncan: A Special Issue*). Tucson, Ariz.: Ironwood Press, Fall 1983. Painting, *The Enamord Mage: Translation #6*, for magazine cover.

Jess: Paste-Ups (and Assemblies) 1951–1983. Sarasota, Fl.: The John and Mable Ringling Museum of Art, 1984. Wraparound cover collage.

Robert Duncan: A Descriptive Bibliography. Santa Rosa, Ca.: Black Sparrow Press, 1986. Frontispiece collage (originally intended for Duncan's *The Truth & Life of Myth*) for book by Robert Bertholf.

Critical Dreams. Berkeley, Ca.: Poltroon Press, 1986. Writings and drawings. Edition of 120 copies signed by Jess.

Zyzzyva, The Last Word: West Coast Writers & Artists. San Francisco: Zyzzyva, Inc., 1989. Collages, *Emblems for Robert Duncan*, and cover.

Notebook Poems: 1953. San Francisco: San Francisco State University, The Press in Tuscany Alley, 1991. Drawings for poems by Robert Duncan.

***o·blēk: A Journal of Language Arts** 10*. Stockbridge, Mass.: The Garlic Press, Fall 1991. Wraparound cover for magazine edited by Peter Gizzi and Connell McGrath.

Mars. Berkeley, Ca.: Listening Chamber, 1994. Wraparound cover for poems by Norma Cole.

Mirage #4/Period[ical] 1. San Francisco: Dodie Bellamy and Kevin Killian, May 1994. Photographic image for magazine edited by Dodie Bellamy and Kevin Killian.

Entropicas, Catasters & Doubtful Fragments, Morning Star Folio 6/4. Edinburgh: Alec Finlay, 1995. Collage for poem by Norma Cole, published as a broadside edition.

Zyzzyva, The Last Word: West Coast Writers & Artists. San Francisco: Zyzzyva, Inc., Winter 1997. Cover collage.

Boxkite 1. Sydney, Australia: The Poetics Foundation, 1997. Wraparound cover collage for periodical edited by James Taylor.

Tolling Elves 10. London: Thomas Evans, September 2003. Collage detail from *Alone in a Crowd* for mail-out magazine edited by Thomas Evans.

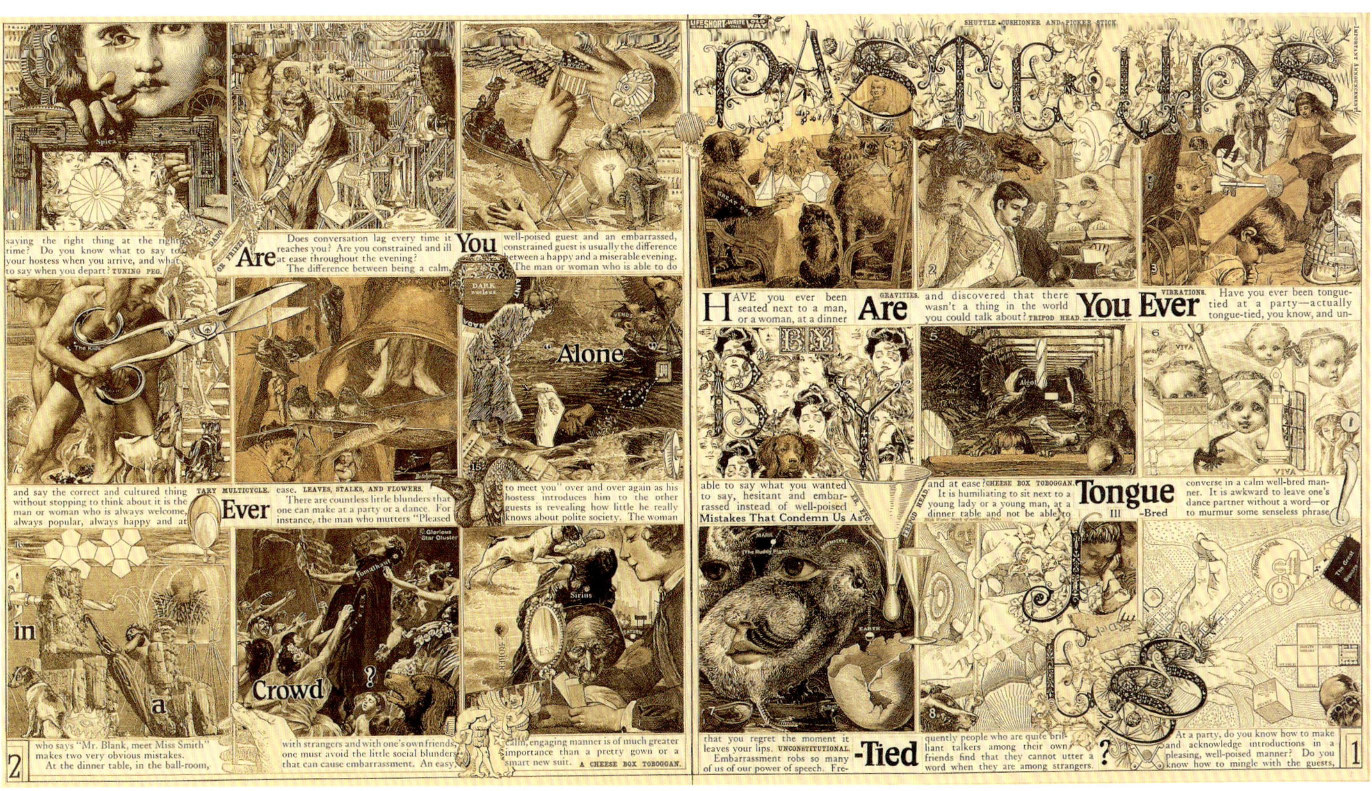

Fig. 87 Jess, *Alone in a Crowd*, 1968.
Collage, 24 ³/₄ x 31 ¹/₂ in. (62.9 x 80 cm).
Private collection, San Francisco

EXHIBITION CHECKLIST

Note: *blue* titles indicate unique objects, such as paintings, drawings, collages, or original book designs; all other entries are books, ephemera, and other printed matter. Entries appear in chronological order, except when the entry for a related item produced later immediately follows the entry for its corresponding object. For all entries, height precedes width precedes depth. "Partial tour" indicates a work not exhibited at all venues.

Jess
Open-Mouthed but Relaxed, 1952
Collage
10 ³/₄ x 16 ¹/₂ in. (27.3 x 41.9 cm)
The Poetry Collection, State University of New York at Buffalo
(page 24)

Jess and Robert Duncan
Boob #1, 1952
Collage
12 ⁷/₈ x 16 ⁵/₈ in. (32.7 x 42.2 cm)
Courtesy Odyssia Gallery, New York
(page 20)

Jess and Robert Duncan
Boob #1
San Francisco: self-published, 1952
Broadside
8 ¹/₂ x 11 in. (21.6 x 27.9 cm)
The Poetry Collection, State University of New York at Buffalo

Jess and Robert Duncan
Boob #2
San Francisco: self-published, 1952
Broadside
8 ¹/₂ x 11 in. (21.6 x 27.9 cm)
The Poetry Collection, State University of New York at Buffalo
(page 21)

Jess
Boob #3, 1954
Collage
19 ¹/₂ x 24 ¹/₂ in. (49.5 x 62.2 cm)
Courtesy Odyssia Gallery, New York
(page 21)

Jess
Brimo of Colchis, 1954
Collage
23 x 12 ³/₄ in. (58.4 x 32.4 cm)
Courtesy Odyssia Gallery, New York
(page 73)

Jess
Goddess Because Is Is Falling Asleep, 1954
Collage
14 x 10 ¹/₂ in. (35.6 x 26.7 cm)
Private collection, New York
Partial tour
(page 22)

Claire Mahl, editor
The Artist's View
Tiburon, Ca.: Painters Poets Sculptors, no. 8, 1954
Broadside with cover by Jess
12 ¹/₈ x 9 ¹/₂ in. (30.8 x 24.1 cm)
The Poetry Collection, State University of New York at Buffalo
(page 14)

Robert Creeley, editor
Black Mountain Review
Black Mountain, N.C.: Black Mountain College, no. 4, Winter 1954
Magazine with collage reproduction by Jess, 64 pages
8 ¹/₂ x 6 ¹/₂ in. (21.6 x 16.5 cm)
Collection of Steve Dickison
(page 80)

Jess
And It's Jung by a Gnose, 1955
Collage
13 x 21 in. (33 x 53.3 cm)
Courtesy di Rosa Preserve, Napa
(page 24)

Jess
Mystic Writing VIII, 1955
Wax crayon on paper
12 ¹/₂ x 11 ¹/₂ in. (31.6 x 29.2 cm)
Courtesy Odyssia Gallery, New York
(page 33)

Jess
Mystic Writing XI, 1955
Wax crayon on paper
11 ¹/₈ x 10 ¹/₈ in. (28.3 x 25.7 cm)
Courtesy Odyssia Gallery, New York

Jess
Mystic Writing XII, 1955
Wax crayon on paper
11 x 10 ³/₄ in. (27.9 x 27.3 cm)
Courtesy Odyssia Gallery, New York
(page 33)

Jess
Land of the Mangaboos, 1955
Oil on burlap, mounted on plywood
24 x 38 ¹/₂ in. (61 x 97.8 cm)
Private collection
(page 60)

Jess
When My Ship Come Sin, 1955
Collage
25 x 30 in. (63.5 x 76.2 cm)
Gift of Federico and Odyssia Skouras Quadrani (class of 1954 in honor of Professor Peter Viereck). Mount Holyoke College Art Museum, South Hadley, Massachusetts
Partial tour
(page 6)

Jess
The Nasturtium that Dissolved the World: Imaginary Portrait #13: Denise Levertov, 1955
Oil on canvas
43 x 30 in. (109.2 x 76.2 cm)
Courtesy Odyssia Gallery, New York
(page 29)

Jess
Tintagel: A Castle Spun from Yarn, 1955
Oil on canvas
48 x 40 in. (121.9 x 101.6 cm)
Courtesy Odyssia Gallery, New York
(page 28)

Jess
Jess's Didactic Nickelodeon, Series Two,
"The Guardian Angels' Guidebook", 1955
37 collages
20 1/2 x 15 1/2 in. (52 x 39.4 cm) each
Courtesy Odyssia Gallery, New York
(pages 35, 36, 37)

Lawrence Jordan
The 40 and 1 Nights, or Jess's Didactic
Nickelodeon, 1955–62
16 mm film (transferred to DVD), color,
sound; 5:19 min.
Collection of Lawrence Jordan; courtesy
Monaco Digital Film Labs, San Francisco
(page 34)

Jess
Caesar's Gate, 1955/1972
Box with 17 collages (16 from 1955,
1 from 1972)
13 1/2 x 9 x 2 1/8 in. (34.3 x 22.9 x 5.4 cm)
overall
Courtesy Odyssia Gallery, New York
(pages 53, 54, 55)

Robert Duncan and Jess
Caesar's Gate
Palma de Mallorca, Spain:
The Divers Press, 1955
Special edition book with original collages
by Jess, 57 pages
8 5/8 x 6 5/8 in. (21.8 x 16.8 cm)
The Poetry Collection, State University
of New York at Buffalo
(page 56)

Robert Duncan
Caesar's Gate
Berkeley, California: Sand Dollar, 1972–73
Cloth-bound book with wraparound jacket
and collage reproductions by Jess, 80 pages
8 3/4 x 6 5/8 in. (22.2 x 16.8 cm)
Collection of Steve Dickison
(page 57)

Jess
Goddess Because II, 1956
Collage
15 1/2 x 19 in. (39.4 x 48.3 cm)
Weatherspoon Art Museum, University
of North Carolina at Greensboro,
Museum purchase with funds from
the Benefactors Fund, 2002
Partial tour
(page 23)

Jess
Tricky Cad: Case IV, 1957
Collage book
9 1/2 x 5 1/2 in. (24.1 x 14 cm)
Courtesy Odyssia Gallery, New York
(pages 12, 25)

Jess
The Marsh King's Daughter in Egypt, 1958
Oil on board
13 1/2 x 9 1/2 in. (34.3 x 24.1 cm)
Collection of Laree Hulshoff
(page 17)

Jess
The Adam Family in Nesbittland:
Imaginary Portrait #18: Helen Adam, 1958
Oil on canvas, mounted on wooden door,
metal hardware, fabric, and rope
40 x 38 in. (101.6 x 96.5 cm)
Courtesy Odyssia Gallery, New York
(page 30)

Jess
Untitled (cover for *5 Poems* by
Denise Levertov), 1958
Ink on paper
17 x 13 in. (43.2 x 33 cm)
Courtesy Odyssia Gallery, New York
(page 95)

Denise Levertov
5 Poems
San Francisco: White Rabbit Press, 1958
Paperbound book with cover and
illustrations by Jess, stapled, n.p.
8 1/2 x 6 1/2 in. (21.6 x 16.5 cm)
Collection of Christopher Wagstaff,
Berkeley

Helen Adam
The Queen o' Crow Castle: A Ballad for
Jess Collins
San Francisco: White Rabbit Press, 1958
Book with cover and illustrations by Jess,
sewn in paper wrappers, 16 pages
8 1/2 x 6 1/2 in. (21.6 x 16.5 cm)
Collection of Dodie Bellamy and
Kevin Killian, San Francisco
(page 89)

Jess
Collage for Paste-Ups and Assemblies
at Dilexi Gallery, 1959
Collage
20 1/8 x 15 7/8 in. (51.5 x 40.5 cm)
Collection of Jim Newman and Jane Ivory
(page 94)

Jess
The Fox Hunt Is Over, 1959
Collage and ink on board
11 3/4 x 8 1/2 in. (29.8 x 21.6 cm)
Courtesy Odyssia Gallery, New York
(page 88)

Jack Spicer
Billy the Kid
Stinson Beach, California: Enkidu Surrogate,
1959
Book with cover and illustrations by Jess,
bound in paper wrappers, stapled, 16 pages
8 1/2 x 6 1/2 in. (21.6 x 16.5 cm)
Collection of Dodie Bellamy and
Kevin Killian, San Francisco
(page 98)

Jack Spicer, editor, and Fran Herndon,
art editor
J
San Francisco: Jack Spicer, no. 5, 1959
Magazine with hand-glittered cardstock
cover and illustrations by Jess, 16 pages
11 x 8 1/2 in. (27.9 x 21.6 cm)
Collection of Thomas Evans and Lisa Jarnot
(page 46)

Jess
Narkissos Notebook, 1959–90
Annotated notebook with additional papers,
bound in cardboard, n.p.
11 1/2 x 10 x 2 1/4 in. (29.2 x 25.4 x 5.7 cm)
Courtesy Odyssia Gallery, New York

Jess
Narkissos: The Last Translation, 1978/1991
Graphite on primed linen
70 x 60 in. (177.8 x 152.4 cm)
The Museum of Modern Art, New York.
Gift of Odyssia Skouras, 2005
(page 64)

Jess
O!
New York: Hawk's Well Press, 1960
Book bound in paper and stapled, 16 pages
8 1/4 x 5 1/4 in. (21 x 13.3 cm)
Collection of Jerome and Diane Rothenberg,
Encinitas, California
(page 39)

Jerome Rothenberg and Steven Clay, editors
*A Book of the Book: Some Works &
Projections About the Book & Writing*
(Contains a complete facsimile of *O!*)
New York: Granary Books, 2000
Paperback book, 537 pages
10 x 6 1/2 in. (25.4 x 16.5 cm)
Collection of Jerome Rothenberg,
Encinitas, California

Jess
The Vinegar Egret's Comick Valentyne,
ca. 1960
Ink on paper
13 1/2 x 10 3/4 in. (34.3 x 27.3 cm)
Courtesy Odyssia Gallery, New York
(page 27)

Jess
Ex Libris, ca. 1960
Ink on paper, mounted on board
(drawing for a bookplate)
13 7/8 x 11 in. (35.3 x 27.9 cm)
Courtesy Odyssia Gallery, New York
(page 52)

Jess
Echo's Wake, Part IV, 1961/1966
Collage
10 1/4 x 14 1/2 in. (26 x 36.8 cm)
Collection of Paule Anglim, San Francisco
(page 66)

Jess
Echo's Wake: Part V, 1966
Collage
17 1/2 x 19 in. (44.5 x 48.3 cm)
The JPMorgan Chase Art Collection
(page 67)

Jess
Echo's Wake, Part VI, 1961/1966
Collage
18 1/2 x 14 1/2 in. (47 x 36.8 cm)
Courtesy Odyssia Gallery, New York
(page 68)

Jess
*A Post-mortem: Echo's Dying, Dying,
into Echo's Wake: '61–'66*, 1966
Ink on photograph and cardboard in
frame with crayon on glass
12 1/4 x 11 1/2 in. (31.1 x 29.2 cm)
Courtesy Odyssia Gallery, New York
(page 69)

Jess
The Dios Kuroi, 1963
Collage book, 9 pages
9 1/2 x 6 1/2 in. (24.1 x 16.5 cm)
Los Angeles County Museum of Art,
Prints and Drawings Deaccession Fund
Partial tour
(page 44)

Jess
Poet's Coffeepot, 1963
Assemblage
17 1/2 x 6 x 6 in. (44.5 x 15.2 x 15.2 cm)
Collection of Robert Glück, San Francisco
(page 44)

Jess
Petals of Paint, 1964
Oil on plywood
16 x 12 1/4 in. (40.6 x 31.1 cm)
Private collection
(page 31)

Helen Adam
Ballads
New York: Arcadia Press, 1964
Paperbound book with cover and
illustrations by Jess, stapled, n.p.
7 1/2 x 5 1/2 in. (19 x 14 cm)
Collection of Christopher Wagstaff,
Berkeley

Diane di Prima and LeRoi Jones, editors;
Alan Marlowe, guest editor
The Floating Bear: A Newsletter
New York: The Poets Press, no. 31, June 1965
Magazine with cover by Jess, 12 pages
11 x 8 1/2 (27.9 x 21.6 cm)
The Poetry Collection, State University
of New York at Buffalo
(page 47)

Jess
From Force of Habit, 1966
Collage book, 10 pages
8 x 5 3/4 x 1/8 in. (20.3 x 14.6 x .3 cm)
Courtesy Odyssia Gallery, New York
(page 33)

Jess
*Fig. 3—Ida, Duncan, and I:
Translation #18*, 1966
Oil on canvas, mounted on wood
12 x 12 in. (30.5 x 30.5 cm)
Courtesy the Pennsylvania Academy
of Fine Arts, Philadelphia. Alexander
Harrison Fund
(page 32)

Jess
*Decoration from A Book of Resemblances
by Robert Duncan*, 1966
Ink on paper
8 3/4 x 6 3/4 in. (22.2 x 17.1 cm)
Private collection
(page 59)

Jess
*Untitled ("An Essay at War") from A Book
of Resemblances*, 1966
Ink on paper
Two sheets, each 21 1/2 x 13 in. (54.6 x 33 cm)
Private collection
(page 59)

Jess
*Untitled ("An Imaginary War Elegy")
from A Book of Resemblances*, ca. 1966
Ink on paper
13 x 10 1/2 in. (33 x 26.7 cm)
Collection of Stephen D. Burton,
Tucson, Arizona
(page 47)

Robert Duncan
A Book of Resemblances: Poems: 1950–1953
New Haven, Connecticut: Henry Wenning,
1966
Hardbound book with embossed cover and
illustrations by Jess, 91 pages
17 1/2 x 13 in. (44.5 x 33 cm)
Collection of Michael Palmer and Cathy
Simon
(page 58)

Jess
Once Upon a Time . . . For Robert, 1966
Collage
10 1/2 x 6 3/4 in. (26.7 x 17.1 cm)
Collection of Mr. and Mrs. Federico Quadrani,
New York
(page 83)

Jerome Rothenberg and David Antin, editors
some/thing
New York: Jerome Rothenberg and
David Antin, vol. 2, no. 1, Winter 1966
Magazine with collage reproduction
by Jess and perforated cover, n.p.
8 1/4 x 5 1/4 in. (21 x 13.3 cm)
Collection of Jerome Rothenberg,
Encinitas, California

Jerome Rothenberg and David Antin, editors
some/thing
New York: Jerome Rothenberg and
David Antin, vol. 2, no. 1, Winter 1966
Magazine with collage reproduction
by Jess and cardboard cover, n.p.
8 1/4 x 5 1/4 in. (21 x 13.3 cm)
Collection of Jerome Rothenberg,
Encinitas, California
(page 46)

Robert Duncan and Jess
The Cat and the Blackbird
San Francisco: White Rabbit Press, 1967
Book with cover and illustrations by Jess,
bound in glossy paper with plastic foldout
spine, n.p.
12 1/4 x 9 1/4 (31.1 x 23.5 cm)
Private collection
(page 99)

Jess
Alone in a Crowd, 1968
Collage
24 3/4 x 31 1/2 in. (62.9 x 80 cm)
Private collection, San Francisco
Partial tour
(page 105)

Joe Dunn
The Better Dream House
San Francisco: White Rabbit Press, 1968
Book with cover by Jess, bound in paper
wrappers, 36 pages
9 1/4 x 6 3/4 (23.5 x 17.1 cm)
The Poetry Collection, State University
of New York at Buffalo
(page 40)

Clayton Eshleman, editor
Caterpillar
Sherman Oaks, California: Clayton
Eshleman, no. 8/9, October 1969
Magazine with cover by Jess, 256 pages
7 x 5 1/2 in. (17.8 x 14 cm)
Collection of Steve Dickison
(page 91)

Julia Newman, editor
The Tenth Muse
San Francisco: The Tenth Muse, no. 26, 1969
Catalogue with cover by Jess, with loose-
leaf paper and cardstock cover, 29 pages
11 x 8 1/2 in. (27.9 x 21.6 cm)
Collection of Christopher Wagstaff, Berkeley
(page 102)

Jess Collins Reading "Songs"
San Francisco: The Tenth Muse, 1969–70
Audio recording, 26:23 min.
Courtesy the Bancroft Library, University
of California, Berkeley

Jess
*Imaginary Dummy of the Catalogue for
"Translations by Jess"*, 1969–71
Catalogue proof with handwritten
notations and inset letter, 45 pages
14 x 11 1/2 x 1/2 in. (35.6 x 29.2 x 1.3 cm)
Courtesy Odyssia Gallery, New York
(pages 41, 100)

Jess
*Gallowsongs: Galgenlieder by Christian
Morgenstern, Versions by Jess*
Los Angeles: Black Sparrow Press, 1970
Book bolted in paper wrappers, n.p.
11 1/4 x 8 3/4 in. (28.6 x 22.2 cm)
Collection of Dodie Bellamy and
Kevin Killian, San Francisco
(page 60)

Jess
*Robert Duncan Reading at Le Conte
Auditorium*, 1970
Collage
30 1/4 x 38 1/4 in. (76.8 x 97.2 cm)
University of California, Berkeley Art
Museum; gift of the artist
Partial tour
(page 79)

Jess
*Announcement for Robert Duncan Reading
at Le Conte Auditorium*, 1970
Broadside
23 1/16 x 29 1/16 in. (60 x 75.2 cm)
The Poetry Collection, State University
of New York at Buffalo

Jess
Mort and Marge: Translation #26, 1971
Oil on canvas, mounted on wood
30 x 20 in. (76.2 x 50.8 cm)
Courtesy Odyssia Gallery, New York
(page 101)

Jess
Translations
Los Angeles: Black Sparrow Press, 1971
Clothbound book, 44 pages
10 3/4 x 8 1/8 in. (27.3 x 20.7 cm)
The Poetry Collection, State University
of New York at Buffalo

Jess
Paste-Ups by Jess, 1971
Collage
22 x 28 in. (55.9 x 71.1 cm)
Courtesy Odyssia Gallery, New York
(page 18)

Jess
Paste-Ups by Jess
New York: Odyssia Gallery, 1971
Exhibition poster
20 1/2 x 26 in. (52.1 x 66 cm)
Courtesy Odyssia Gallery, New York

Jess
Notice. No Eggs Required. By Order, 1972
Collage
7 1/2 x 12 in. (19 x 30.5 cm)
Collection of Robert M. Murdock, New York
(pages 48, 49)

Clayton Eshleman, editor
Caterpillar
Sherman Oaks, California: Clayton
Eshleman, no. 18, April 1972
Magazine with cover by Jess, 128 pages
7 x 5 1/4 in. (17.8 x 13.3 cm)
The Poetry Collection, State University
of New York at Buffalo

Jess
Deranged Stereopticon, 1974
Collage
15 1/2 x 34 1/2 in. (39.4 x 87.6 cm)
Courtesy Odyssia Gallery, New York
(page 74)

Jess
Cover for The Mutabilities, 1975
Collage
22 x 24 3/8 in. (55.9 x 62 cm)
The JPMorgan Chase Art Collection
(page 42)

Michael Davidson
The Mutabilities & the Foul Papers
Berkeley, California: Sand Dollar, 1976
Perfect-bound book with wraparound
jacket by Jess, 80 pages
9 x 6 in. (22.9 x 15.2 cm)
Collection of Steve Dickison

Jess
Cover for Credences 3, 1976
Collage
8 ¹/₂ x 14 in. (21.6 x 35.6 cm)
Collection of Anne and Robert Bertholf,
Buffalo, New York
(page 92)

Robert Bertholf, editor
Credences
Kent, Ohio: Credences Press, no. 3,
May 1976
Magazine with cover by Jess, 128 pages
8 ¹/₂ x 7 in. (21.6 x 17.8 cm)
The Poetry Collection, State University
of New York at Buffalo

Jess
Cover for A Lesbian Estate, 1977
Collage
13 ³/₄ x 19 ³/₄ in. (34.9 x 50.2 cm)
The Museum of Modern Art, New York.
The Judith Rothschild Foundation
Contemporary Drawings Collection Gift,
2005
(page 97)

Lynn Lonidier
A Lesbian Estate: Poems 1970–1973
South San Francisco: Manroot, 1977
Perfect-bound book with cover by Jess,
88 pages
10 x 7 in. (25.4 x 17.8 cm)
Collection of Steve Dickison

Jess
Cover for Credences 8/9, 1980
Collage
10 ¹/₂ x 14 in. (26.7 x 35.6 cm)
Collection of Anne and Robert Bertholf,
Buffalo, New York
(page 82)

Robert Bertholf, editor
Credences
Kent, Ohio: Credences Press, no. 8/9, 1980
Magazine with cover by Jess, 175 pages
8 ¹/₂ x 7 in. (21.6 x 17.8 cm)
Collection of Anne and Robert Bertholf,
Buffalo, New York

Jess
*Jess: Paste-Ups (and Assemblies)
1951–1983*, 1984
Collage
10 ¹/₄ x 21 in. (26 x 53.3 cm)
Private collection
Partial tour
(page 19)

Michael Auping
Jess: Paste-Ups (and Assemblies) 1951–1983
Sarasota, Florida: The John and Mable
Ringling Museum of Art, 1984
Exhibition catalogue with cover by Jess,
bound in paper wrappers, 157 pages
10 x 10 in. (25.4 x 25.4 cm)
Collection of Christopher Wagstaff,
Berkeley
(page 19)

Jess
Critical Dreams
Berkeley, California: Poltroon Press, 1986
Clothbound book with paper wrappers,
24 pages
11 ⁵/₈ x 7 ¹/₈ in. (30 x 18.4 cm)
Courtesy Turtle Island Book Shop, Berkeley

Jess
Emblems for Robert Duncan I, 1989
7 collages
6 ¹/₄ x 5 ⁵/₈ in. (15.9 x 14.3 cm) each
Courtesy Odyssia Gallery, New York
(pages 85, 86, 87)

Jess
Cover for o·blēk, 1991
Collage
10 ¹/₂ x 14 ¹/₂ in. (26.7 x 36.8 cm)
Collection of Laree Hulshoff
(pages 8, 45)

Peter Gizzi and Connell McGrath, editors
o·blēk: A Journal of Language Arts
Stockbridge, Mass.: Garlic Press, no. 10,
Fall 1991
Journal with cover by Jess, subscription
card laid in, 212 pages
7 ¹/₂ x 5 ¹/₂ in. (19.1 x 14 cm)
Collection of Dodie Bellamy and
Kevin Killian, San Francisco
(page 45)

Jess
Dyslecstasy, 1991
Collage
36 x 24 in. (91.4 x 61 cm)
Private collection, San Francisco
Partial tour
(cover, page 70)

Jess
Bookcover for Norma Cole (Mars), 1993
Collage
8 ¹/₄ x 12 ³/₄ in. (21 x 32.4 cm)
Collection of Richard Harris
(page 2, 43)

Norma Cole
Mars
Berkeley, California: Listening Chamber,
1994
Perfect-bound book, 120 pages
8 x 6 in. (20.3 x 15.2 cm)
Collection of Steve Dickison
(page 43)

Jess
Song of the Pied Parrot, 1994
Ink on paper, letterpress edition
18 x 12 in. (45.7 x 30.5 cm)
Collection of Christopher Wagstaff,
Berkeley

All images of work by Jess © The Jess Collins Trust, Berkeley, CA

Jon Abbott, courtesy Odyssia Gallery, New York: figs. 38, 73, 87; Ray Andrews, courtesy the Des Moines Art Center: fig. 5; © 2007 Artists Rights Society (ARS), New York / ADAGP, Paris: fig. 30; Benjamin Blackwell: fig. 37; Benjamin Blackwell, courtesy the University of California, Berkeley Art Museum: fig. 68; Courtesy Daria K. Conservation, New York: fig. 45; D. James Dee, courtesy Odyssia Gallery, New York: cover, detail page 2, detail page 8, figs. 19, 35, 57, 62, 64, 85; D. James Dee, courtesy the Weatherspoon Art Museum, University of North Carolina at Greensboro: fig. 13; Courtesy Michael Duncan, Los Angeles: figs. 3, 32, 83; Ali Elai, Camerarts, Inc., New York: figs. 8, 31, 36, 40, 41, 42, 51, 52, 56, 70, 76, 77, 82, 86; Tom Van Eynde: fig. 34; Courtesy Gallery Paule Anglim, San Francisco: fig. 60; Wilson Graham: figs. 23, 43, 53, 54, 55, 79; Courtesy the JPMorgan Chase Art Collection: fig. 61; Barbara Katus, courtesy the Pennsylvania Academy of Fine Arts: fig. 24; Stefan Kirkeby, courtesy the di Rosa Preserve, Napa: fig. 15; Courtesy the Mount Holyoke College Art Museum, South Hadley, Massachusetts: fig. 1; Digital image © The Museum of Modern Art/Licensed by SCALA / Art Resource, NY: fig. 81; Courtesy Odyssia Gallery, New York: figs. 6, 9, 11, 16, 18, 20, 21, 22, 25, 26, 27, 29, 33, 48, 49, 59, 63, 65, 66, 74, 75, 80, 84; PHOCASSO/J.W.White, courtesy Hackett-Freedman Gallery, San Francisco: fig. 12; Courtesy The Poetry Collection, University Libraries, University at Buffalo, The State University of New York: figs. 14, 50, 67, 69, 71; Courtesy the San Francisco Museum of Modern Art: fig. 58; Steve Tatum, courtesy the University of Iowa Museum of Art: fig. 17; James A. Ulrich: figs. 2, 4, 10, 39, 44, 46, 47, 72, 78; David Wharton Photography, courtesy the Modern Art Museum of Fort Worth: fig. 7